TWAYNE'S
FILMMAKERS SERIES

Frank Beaver, Editor

CLAY ANIMATION
American Highlights
1908 to the Present

Clay Animation

American Highlights 1908 to the Present

Michael Frierson

TWAYNE PUBLISHERS • NEW YORK
MAXWELL MACMILLAN CANADA • TORONTO
MAXWELL MACMILLAN INTERNATIONAL •
NEW YORK • OXFORD • SINGAPORE • SYDNEY

Twayne's Filmmakers Series

Clay Animation
Michael Frierson

Twayne Publishers
Macmillan Publishing Company
866 Third Avenue
New York, New York 10022

Maxwell Macmillan Canada, Inc.
1200 Eglinton Avenue East
Suite 200
Don Mills, Ontario M3C3NI

Library of Congress Cataloging-in-Publication Data
Frierson, Michael.
Clay animation / Michael Frierson
p. cm. — (Twayne's filmmakers series)
Includes filmographies, bibliographical references, and index.
ISBN 0-8057-9327-5 (alk. paper). — ISBN 0-8057-9328-3 (pbk.: alk. paper)
1. Animation (Cinematography)—United States—History—20th century.
2. Clay animation films—United States—History —20th century. I. Title.
II. Series.
TR897.5.F75 1994
791.43'3—dc20 93-38644
CIP

The paper used in this publication meets the minimum requirements of American National Standard for Information Sciences—Permanence of Paper for Printed Library Materials. ANSI Z3948-1984. ∞

10 9 8 7 6 5 4 3 2 1 (hc)
10 9 8 7 6 5 4 3 2 1 (pb)

Printed in the United States of America

For my parents, Dargan and Josephine,
who have given me everything I needed to live,
and
For Marianne, at the beginning of her new life

Contents

Foreword

Of all the contemporary arts, the motion picture is particularly timely and diverse as a popular culture enterprise. This lively art form cleverly combines storytelling with photography to achieve what has been a quintessential twentieth century phenomenon. Individual as well as national and cultural interests have made the medium an unusually varied one for artistic expression and analysis. Films have been exploted for commercial gain, for political purposes, for experimentation, and for self-exploration. The various responses to the motion picture have given rise to different labels for both the fun and the seriousness with which this art form has been received, ranging from "the movies" to "cinema." These labels hint at both the theoretical and sociological parameters of the film medium.

A collective art, the motion picture has nevertheless allowed individual genius to flourish in all its artistic and technical areas: directing, screenwriting, cinematography, acting, editing. The medium also encompasses many genres beyond the narrative film, including documentary, animated, and avant-garde expression. The range and diversity of motion pictures suggest rich opportunities for appreciation and for study.

The Twayne Filmmakers Series examines the full panorama of motion picture history and art. Many studies are auteur-oriented and elucidate the work of individual directors whose ideas and cinematic styles make them authors of their films. Other studies examine film movements and genres or analyze cinema from a national perspective. The series seeks to illuminate all the many aspects of film for the film student, the scholar, and the general reader.

Frank Beaver

Preface

Cel animation's domination over other animation techniques was firmly established by 1931. That year, the Academy of Motion Picture Arts and Sciences awarded its first Oscar for animation, "Best Cartoon," and proceeded to hand it to Walt Disney ten out of the next eleven years for some brilliant animation that also added a wholesome luster to an industry tarnished by the scandals of the 1920s.

But cel's domination had begun much earlier. Between 1915 and 1917, cel production houses sprang up to fill the demand for theatrical shorts. Specialization of labor not only made cel animation an attractive, cost-effective medium but also fit the emerging ideology of the film industry, a factory system that was turning out a product on the East Coast and expanding toward its new Mecca on the West Coast—Hollywood. For roughly four decades (1920–1960), cartoons rolled off the assembly line, tightly packaged in the style of the particular studio cartoon unit from which they emerged. The studio cartoon reigned supreme. Freedom of expression was limited to the relatively narrow bounds established by the studios, which had singlehandedly given birth to the cel animation industry but had trivialized it from the beginning. So it happened in America that "cartoon" became synonymous with "animated film," a misnomer convenient for the major studios, but one that ignored the existence of other forms of animation, particularly three-dimensional forms. As a rule, three-dimensional animation has been a neglected art form in American animation.

Although three-dimensional animation has existed since the very earliest days of filmmaking, it has been used in a relatively small number of films, none of which have produced stars on the order of theatrical regulars such as Mickey Mouse, Popeye, or Bugs Bunny. The puppet film is one of the more common forms of dimensional animation that quickly reached a sophisticated level; it came to be widely used in other parts of the world, such as Eastern Europe. Yet, outside of George Pal's "Puppetoons," the films of the finest puppet animators—such as those by Ladislav Starevich and Jiri Trnka—are largely unseen by American audiences.

Three-dimensional animation using clay figures is no exception, even though films incorporating animated clay were being produced in the United States as early as 1908. It was not until 1974, when Bob Gardiner and Will Vinton's clay film *Closed Mondays* (1974) won the Academy Award, that audiences took note of a clay animation revival that had been under way for some time among independent filmmakers. The last two decades have brought the rebirth of Gumby in a new television series, the production of the first clay animated feature film, and the huge success of Will Vinton's California Raisins. Clay animation has developed from a cottage industry into one as visible as the cel animation industry, if not as pervasive. Clay animation has finally arrived as an art form: it has permeated American culture through short and feature films, television programming, commercials, and spin-off merchandise. The resurgence of clay animation has made a basic survey of the medium's history a significant area of film study.

At the same time, the recent scholarly interest in Hollywood studio cartoons has prompted a renewed interest in the broader field of animation history. This revival is evident in the formation of a new scholarly association (Society for Animation Studies) and a scholarly journal (*Animation Journal*), the revival of animation magazines (*Animatrix*, *Animation Magazine*), and the publication of numerous new books in the field. Yet, three-dimensional forms of animation—particularly clay—remain largely ignored in film literature. The purpose of this study is to explore the technique of clay animation and its history in the United States. Against the backdrop of American film and television history, the book presents key films and key figures in the development of the medium, examines their technique, and offers a critical interpretation of the work. One theme of the book is that clay animation is an accessible, low-technology medium that, despite its wide range of potentials, has often been dismissed because it is less suited to division of labor than cel animation.

Accounts of the early history of clay animation are practically nonexistent. Information on early clay films is found primarily in trade magazines, early catalogs of film distributors, and newspaper reviews. The early clay films that still exist are archived in collections in various parts of the country, notably at the Motion Picture, Broadcasting, and Recorded Sound Division of the Library of Congress, at the UCLA Film and Television Archives, and in the International Museum of Photography at the George Eastman House. Primary information about contemporary clay animators was gathered through interviews. In all cases, a close reading of the films was used when prints were available. My method involved constructing a complete log for the films, noting the scope of the shot, camera angle, camera movement, action, and duration. I have tried throughout to accurately describe and analyze the works based on the key elements that are noted in these logs.

There is some confusion surrounding the term "clay animated film." The obvious problem is that clay films generally do not use "clay" at all—that is, wet clay, clay made from dirt, pottery clay—but oil-based modeling materials, usually plasticine. Frequently, it is impossible to tell what sort of material was used in making a film. So I am using the term "clay animation" to encompass any film made that animates nonhardening modeling material. "Clay" in this book usually means plasticine, or other nonhardening materials, but it can also refer in some contexts to wet clay. When this latter usage is required, I sometimes specify "pottery" or "wet" clay, though the usage should be clear from the context. In addition, the term "clay animated film" should be reserved for those films that, in the main, are produced using the technique. Many early works in clay are live-action films that incorporate clay animated segments; though they are clearly within the scope of this work, I have tried to identify them restrictively as "trick films" or as films "containing clay animation."

Another problematic area in this study is defining authorship of the films. In clay animation, there is a continuum of authorship, extending from artists who work alone to larger organizations that function more like Hollywood animation studios. Some clay animators—Helena Smith Dayton and Bruce Bickford, for instance—have controlled almost every aspect of their work. In the center of the continuum lie examples like the early "Gumby" series. It is clear that the driving creative force behind these works was Art Clokey, who created the character, even though Pete Kleinow and Ray Peck wrote and directed approximately one-third of the early episodes. The identities of the clay artists who produced the very early clay films and their roles in the production organization are simply unknown. In these cases, I have assumed that the production followed the general pattern of the period, the so-called cameraman system wherein a single cinematographer was ultimately responsible for the film but worked collaboratively with crew and clay artist to create the film. Thus, though Billy Bitzer was the cameraman on *The Sculptor's Nightmare* (1908), it is clear from the quality of the sculptures that he worked with a clay artist to animate the film. In contrast, it seems safe to attribute the crude clay animation in *Chew Chew Land* (1910) to James Stuart Blackton, an accomplished animator and trick film director. In the later "Gumby" series, and in later Claymation® films, screen credits suggest increasing specialization at those studios, and it follows that particular directors or animation directors may have exerted more control over specific works. Detailed filmographies can be useful in suggesting the person responsible for specific aspects of these works.

I have tried to be circumspect in attributing authorship to some of the films discussed. For example, I always credit Gardiner and Vinton for *Closed Mondays*. Though there is some debate over whose vision the film actually represents, I believe this is the correct attribution, since I have difficulty imagining what concrete evidence could definitively resolve the issue. Similarly, *Monsters of the Past* from the *Pathe Review* of 1928 contains clay animation but goes no further than attributing the *sculptures* to Virginia May. It is possible that (1) the insert title giving that attribution was a ruse, and/or (2) someone else animated the sculptures. But having shot and directed clay animated films myself, I know that sculptors are best equipped to manipulate their own constructions. It therefore seems highly likely that Virginia May was the animator for that film. Given the range of settings that gave birth to these films and the dearth of hard information about their production, we may never unequivocally establish authorship for many of these works.

This is the first historical survey of clay animation in the United States, and, regrettably, many films and figures of interest have been left out. Ashley Miller, Lew Cook, Joseph Sunn, Charlie Bowers, Douglass Crockwell, Elliot Noyes, Jimmy Picker, Art Pierson, Paul Boyington, and Tim Hittle are all significant contributors to the medium for one reason or another who await further research and analysis. I hope this book will stimulate others to research these and other neglected clay artists.

Acknowledgments

I want to acknowledge the contributions of many people who made this work possible. Dr. Frank Beaver, the series editor, has been a model, a mentor, and a friend to me for many years; our relationship is established on the unshakable foundation that we are both from North Carolina. Mark Zadrozny from Twayne Publishers shared his professional insight on many problems I encountered along the way. Dr. David Batcheller and Dr. Robert Hansen of the Department of Communication and Theater, as well as the Research Council of the University of North Carolina at Greensboro, have given me solid support and encouragement to write this book. Many colleagues generously shared their unique cache of information on film and animation history, especially Karl Cohen, Louise Beaudet of Cinématheque Québecoise, Paolo Cherchi-Usai of the George Eastman House, Eileen Bowser of the Museum of Modern Art, Rosemary Hanes and Madeline Matz of the Motion Picture, Broadcasting, and Recorded Sound Division of the Library of Congress, Cecile Starr, Jerry Fialka, Harvey Deneroff, Mark Langer, Maureen Furniss, Todd McMahon, and Glenn Myrent of La Cinématheque Française, Jerry Gulding at the UCLA Film and Television Archives, Jeanne Bennett-Schultz of the Will Vinton Productions Archive, and Jane Hockings of the British Film Institute. Barry Bruce, John Lemmon, Tim Hittle, Joan Gratz, and David Daniels told me everything they know about the current scene in clay animation. The reference department at Jackson Library answered innumerable questions of every kind for me, but the work of Kathy Crowe, Nancy Fogarty, and Mark "Some Guy Named Gumby Just Called Here for You" Schumacher deserve special thanks. Gaylor Callahan from the interlibrary loan office found everything I requested, no matter how obscure. At many junctures, graduate assistants did unenviable but essential tasks of every kind, and I particularly want to thank David Randall, Brett Ingram, Chris Ndingwan, Jay Bushman, and Janice Janostak for their help. My brother Dargan helped me with computer problems, my brother John did research for me in New York, and my sister Marianne proofed and rewrote many awkward passages. Finally, I want to thank my wife Martha, an accomplished sculptor and animator, for her invaluable insight on the clay aesthetic.

Chronology of Clay Animation in the United States

c. 1897 Plasticine invented. William Harbutt publishes *Harbutt's Plastic Method and the Use of Plasticine in the Arts of Writing, Drawing, and Modelling in Educational Work* (1897).

1902 *Fun in a Bakery Shop*, a film that uses clay for "lightning sculpting," released.

1908 *A Sculptor's Welsh Rarebit Nightmare*, an early trick film that uses animated clay sculpture, released in February. *The Sculptor's Nightmare*, a trick film shot by Billy Bitzer with animated clay sculpture, released in May.

1910 James Stuart Blackton produces *Chew Chew Land; or, The Adventures of Dollie and Jim*.

1916 *Universal Screen Magazine* releases Willie Hopkins's first clay animated segment, on 8 December. Hopkins goes on to produce at least 53 more "Miracles in Mud." *Scientific American* publishes an account on 16 December of the work of Helena Smith Dayton, the first-known woman clay animator.

1917 Educational Film Corporation of America releases Helena Smith Dayton's *Romeo and Juliet*.

1921 Clay animation appears in *Modeling*, an "Out of the Inkwell" production from the Fleischer Brothers Studio.

1923 Buster Keaton makes his entrance in *Three Ages* on the back of a clay animated dinosaur.

1928 Virginia May animates clay dinosaurs in a segment for the *Pathe Review*.

1931 Academy of Motion Picture Arts and Sciences awards first Oscar for "Best Cartoon."

1948 *No Credit*, an abstract clay film produced by Leonard Tregillus, Jack Chambers, and Ralph Luce, released.

1953 Art Clokey produces *Gumbasia*.

1956	Gumby episodes appear on "The Howdy Doody Show," beginning 16 June.
1957	"Gumby," a half-hour television show hosted by Scotty McKee, airs from 23 March until 16 November on NBC.
1966	Elliot Noyes produces *Clay: Origin of the Species* at the Carpenter Center, Harvard University.
1971	Bruce Bickford begins animating *Last Battle on Flat Earth.*
1974	*Closed Mondays*, a film by Bob Gardiner and Will Vinton, is released and wins the Academy Award for "Best Animated Short Film."
1976	Will Vinton adapts a Leo Tolstoy short story in *Martin the Cobbler.*
1978	*Jimmy the C*, a film by Jimmy Picker and Robert Grossman, spoofs President Carter. Will Vinton and Susan Shadburne's documentary *Claymation®* released.
1979	Frank Zappa releases *Baby Snakes*, a concert film with clay animation by Bruce Bickford. Tim Hittle begins animating his recurring character Jay Clay.
1981	Will Vinton obtains trademark on *Claymation®*.
1984	Jimmy Picker wins Academy Award for *Sundae in New York.*
1985	*The Adventures of Mark Twain* (Vinton), first clay animated feature film, released. David Daniels produces *Buzz Box* as a thesis project at California Institute of the Arts. Perfects "strata-cut" animation.
1986	Vinton studio produces the first California Raisins television commercial. "Penny Cartoons" (Aardman Animations) appear on "Pee Wee's Playhouse."
1987	Strata-cut segments by David Daniels—"The Declaration of Independence" and "Christopher Columbus" appear on "Pee Wee's Playhouse."
1989	"Michael Raisin," based on Michael Jackson, is produced by Vinton studio.
1990	Joan Gratz's clay painting appears in United Airlines ad, "Natural." Nick Park's *Creature Comforts* (Aardman Animations) wins the Academy Award for "Best Animated Short Film."
1991	Tim Hittle produces *The Potato Hunter* with Jay Clay.
1993	Joan Gratz's *Mona Lisa Descending a Staircase* wins the Academy Award for "Best Animated Short Film."

1

The Technique of Clay Animation

In 1908, Etienne Arnaud, interviewed in a French mass-circulation magazine called *Lectures Pour Tous*, described the clay animation segment of the trick film *La Statue*: "Take a statue modeled in clay. With successive touches of the thumb, deform it until it is only a mass and with each change, expose one frame."[1] This brief account was probably the first attempt to explain how clay animation is done. In 1978 Will Vinton made a documentary film explaining the process of clay animation, which he had refined. The title of that film was *Claymation®*, a word synthesized from the obvious roots that became Vinton's registered trademark. In the intervening 70 years, clay animation remained a relatively obscure technique, largely unseen by audiences and largely unexamined by film scholars, for it was only in the late 1980s that clay animation become a large-scale, mass-media phenomenon.

Where the clay technique has been treated in the mass media, it has—like all animation methods—suffered from an undue focus on process, a stultifying attention to the mechanics of how the films are made. Over the years, in countless newspaper and magazine articles, animators have played to the popular curiosity about how animation is produced, re-creating for each new generation of filmgoers a myth of the artist as Pygmalion: an ingenious creator who can breathe life into the inanimate using a kind of magical process that is extremely laborious and inaccessible to common people.[2] While enjoying their privileged status among filmmakers, animators have inadvertently shifted the focus from their work, trading real critical analysis of their films for short discussions of their techniques. Serious inquiry into the body of animated films has only scratched the surface, while the literature of animation is littered with "how-they-do-it" articles.

Although this chapter will deal with the clay technique, my aim is to move beyond the traditional accounts of process and breezy popular explanations of magazines and documentaries like *Claymation®* and to find a middle ground between description of technique and the aesthetic imposed by that technique. This approach aims to uncover how the process imposes and unlocks the clay aesthetic, to illuminate the inherent advantages and disadvantages in the medium, and to give some hint of the artistry required to make a successful film.

Clearly, clay shares many traits with other dimensional animation forms. Those traits that overlap and are more thoroughly dealt with elsewhere—particularly in Bruce Holman's excellent book *The History of Puppet Animation in the Cinema* (1975)[3]—will be only briefly examined here.

HOW CLAY IS ANIMATED: ADVANTAGES AND LIMITATIONS

Every technique of animation offers advantages and disadvantages and has its unique problems and solutions. Three examples will illustrate. In spite of the huge effort Walt Disney spent perfecting the multiplane camera, the problem of simulating a camera dollying into a scene remains inherent in the cel medium. Second, although the cel animator can very easily achieve the motion of a character jumping into the air by using a few drawings, the same action obviously presents serious technical problems for the animator using puppets or clay. And finally, when one uses the technique of drawing directly on film stock, the problem of registering one drawing precisely in the same spot over successive frames makes the static shot the most difficult to achieve, rather than the easiest shot, as it is with other animation methods. Animation of clay figures shares many of its most obvious advantages with other dimensional forms: the figures move in three-dimensional space, create their own perspective, and cast their own shadows.

Clay is animated with relative ease. A mass of clay is animated by filming one frame at a time and by changing either the position of the mass in the frame or its appearance relative to some previous frame. Both of these methods can be very simple. A mass of clay—in any shape—can simply be moved between exposures to animate it, just as other objects are pixilated. Since clay is a plastic medium, there are many ways to change its appearance: it can be rolled, flattened, twisted, carved, kneaded, folded, smeared, ad infinitum. Clay can be animated using simple geometric objects, as in *Gumbasia* (Clokey, 1953), or by using human or animal characters, as in *Closed Mondays* (Gardiner and Vinton, 1974). Clay may also be animated in relief under a conventional rostrum camera, as in *The Fable of He and She* (Noyes, 1974) and the "Penny Cartoon" series (Aardman Animations/ Broadcast Arts, 1986–90) from "Pee Wee's Playhouse." Clay vignettes can also be constructed and embedded by the so-called strata-cut method into "loaves," then cut away a layer at a time and filmed in stop motion, as in "The Declaration of Independence" (Daniels, 1987) and "Christopher Columbus" (Daniels, 1987) segments from "Pee Wee's Playhouse." Discussed later in this chapter, this technique is similar to the one pioneered by Oskar Fischinger in his sliced-wax films, *Wax Experiments* (1921–26).[4] In short, clay is adaptable to many different forms of incremental manipulation.

Yet, like other methods of animation, clay does have its limitations, notably, its inherent weight and the difficulty in achieving deeply saturated colors. The sheer weight of clay makes larger clay forms sag, sometimes imperceptibly, over successive frames during filming. When projected, such sagging is often clearly visible to the viewer. While the cel animator has at his or her disposal a complete range of richly saturated colors, those who work with plasticine must accept it for what it is, a low-saturation medium. Because of the density of plasticine, it can hold only so much pigment and its surface tends to soak up rather than reflect light, creating a rather limited range of saturated colors.

THE CLAY ANIMATION PROCESS

Preproduction

Recognizing that the medium offers possibilities and imposes constraints, the clay animator sets out to realize a vision. In the process, the animator brings that vision from an abstract notion (one that poses more questions than answers) to a well-developed script and storyboard, and ultimately into an object: a film of a fixed length, with a certain number of images, shots, and scenes. Examining the major stages in this evolution will clarify how the animator proceeds.

The standard breakdown of live-action filmmaking applies, with some notable differences. The preproduction (or planning) stage, involving as it does the primary work of conceptualization and organization of the means to make the film, is frequently more precise and detailed in animation than in live-action filmmaking. The production (or shooting) stage, in which the incremental visuals are recorded on film, is laborious but requires fewer creative decisions than live action and almost no retakes. The postproduction (or editing) stage, in which the scenes are cut together and the sound track is finalized, is much simpler in animation because the selection of shots is nonexistent or extremely limited compared to live action. Since postproduction of clay animated films is relatively straightforward, it will not be dealt with here; rather, our focus will be on the most creative stage—preproduction—and on some aspects of shooting clay animation.

Animation is unlike live action in two fundamental ways. First, changes are routinely made and new approaches experimented with during live-action shooting; by contrast, the animator generally follows a log sheet to film each frame according to an established plan. Cel animation is particularly inflexible at the shooting stage, since the artwork must be complete before filming begins. Other animation techniques that create the visuals before the camera—such as sand, clay, or puppets—allow occasional variation from the log sheet, but few artists have resorted to pure improvisation during production. Second, while scenes are routinely cut, refined, and recut during the postproduction stage of live-action films, the animator generally has little or no choice of shots and simply assembles the good takes.

Thus, in animation almost all of the creative decisions are made in the preproduction stage, and the remainder of the process is, in a sense, "donkey work" aimed at bringing those decisions to fruition, though it should be noted that in practice these steps often are not discrete or clear-cut. The design for sets, characters, and sound track may all be moving forward simultaneously and influencing each other at every step. A single change in character design, for instance, may have consequences in the set construction, the recording of the audio track, or the planning of a particular camera angle.

An anonymous writer employed by Disney in the heyday of studio animation has said, "Animation is where screen direction gets down to matters of detail unheard of in live action. In animation you deal with the glint in the eye, the twitch of an eyebrow, the tic of a muscle. You're dealing with microscopic fractions if you want to."[5] Generally, the goal of preproduction for a clay animated film, as with other forms of animation, is to *pre*-visualize the finished product—in all its minute details. Careful previsualization ensures that the action will be animated as precisely as possible and the film shot as efficiently as possible. The goal is to avoid reshoots and to guarantee that the laborious animation process produces footage that is included in the final film—in other words, to keep the shooting ratio as close to 1:1 as possible.

During preproduction, the designer-animator makes concrete decisions about the film's aesthestic. The overriding concern is to mold every production element—character, set, sound design—to support the film's thematic or aesthetic end. In mainstream clay films, the designer-animator must first reach an understanding of the script's overall intent through repeated readings and discussion with other members of the production team. To paraphrase Sergei Eisenstein, the designer is embedding within each shot "overtones" or secondary stimuli that support the film's thematic development.

At the preproduction stage, a central concern for the clay animator is how clay will be depicted within the film frame. Abstract work may admit some of the natural qualities of clay—its sculptability, its plasticness, its natural affinity for metamorphosis—and be unconcerned with refined surfaces, with avoiding fingerprints or stray scorings in the clay, with the need for armatures, or even with the need for figures at all. More traditional work must create and "costume" characters—often human characters—to meet the needs of a specific narrative. With either end in mind, during preproduction the designer-animator explores and refines the look and feel of the final film.

At this stage, the animator usually hopes to create the most complete image of how the final film will appear, often down to "the glint in the eye," before expending any effort on the actual animation. Depending on the nature of the piece, describing the action—whether in a simple story line or in a full-blown script—is clearly the first step. Traditionally, a storyboard follows: a series of drawings that portray key images, actions, or moments in the film, with some indication of how the sound track will interact with those images.

An innovation credited to Webb Smith at the Disney studio in the early 1930s,[6] the storyboard has become a standard tool—in television commercials, in feature films, and throughout the film and video industry—for visualizing filmed sequences on paper, and an indispensable one for animators faced with the task of creating a film one frame at a time. One advantage of three-dimensional forms of animation is that *drawn* storyboards are not always essential. Storyboards for clay animation, as with other three-dimensional forms, can be created using still photographs of rough characters posing in rough versions of the settings for the final film. Studying actual photographs of the characters placed in roughed-out settings, the animator gains a better sense of their look in the final film, as well as a concrete feel for the possibilities and problems the design will present during filming.

Character Design and Construction

One of the central problems to be faced in preproduction is the design and execution of clay characters that not only meet the needs of the script but can reasonably be animated. With the scenes in mind, the animator usually produces a series of sketches of the character, followed by "sketches" in clay, refining both the look and the technical needs of the design. Will the character require arms, eyes, and other human features? If arms are needed, will the character have them at all times or simply "grow" them when needed? Will the character need legs? Or will a simple gliding motion across the floor suffice? Designs that eliminate the need for bipedal locomotion are often advantageous: a character poised in midstride is often unstable, and the repeated movements of a walk cycle can cause cracking and stress. If the character must walk like a human, then designs with a low center of gravity—heavy legs and feet—may help balance it at key points in the walking cycle. And throughout traditional character animation, designs that reduce or eliminate sagging are preferred, though more fluid work, like that of Bruce Bickford (*Baby Snakes*, 1979), capitalizes on that characteristic of clay.

Will the eyes, the expressive locus of the face, have to move or change in size or shape to express certain ideas? Eyes for characters are often made from plastic or wooden beads, and a pin tool or small nail in the center hole allows them to be turned to look around. Smaller or larger beads can be used in the face over successive frames to create a hateful narrowing of the eyes or a look of wide-eyed surprise. Will a mustache make the filming of lip-sync dialogue simpler? In the "Celebrated Jumping Frog of Calaveras County" segment of *The Adventures of Mark Twain* (Vinton, 1985), the huge, exaggerated mustaches envisioned for the old miners led the character designer, Barry Bruce, to develop a series of mustaches that could be substituted in to approximate lip sync, an adaptation of the replacement method of animation popularized by George Pal's "Puppetoons" (Figure 1.1). Does the character need a hat to suggest a particular setting, or would a hat present insurmountable lighting problems during filming? The animator continually balances the concerns of design with those of production as he or she refines a character. Barry Bruce describes the initial steps of this process: "When we begin character work, one of the first stages we go through is a kind of sketch stage, where we do a lot of drawings, thinking about the characters, slowly trying to settle into a general framework of what we want the characters to look like."[7]

After the drawings are completed, the designer may produce another series of clay sketches of the character to resolve any problems that may emerge as the drawings are translated from a two-dimensional into a three-dimensional medium. For some prototypes and for final models, construction usually begins with some form of armature, a device that gives skeletal support to the figure. Armatures allow the figures to be moved incrementally and to hold positions during filming without sagging, all in a manner that mimics fluid, live-action movement. Flexible wire or aluminum foil wrapped or molded into the underlying structure of the figure is the most accessible and frequently used; these forms support the arms, legs, and joints that will be manipulated during filming. Both are limited, however, because they become brittle with use and frequently break through the surface of the clay as it becomes soft under the lights.

Puppet animators have worked for many years at perfecting sophisticated armatures that precisely mimic the skeletal movements of the human figure: hinged metal joints allow the replication of knee movement, while ball-and-socket joints of metal or nylon replicate movements of shoulders and hips. These armatures, many of them quite complex, are also now used in clay animation. They must be custom-machined and so are more likely to be used in high-budget productions. Will Vinton, for example, says, "We've gone through a lot of different armatures. We went from crummy wire armatures to sophisticated nylon-and-steel ball-and-socket armatures, back to very sophisticated wire armatures. What we use now is a plug-in type, of brass and lead" (Vetter, 78). Vinton's method, clearly one of the more sophisticated, is to use heavy lead wire for character parts that must bend and a system of set screws and brass connectors to lock those parts together, allowing the replacement of any piece of the armature that may be wearing out during a scene.

Figure 1.1 Character design by Barry Bruce for *The Adventures of Mark Twain* that minimizes the need to animate lip sync. Courtesy of Will Vinton Productions Archive. © Will Vinton Productions, Inc. All rights reserved. Claymation® is a registered trademark of Will Vinton Productions.

Waste clay—clay from previous scenes or previous productions—is often used to create the basic shape of the figure around the armature. Applying thinly rolled sheets of clay in different colors, the designer-animator next creates the "skin," or outer surface of the figure. The animator must decide whether to use his or her fingers in sculpting this outer layer, since the clay surface picks up fingerprints and gives a clue to the object's scale. Some animators, like Bickford, reveal the natural, "crude" surface quality of the material by poking, stretching, and tearing the clay with fingers and tools, occasionally relying on texture and perspective to distinguish objects more than color. Others in the Vinton school use sculpting tools to maintain a meticulously clean, smooth texture. Plasticine is by nature smooth, so the animator must often mix it with sand or other materials like crushed walnut shells to alter its puttylike consistency enough to mimic natural textures. Clay is often melted and mixed together, or mixed with oil paint, in specific ratios or "recipes" to create custom colors. In longer productions, these recipes maintain the color consistency of the various clays as characters are rebuilt, repaired, or replaced during filming.

Once a character is built, it must be costumed in much the same way live actors are outfitted. Articles of clothing are made from thin clay slabs or from nonclay materials with their own level of detail, such as cloth, human hair, or wire. Small plastic parts like sunglasses, hats, or shoes may be added. One of the advantages that clay animation shares with other three-dimensional animation forms is that it can capitalize on the level of detail inherent in these nonclay materials. If a piece of cloth or miniature clothing is used to costume Gumby, for example, the level of detail in that item is brought to each frame of the film with no extra work on the part of the animator. By contrast, the details of Popeye's sailor suit—its buttons, its wrinkles, its shoelaces—must be drawn and redrawn for every cel used in a Popeye film. Even early clay films, such those made by Helena Smith Dayton in 1916, used real doll clothes and human hair to add realism to their designs, and the original "Gumby" series (1956–57) made extensive use of nonclay materials in its set and character design.[8] This issue will be dealt with in more detail later.

Occasionally, the designer must create models of varying scale for the extreme long shots or extreme close-ups called for in the storyboard. Shot in the appropriate setting, small-scale characters—say, an inch high or less, and sparsely detailed—can suggest distance in extreme long shots. Conversely, large-scale characters are often more expressive in close-up. In *Closed Mondays*, for example, there are both small- and large-scale characters. In one shot, a miniature wino suggests the central character has moved inside a gallery painting, and later a life-size bust is used to lip-sync a crucial line, "Blabbermouth computer!" Here, the life-size human head facilitated very precise lip sync, though busts one-half life size or smaller are more common in Vinton's work. These special large-scale models are often shot against the same sets used for the ordinary characters. The designer-animator "cheats" the shot by clever camera placement within the set or by selective focus that renders the background in soft focus. Similarly, special models may be used whenever a full shot is not required. Looking at the storyboard for the first clay feature film, *The Adventures of Mark Twain*, animators at the Vinton studio noticed that "about 80% of all the shots were medium close-ups of the characters" (Vetter, 78). To avoid the problems of animating a human walk, models were constructed with traditional armatures from the waist up but with heavy metal bases, permitting the character a full range of upper body movements and the simulation of walks and turns within the appropriate camera framing.

Set Design

Clay films demonstrate an astonishingly wide range of settings: from the simplest backdrops of seamless paper in *Clay: Origin of the Species* (Noyes, 1966) to a complete Russian village in *Martin the Cobbler* (Vinton, 1976); from a real apartment kitchen in Bloomington, Indiana, in *Jay Clay Gets Depressed* (Hittle, 1980) to an underground worm burrow in the "Gumby" episode "As the Worm Turns" (Clokey, 1988).

Preproduction set design in clay animation involves many of the same steps as character design: working with the director, the designer previsualizes the set through sketches and prototypes. Clay set design also naturally shares many of the basic principles of theater and live-action set design. The basic goal of the set designer (who may also be the animator) is to translate the settings of the script into concrete designs that establish time, place, and mood, that sustain the action, and that reinforce the film's meaning. The set designer works with the production team through discussions of the script and through evolving sketches or models that detail more and more explicitly the technical requirements of each scene. The designer uncovers the script's technical requirements: number and placement of exits and entrances, space requirements for the number of clay characters within each scene, the animator's physical access to every item on the set that must be moved, and so forth.

The designer of sets for animated films must pay special attention to the peculiar needs of the medium and must anticipate certain problems—both technical and aesthetic—that will arise during production. First, the design must account for the placement of lights and cameras on the set. Given the task of lighting very small areas with small instruments—"lighting to scale"—the animator must use every possible means for controlling the light, including small "inky-dinkies," "barn doors," "snoots," and "flags" to carefully place the light and shadow areas on the set. In recent years, the overall illumination level required for filming has decreased owing to the use of faster film stocks and longer exposure times, which in animation are typically much longer than the standard 1/50 of a second produced by filming at sound speed. Lower illumination levels help keep the clay from sweating or turning mushy.

The need for backlighting to separate figures from the background, as well as the peculiarities of lighting to scale, must also be addressed by the designer. If the instruments suspended above the set and out of camera range cannot achieve the needed effect, the designer must make special accommodations to conceal instruments within the set.

Similarly, having to place the camera at or below the eye level of a miniature character presents continual problems that need the serious consideration of the set designer. When small-scale characters are shot from above their eye level, the camera angle tends to destroy the illusion that they are full-size and reveals them for what they are: clay characters sitting on a tabletop. Noting a similar effect in puppet animation, Holman says, "Shooting puppets from their own eye-level gives the audience a feeling of presence—from this point of view they are the same size as the puppets. Shooting from above, the normal viewpoint one would have when looking at miniature puppets, tends to make the audience conscious of the fact that the figures are indeed miniatures" (67).

Since most tripods are made to place the camera somewhere between knee and head height for the camera operator, it is common for dimensional animation sets to be built higher than the average tabletop level, ensuring—at least when the camera remains at the outer edge of the set—that the lens is placed low enough. Alternatively, a "high hat"—a tripod with short legs—placed atop apple boxes [a grip term for a small box or riser] can be used to bring the camera to the proper height if the set is placed on an ordinary tabletop. In general, the goal is to get the camera lens close to the action and placed virtually at the set's floor level.[9] Some set designers deal with the problem of camera-to-set height by making the set movable so that it can be placed on supports of varying height to accommodate the tripod height.

As scenes are broken out into shots, a new problem arises: the camera must be moved within the mise-en-scène, much as in live-action filmmaking. Typically, the camera must be moved from the edge of the set *onto* the set to get an over-the-shoulder or point-of-view shot.[10] The advantage for the designer of sets for both live-action and animation is that the problem of audience sight lines, which must be dealt with in theatrical productions, does not exist. But moving the camera onto a miniature set immediately presents other complications. Given that the distance from the base of the camera to the middle of the lens in most film cameras is several inches—the same height as most clay characters—even the shortest high hat or the simplest tripod head will automatically raise the camera above their eye level. If the animator forgoes both and simply mounts the base of the camera onto the set, the production of smooth, incremental camera movements becomes difficult, if not impossible.

The set designer may facilitate proper camera placements within the mise-en-scène by designing the set with removable floor segments, trapdoors, or removable walls, increasing the camera's range across the set. Moreover, because of film's ability to create its own geography, the audience need not be given a single view of the entire set. Thus, a designer could, if necessary, create the sense of any space through a series of discrete backdrops without ever constructing one unified set. Such creative geography is more often used by the set designer to film inserts. If the main set does not permit a closer placement of the camera, tighter shots can be "cheated" against discrete backdrops—simple plywood walls with similar colors, textures, and details—that suggest the larger space. Clearly, creating stand-in sets, no matter how little detail they re-create from the original, is an approach that requires a certain duplication of effort in both construction and lighting.

For high-budget productions, the development of periscopic, snorkel, or so-called probe lenses has facilitated a wider range of camera placements. Like periscopes, these lenses allow the camera a point of view displaced from the camera body's line of sight. While the smaller, more maneuverable lens can be extended onto the set, it can still funnel light to the bulky camera body, wherever it is mounted. In a typical arrangement, the camera body is actually suspended above the set on a boom, and the periscopic lens extended into difficult-to-reach areas of the set. When used in conjunction with motion control devices that facilitate a wide array of incremental camera movements, these lenses and mounts have substantially increased the camera's access to different types of shots from anywhere on the miniature set.

Another problem the set designer must anticipate is registration, or the maintenance of a rigid spatial relationship between camera, set, and set pieces. Given the difficulties in maneuvering the animator's hands and arms about on a miniature set, designs that minimize unwanted shifting between frames are crucial. Set pieces that are not rigid or firmly attached will almost inevitably sag or be jarred slightly out of position during animation. When projected, the unwanted movement is accentuated: set pieces appear to quickly droop or jump about. Typically, problems arise with material that is easily wrinkled, like taffeta, or ruffled, like carpeting with deep pile. In the final film, these kinds of materials may appear to be constantly twitching because they were moved inadvertently by the animator between frames. These registration problems can be avoided by meticulous preproduction planning, by "nailing down" every set piece that will not move during filming, and by using extreme care during animation.

Finally, the set designer faces problems in creating depth and detail in a small-scale set. On a set built to the scale 1" = 12", a 10-foot-square room is only 10" deep and may appear to be quite flat from the camera's point of view. Following the lead of set designers in theater and live-action films, the animation set designer will frequently force the perspective of the scene by building the set so that the distant lines converge somewhat and distant objects are reduced in size. Depth in sets with normal or forced perspective may be enhanced through the use of a wide-angle lens, which accentuates depth in the frame and allows the animator to play with the lower areas of the frame, stretching and accentuating the floor in the composition and thereby adding depth to the composition.

Likewise, articulation of the foreground has long been recognized in live-action filmmaking, and even in other forms of animation, as a sure method for adding a sense of depth to the frame. For example, Disney opens *The Old Mill* (1937) with a simulated dolly movement through some foreground vegetation, giving the audience a sense of "approaching" the unfolding scene—the multiplane effect.[11] Given the perspective inherent in three-dimensional sets, articulation of the foreground is easily achieved by, for example, simply shooting through foreground windows or doors, placing plants and other set pieces in the foreground, or moving the camera so that the difference in parallax between foreground and background is observed.

Establishing a certain level of detail in the set is a double-edged sword for the designer. The first decision to be made is whether to create a set from scratch or to use existing miniatures of furniture, appliances, toys, bicycles, automobiles, trees, shrubbery, telephone poles, fire hydrants, and so forth. Will Vinton's early work and Art Clokey's "Gumby" present the extremes of each approach: Vinton's approach, heavily reliant on clay or clay-covered objects in the set design, is purist; Clokey's films from the 1950s are littered with recognizable toys, imitation plastic plants, and store-bought miniatures (see Figs. 1.2 and 1.3). Although railroad hobby shops and doll house suppliers can save the effort involved in the construction of set pieces by providing a surprising range of miniatures, they tend to be identifiable as manufactured items, particularly if they are isolated elements within the mise-en-scène. Moreover, Vinton argues that the inclusion of nonclay materials may actually work to the film's *disadvantage*, causing the viewer to "decode" scale and construction methods within the mise-en-scène and to become aware of the animation process. Thus, the viewer is unable to suspend disbelief, to be drawn into the world created by the film.[12]

The purist aesthetic of Vinton's "full-clay" worlds notwithstanding, the success of clay shorts more often hinges on the quality of the narrative and the skill of the animator in breathing life into the figure, rather than on the cohesiveness of the mise-en-scène. And in some clay shorts, like Hittle's *The Potato Hunter* (1991), a disjointed mélange of materials within the mise-en-scène actually adds another layer of meaning. Hittle's set design—a flat landscape of cheap paneling sparsely littered with windup tin birds, vacuum cleaner attachments, doll heads, bones, poker chips, buttons, starfish, bricks, cow skulls, wooden spoons, and bent spray-paint cans—creates a surreal, postmodern landscape that comments on the central character's hunt for food. In this landscape, Jay Clay's tribal hunt of a herd of potatoes is at once humorous and mythic, a tongue-in-cheek, postapocalyptic battle of survival. Because the inclusion of nonclay materials becomes visually prominent in the mise-en-scène, it is often an early and fun-

Figure 1.2 Creating depth and detail in clay: *Martin the Cobbler*. Courtesy of Will Vinton Productions Archive.

Figure 1.3 Simple set from an early "Gumby" episode. Courtesy of Art Clokey.

damental aesthetic decision for the clay animator. If he or she decides on an overall style that includes nonclay items, the question becomes one of the proper mix of construction materials that will bring the design to life. Just as the designer of clay characters may include nonclay items for color and detail, materials such as fabrics, wallpaper, stucco, flooring materials, wood, and so forth, may be used to dress a set. Existing materials can be useful in establishing time, place, or mood. For example, a fine print calico material used for curtains or tablecloths suggests early, rural America, while a wall treatment of miniature stones creates a cold, austere atmosphere. Such materials supply a richness of colors, textures, and patterns, but like all elements of a miniature set, they must be well crafted, since slight imperfections are magnified many times by the camera. To that end, many designers have found that a variety of modeling materials sold by craft stores are very useful for the manufacture of miniature set pieces, props, and architectural details. These materials—sold under the brand name Sculpey—can easily be sculpted, "fired" in an ordinary oven into a hard material, and then cut, drilled, sanded, painted, and so forth. Because they are rigid after they are baked, these materials do not sag or droop like ordinary plasticine and are less prone to registration problems during production. Whether the designer chooses to construct needed items from clay, oven-fired modeling materials, or nonclay materials, the level of craftsmanship will be evident when the image is projected and enlarged a hundredfold in the final film.

Preproduction Sound

Like other forms of animation, clay films are ordinarily "presynched": the audio is recorded before the images are produced and the animation is "shot to the track." The images generated conform to the timing of the existing audio, which is mapped out with precision during preproduction. While there is no single presynching method, if the film contains dialogue much of the action will be keyed to that track because the voice track usually conveys the most specific information in the sound track and therefore is most often recorded first.

The voice track is then transferred to 16mm "mag," or magnetic film, which is sprocketed audiotape in the format of 16mm film. With the audio in this format, the animator can play it back and forth over a sound head so that the beginning and end "frame" for each word—or each syllable, if need be—can be marked directly onto the mag track. Because the mag has sprocket holes, the duration of any word is thereby determined in discrete units, *in frames*. Using the sync block—the standard editing device for creating synchronized tracks in live-action filmmaking—the animator can then count the track frame by frame and record the dialogue on a log sheet, a chart representing every frame of the scene. If the mag track for a given scene runs 10 feet, 13 frames (or 413 frames), the animator must generate 413 images to cover that scene. The log sheet allows the animator to know at the preproduction stage what is occurring at each frame of the voice track (or any other track that the action is being keyed to) and to use this precise knowledge to refine the script's description of the action. Typically, a completed log sheet indicates for each frame of sound what will be happening in the picture portion. At frame 80, for example, the log sheet may indicate: "Character begins to turn doorknob; start smile upwards." By following the log sheet, the animator creates action that corresponds to the track, producing a one-to-one correspondence between sound frames in the mag track and picture frames in the camera. This process will provide synchronization when the film is edited.

Presynching is the best way to achieve the incredibly precise synchronization between picture and sound that, for audiences, is one of the most entertaining aspects of animation. For the animator, presynching also helps solve one of the most difficult problems encountered during shooting: how to pace the action, or more precisely, how to determine the extent of each incremental movement. Once a voice or music track has been recorded and logged, it becomes a concrete determinant of when key actions must take place. The animator can then extrapolate where other actions must occur relative to those points. Using our example above, if "character begins to turn doorknob; start smile upwards" occurs at frame 80, the animator knows that the character must get to the door, come to a stop, and place his hand on the doorknob by frame 80. If the log sheet also indicates that "character sets cup on the table" at frame 30, then the animator can refine an increasingly precise description of the intervening 50 frames. Obviously, the character must rise and get to the door in 50 frames. Assuming he moves steadily, he must be up and halfway to the door in 25 frames. Therefore, he must be *halfway to that halfway point* in 12 frames, and so forth.

During the shooting of the scene in our example, the animator may find it impossible to get the character smoothly up and to the door in the allotted 50 frames. If so, a note is made on the log sheet and additional frames of sound equal to the number of frames the animator has varied from the log sheet will have to be inserted into the track to maintain synch. But ordinarily this problem is not encountered, and presynchronization, by dictating the key points of action and the spacing between these points, greatly reduces the ambiguity of pacing and incremental movement during shooting.

Sound effects in animation are used as a source of aesthetic energy or, as in live action, simply to complete the outer orientation—the spatial and temporal setting—established by the visuals.[13] Classic Hollywood studio cartoons contain the most obvious use of sound effects to establish the energy of a scene, and sound tracks for scenes that are entirely constructed from "boinks," "petangs," "pings," and "kerthuds" are not uncommon. Regardless of the production technique, when these sounds are the primary determinants of a scene's pacing, they are recorded prior to shooting and logged like a voice track; the animation is then shot to the effects track.

When used as outer orientation or "scene setting," however, sound effects are often added in postproduction, since they are rarely the primary determinant of a scene's pacing. If the animator is shooting to the voice track, particular actions in the picture that require an effect—such as doors closing, gunshots, telephones ringing, and so forth—are simply cut into the effects track at the appropriate frame.

Music for the film may be nonsynchronous, presynchronized, or postsynchronized. Nonsynchronous music has not been carefully timed to fit the picture. Typically, it is preexisting music that is selected and simply placed against the picture. Because music and film are both "time arts," it is inevitable that any selection will synchronize with the picture at random points, and even nonsynchronous music serves as a "bed" for the action throughout.

Music is presynchronized by transferring the music track to sprocketed mag tape and playing it in a sync block to find key passages in the track and/or the overall rhythm of the piece. When instrumentation stands out in the music—a trumpet blare, a cymbal crash, a trill in the wind section—such passages can be counted and logged in the same way that dialogue is, and action is then shot to punctuate that particular moment. If the action must synch to the beat, the mag tape is played back at sound speed in a sync block or similar device and a felt marker is placed next to the sound head and tapped in rhythm with the piece. The marks can then be counted and logged; they usually reveal a loose pattern: a beat every fourth, seventh, twelfth frame, and so forth. Action may then be shot to match that rhythm.

To postsynchronize music, the animator may simply accent the actions occurring every 4th, 7th, 12th frame, and so forth, thereby establishing a metronomic tempo in the picture that music can be written to fit.

Production

Like puppet animation and other three-dimensional animation forms, animating clay is slow and painstaking work, but no more so than other handicrafts like embroidery or lacemaking, crafts that require patience, fine motor skills, and concentration. From the beginning, the difficulty of clay animation has often been the focus of popular accounts, which invariably calculate the number of individual frames that must be generated, the number of individual characters that must be moved for each of those frames, and on and on until animating a short film seems to be an overwhelming, unending task. But as noted above, most of the creative work is done at the preproduction stage, and the shooting and editing of animated films is a straightforward process that has largely been determined ahead of time. The physical animation of a scene can best be described as semiskilled labor.

With storyboard and log sheet completed, set and characters built, lights hung and trimmed, camera loaded and mounted, the clay animator is ready to begin animating a scene. The process is long but not unpleasant, tedious but with easily quantifiable results. Susan Pitt offers a poetic description of the move-and-shoot process of constructing a world frame by frame, of creating filmic time one instant at a time, of building a chain of images that will come to life in the projector: "One's mind, one's creativity, takes the highway of frames constructing each view like a sped-up, slowed-down architecture, building a long dream of flashing windows for other eyes to see."[14] The real challenge for the clay animator is to visualize this "sped-up, slowed-down architecture," to move back and forth between the mental image of a movement in real time and that same motion in increments. Like other forms of animation, smooth, lifelike clay animation involves more than the deconstruction of a movement into equal parts; it requires a sense of pace, of where and when an action pauses, of how a movement is "squashed" and "stretched" and "faired." These last three concepts evolved in the 1930s in the work of traditional cel animators. In trying to mimic natural, smooth motion, cel animators discovered that many character positions have to be drawn with exaggerated elasticity—"squashed" and "stretched"—and that the incremental movements near the beginning and ending positions of an action need to be smaller—"faired"—to match the natural acceleration and deceleration of movements at these points.[15]

As the clay animator proceeds, he or she incorporates these principles intuitively into a running calculation of what actions the character has recently completed, where the character is now, what the log sheet indicates the upcoming action will be, and the number of frames allotted until the next crucial point of action. The clay animator is always working toward the next key bit of action, trying to make the action proceed in the proper time and space to hit that next action at the frame indicated. This aspect of shooting dimensional animation is fundamentally different from shooting cel animation. The action of a cel animation is already "fixed" at the shooting stage because altering an action would require backtracking to generate more drawings. Dimensional animation, on the other hand, is being created before the camera, and there are no preexisting "fixed" positions (Holman, 50). Although the dimensional animator has a log sheet, he or she can still make changes as the action unfolds on the set. Acting on a momentary insight, the animator may choose to vary from the log sheet and extend, exaggerate, hold, or shorten a particular movement, or even to improvise a bit of stage business. Depending on how far these actions vary from the log sheet, they may necessitate an adjustment in the sound track. If an animator "gets behind" the log sheet, he or she can make up the difference at some point down the line, adjusting the timing of a scene as it proceeds.

This flexibility, however, has its disadvantages. Unlike the cel animator, who may refer back to a previous sequence of drawings, in clay no reference exists for previous frames. In Holman's words, "[A]t the time of filming, the puppet's previous movements exist only in the animator's memory and as an invisible latent image on the film" (51). With the advent, however, of "video assist"—the use of video taps to render the image seen through the camera as a video signal—animators now have a method of referencing previous frames. At the Vinton studio, one low-tech application of this idea uses a grease pencil to mark previous character positions directly on a video monitor. But with the introduction of frame storage and digital video, it seems likely that dimensional animation will begin using video to recall previous character positions, for "pencil tests" (as is currently done in cel animation), and ultimately for animation directly to video without the use of film.

A SPECIAL TECHNIQUE IN CLAY ANIMATION: METAMORPHOSIS

The freedom to vary from the log sheet offers the clay animator a unique opportunity for spontaneity: the visually stunning technique known as metamorphosis. Metamorphosis (from the Greek for "change form") is the transformation of one thing into another. Eisenstein identifies a similar phenomenon called "plasmaticness," a "liberation of forms from the laws of logic and forever established stability," and describes some of its manifestations in art and literature from a surprising number of different cultures.[16] Metamorphosis is a technique that has been extensively explored in many animations, even in the earliest films. Emile Cohl, the great French animator, used metamorphoses in a number of his early drawn animations, including *Fantasmagorie* (1908) and *Le Retapeur de Cervelles* (1911). Metamorphosis provides a running sight gag throughout the "Popeye" series (Fleischer Brothers Studio, 1933–42) as the sailor's body parts routinely transform into jackhammers, wrenches, can openers, and so forth. Experimental animators have explored how metamorphosis functions in a range of animation media, notably, Oskar Fischinger with oil on plexiglass in *Motion Painting No. 1* (1947), Alexander Alexeieff and Clare Parker with the pinscreen in *Night on Bald Mountain* (1933), and Caroline Leaf with sand on plexiglass in *The Owl Who Married a Goose* (1974).

Some animation historians actually credit metamorphosis as a key source of the enduring power of experimental animation. "The gradual repression of surprise transformation in later commercial cartoons led to their aesthetic decadence, while its survival in independent nonobjective and non-linear animation has continually nourished their vitality and creative exploration. For example, in films as diverse as the interview *Confessions of a Stardreamer* (1978) and the musical *Bottom's Dream* (1983), John Canemaker's witty and inventive metamorphoses translate what would have been a banal linear illustration into a novel, magical experience."[17]

Suppose the clay animator knows that character A must "metamorphose" into form B over *x* number of frames. The animator usually begins by rotating the character over successive frames and deforming it just slightly, so that a second, more crudely sculpted stand-in character may be substituted in at an early stage, thereby preserving the original character (with only slight deformations) for later scenes. Often the substitute is placed into the sequence at a point when the character is facing away from the camera, making for a smoother transition between the crisply sculpted character and the rough-hewn stand-in. The viewer's eye will accept a significant change between the two because any mismatch in the character design is disguised by the rotation, by the simple match of overall shape and position, and by the rapidity with which the transformation happens at 24 frames per second. Once the substitute is in place, the transformation can begin in larger increments and the animator can work the substitute with a great degree of creative freedom toward the next desired form. Here, the animator can do whatever he or she wants with the clay, a freedom not present in animating lip sync or scenes of character movement. Describing one such metamorphosis sequence, Barry Bruce says, "When the baby changes into the sophisticate in *Claymation®*, where you go through a whole bunch of things in between, that's a whole lot of fun. Essentially, we just sat down. We didn't know what we were going to do. You just do whatever comes next. And it's great to get it back [from the lab]. You don't know what you're going to see. It's nice. I mean, it's much more satisfying [than animating other sequences]."[18] Perhaps the satisfaction derived from free experimentation is one reason metamorphoses recur in Vinton's work, and throughout the body of clay animated films.

When the animator has sketched out a series of key forms that will be identifiable during the transformation, the freedom described here is not so complete. In such sequences, the animator will work toward a particular form, then substitute in the previously completed form, hold or animate it for a period long enough to make it "read" well for the audience, then deform and substitute in another comparable form, continuing the transformation. However the animator proceeds, the overriding concern is to complete the transformation from character A to form B in the requisite number of frames. Outside of those parameters, the range of possible transformations is almost unlimited.

Because of its plasticity, clay is uniquely suited to animating metamorphoses. Unlike a walking sequence, in which the animated movement is easily referenced to a movement in the natural world, metamorphoses are open-ended transformations over successive frames and need not mimic natural movement. The plasticity of clay, the ease with which it can organically change forms, fits the demands of nonnaturalistic transmutations. The impact of seeing a three-dimensional object transform into another object is spellbinding. Metamorphosis has the same element of visual incongruity, of cognitive dissonance, that magic has: the destruction of the static form is in direct opposition to our experience of the natural world.[19]

In his book *The Metamorphoses of Shakespearean Comedy* (1985), William Carroll, discussing the transformation of stage characters, observes, "The proof of transformation is essentially perceptual. A transformation has occurred when something . . . recognizably changes its nature. It requires our ability to mark difference and similarity at once, to remember what was while we realize what is."[20] He later adds, "Metamorphosis is simultaneously both the transgression and the establishment of a boundary. It can be conceptualized only after it has ceased, when we can compare the memory of past and present" (5).

Clearly, metamorphosis in animation shares some of these characteristics. During a clay metamorphosis, viewers are unconsciously marking the similarity of the object from frame to frame as it progressively evolves, as well as the resulting difference, that is, they momentarily recognize other distinct forms during the transformation. While viewing a metamorphosis in the "sped-up, slowed-down architecture" of incremental movement, we see impromptu but recognizable changes in the nature of the object, the continual transgression and reestablishment of spatial boundaries. Metamorphoses are visually stimulating and occupy the mind in an active, extended perceptual game of discovery as the viewer engages the transforming object and finally understands the transmutation in the resulting object. When the transformation is complete (or momentarily completed at a given stage, a "pause" at a recognizable object), the full impact of the change is registered in the unconscious comparison of the present object and the memory of what it was.

CLAY ANIMATION AND THE NATURE OF THREE-DIMENSIONAL ANIMATION

In clay animation particularly, the visual impact of these metamorphic sequences is increased because they are not fluidly transforming *drawings*, as one would find in cel or drawn animation, but fluidly transforming *objects*. In clay metamorphoses, the audience sees a projected photographic image of a tangible object with one of its most fundamental characteristics--its static form—in flux. So clay metamorphoses (and at some level, any dimensionally animated action) benefit from the fundamental realism of cinema by being *an objective recording of raw, three-dimensional reality*. Three aspects of cinematic realism are described in this phrase:

1. Its objectivity: that is, it is mechanically recorded. On this point, the realist theorist André Bazin argues, "The objective nature of photography confers on it a quality of credibility absent from all other picture making. . . . We are forced to accept as real the object reproduced, actually *re*-presented, set before us, that is to say, in space and time."[21]
2. Its rawness: that is, the medium is "effaced" or "transparent"; the viewer is largely unaware of the intervening medium. The object represented by the image appears "real" to the audience, though Bazin argues that one does not see "reality" in films but something very close to it—the "tracing," the "fingerprint," the "asymptote" of reality.
3. Its three-dimensionality: more specifically, the space objects occupy and the space between objects that the clay film "set[s] before us."

Art Clokey, the creator of Gumby, also writes about this third aspect of three-dimensional animation (which he dubs "trimensional animation"):

> Trimensional Animation looks real because it is photography of *spatial reality*. Cartoon animation does not look real because it is photography of an *abstraction*. . . . You can see how abstract a cell [*sic*] drawing is if you compare it to a fine detailed painting by a Dutch Master. . . . In cartoons they are working with a strong handicap of ABSTRACTION; whereas with Trimensional Animation we do not have that basic handicap. Trimensional Animation satisfies our SPATIAL HUNGER without having to resort to tricks that don't really succeed, because our senses feel that the drawing is fake. In this sense Trimensional Animation is far more sensual in its appeal.[22]

Here, Clokey reiterates the notion that a photograph of real space looks more real to us than a photograph of a *drawing* of a "real space." Unlike cel films, which are created on a single plane, dimensional animation, like live-action film, is movement occurring in real space, albeit miniaturized space. So our "spatial hunger," our need to read depth into two-dimensional representations of reality (here, the projected film image), is better satisfied by a dimensional film than by a cel film. The audience for a dimensional film sees a two-dimensional representation (that is, a projected image) of three-dimensional objects (a puppet, a clay character). But when viewing a cel or drawn film, the audience ordinarily sees a two-dimensional representation of a two-dimensional representation (a drawing) of three-dimensional objects. The projected image of a dimensional film is thus only "once removed" from reality, whereas the projected image of a cel film is twice removed from reality. Being only once removed from reality is surely the source of dimensional animation's immediacy and presence.

Clokey notes a second fundamental difference here between drawn and dimensional animation. Most cel animation is an extreme abstraction from reality in that the drawings do not have anywhere near the detail one would find in, say, a photograph. This lack of detail has become more and more prevalent as production costs preclude the use of lavishly detailed background drawings and characters.[23] To paraphrase Art Clokey, there simply are not that many Dutch Masters in the cel animation business today, and so the inherent level of detail in cel does not usually approach the inherent level of detail in dimensional animation.

As we have noted, the detail in a cel film is ordinarily limited to whatever the artist labors to put into it, while dimensional animation's high level of detail is naturally derived from the materials used. Clay films often fall somewhere in between the two, since objects or characters made solely of clay do not ordinarily exhibit much surface detail. Yet even in simple clay films, such as Elliot Noyes's *The Fable of He and She*, the imprints of the animator's fingers are often clearly visible. As a plastic medium, clay readily accepts sculpted detail. Regardless of the level of detail established in a drawn animation, it will remain an abstraction from reality, unable to achieve the level of "transparency" that dimensional animation can. Drawings—whether line drawings or the most realistic paintings of the photorealist school—will always be twice removed from reality.

THREE OTHER SIGNIFICANT TECHNIQUES

Three other methods of clay animation have been less widely used but deserve mention here because they suggest new avenues of development for the medium: clay replacement animation, clay painting, and clay slicing. Clay replacement animation follows the method developed in the 1930s by George Pal, who used wooden puppets and a series of interchangeable body parts that were substituted in over successive frames to suggest movement. Instead of turning and carving the parts from wood as the Pal studio did, clay replacement merely sculpts a series of figures or body parts in clay to create the incremental visuals. As mentioned above, clay replacement has been used effectively in *The Adventures of Mark Twain*, in which a series of mustaches were changed over successive frames to suggest lip-sync dialogue. Clay replacement is also easily adapted to the squash-and-stretch methods of cel, as in John Lemmon's commercial work. Lemmon says, "We don't use [replacement animation] much for cycles, but we do use it for growing, shrinking, or squash and stretch, anything where you would have to move a lot of clay around on a single figure. Replacement animation is useful because it puts the planning at the fabrication stage, instead of leaving it to the production stage. With all of the things you have to deal with during shooting, using replacements gives you one less thing to think about, it frees you up to focus on other things."[24] Lemmon has capitalized on clay replacement to capture the "bouncy" feeling of classic cel animation.

Clay painting has been extensively explored by Joan Gratz, who began using the technique in 1968 and brought clay painting to the Vinton studio beginning with *The Little Prince* (Vinton, 1979). Clay painting is a two-dimensional technique that creates subtly changing colors and a unique fluid motion very different from animating cel or drawn figures. Gratz smears and blends plasticine with fingers and other tools on masonite while photographing the process on an easel (see Figure 1.4). She used the technique in *The Little Prince* for animating dramatic sky backgrounds (later composited with the foreground image) that melt and transform in waves of swirling, impressionistic colors, and in animating a special waltz sequence of the Little Prince and his rose. More recently, Gratz has applied the technique to a United Airlines commercial, "Natural" (1990), which shows a series of metamorphosing clay landscapes, waterscapes, and portraits of United employees, set to "Rhapsody in Blue." The technique demands the skills of a painter rather than those of a sculptor and can result in anything from boldly colored images to more subtle blends of interacting colors (see Figure 1.5). Gratz says, "The main advantage of clay painting is its fluid look. It has some affinities with other forms of animation that are done directly under the camera.

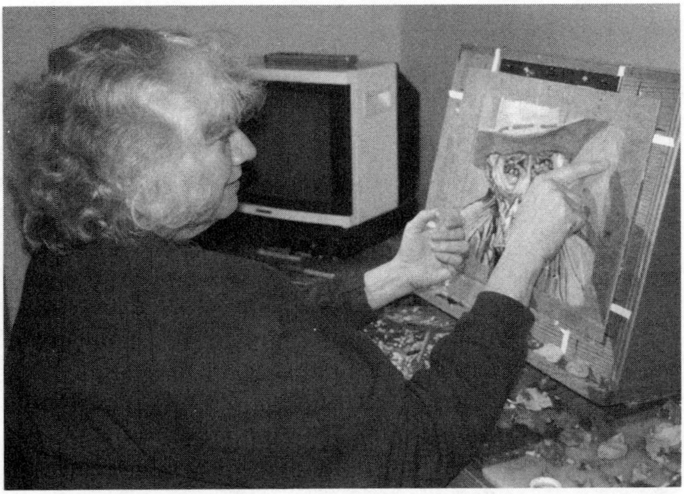

Figure 1.4 Joan Gratz animating her clay paintings. Photo courtesy of the author.

Clay painting can create complex color and give you the texture of brush strokes."[25] Gratz produced a seven-minute Academy Award–winning film entitled *Mona Lisa Descending a Staircase* (Pyramid, 1992) using the clay painting technique (see Figure 1.6). *Mona Lisa* metamorphosizes clay-painted versions of famous paintings to show how painting evolved over the centuries and uses the painterly quality of the technique "to communicate the emotional content of the works" (Gratz interview).

Finally, clay slicing has been used by David Daniels with great impact in segments from "Pee Wee's Playhouse" like "The Declaration of Independence" and "Christopher Columbus," in Peter Gabriel's video *Big Time* (1987), and in Daniels's short film *Buzz Box* (1986). Daniels calls his technique "strata-cut" and constructs long clay "loaves" with three-dimensional visuals embedded within them. Though this construction is laborious, at the production stage the loaf is simply cut into 1/8-inch slices with the camera following (tracking and following focus if shot upright on a set; lowering the camera and following focus if shot on a rostrum camera). Thus, strata-cut is an easy, mechanical process at the production stage. To hit key words or sounds in the track, Daniels simply marks the outside of the loaf

Figure 1.5 One of Joan Gratz's clay painted images from *Creation*. Courtesy of Will Vinton Productions Archive. © Will Vinton Productions, Inc. All rights reserved.

where those key images are embedded, noting where that cut must happen on the log sheet.

Strata-cut scenes have a remarkably fluid feeling, like an electrically vibrating, low-tech computer screen, a kind of flat metamorphosis in sliced rock that is melting down and moving away from the camera like a burning fuse. Daniels says that strata-cut "can fill the frame with continuous, seamless, changing images without the need for figuring out in-betweens. But simple images on the level of icons or logos or hieroglyphics work best because they can be easily read. The moving textures of a strata-cut image can be overpowering to a complex image."[26]

SUMMARY

For the clay animator, preproduction and production involve many of the same tasks of other animation techniques: the struggle with con-

Figure 1.6 Joan Gratz with clay painted images from *Mona Descending a Staircase*, winner of the 1993 Academy Award for "Best Animated Short Film." Photo courtesy of the author.

cept and design in the storyboarding stage, the feeling of slow accomplishment that comes with shooting. Clay presents some unique obstacles—oiliness and weight—but some unique advantages can be reaped from its plasticity and dimensionality. The key to success is determination and ingenuity, for the process is time-consuming but accessible, low-tech but visually striking, tactile and "funky," but fluid. The clay animation process is "really as much a problem-solving process as it is any kind of an art process," according to Barry Bruce. In 1979 Bruce argued, "This isn't a very high-tech field. . . . [W]henever we're doing camera moves and solving all sorts of problems, most of the time there are all sorts of funny pieces of plywood that we tack together that we find lying around on the floor. . . . A lot of our camera moves [crane shots] are pieces of clay being shoved under a piece of plywood with a door hinge on one end of it. It takes a bit more labor, but it works just fine" (Bruce workshop).

Though clay films (particularly from the Vinton studio) have gotten more high-tech in the last decade, the spirit of Rube Goldberg ingenuity and hands-on manipulation that Bruce describes here will likely remain basic to the clay animation process for many years to come. In a typical clay film, the designer's first task is to construct a three-dimensional space and figures that can be animated, remain workable throughout the life of the production, and fulfill the parameters outlined in the script. This basic construction aspect of clay animation will likely remain critical to the process no matter how many high-tech methods are used in the future.

Likewise, an ability to visualize movement in the "sped-up, slowed-down architecture" of animation is crucial to successful animation in clay (as in other media). The observation of movement in the world and the intuitive capacity to express it in a series of incremental poses, holds, accelerations, and decelerations involves more than simply deconstructing motion into smaller parts. The successful animator will continue to express his or her understanding of the character suggested by the script in a series of actions that involve anticipation, takes, holds, overlapping action, and exaggeration, a process that goes far beyond simply moving the character from one pose to the next. The artistry of the sculptor will continue to transcend the construction aspect of the medium, to push the figure into a visually expressive "dance of poses." It seems likely that this struggle between transcendent vision and nuts-and-bolts manipulation will continue to be central to the medium of clay animation, no matter where its evolution ultimately leads.

2

The Invention of Plasticine and Early Clay Films

Historians and critics of the animated cartoon look to the cartoon strip, the flip book, the Zoetrope strip, and the lightning sketch as the forerunners of cartoon animation. Sequential drawings are present in each, and it is not difficult to trace their individual contributions to the development of cartoons. Humorous narratives told sequentially in a mass medium, newspaper strip panels suggested the shots—if not the key drawings—of cartoon animation. John Canemaker has documented numerous examples of cinematic qualities in Winsor McCay's strips,[1] and Donald Crafton has shown how the magazine cartoons of Emile Cohl contain metamorphoses that could easily be translated to film (1990, 78). And though strip characters were not brought to the screen until relatively late—when Winsor McCay made *Little Nemo* in 1911—the comic strip ultimately became a source of popular stock characters and of artists to create the films. Flip books and zoetrope strips brought sequential drawings to life through the phi phenomenon—the optical impression of motion created when objectively stationary images are presented one after another at a sufficiently rapid rate. McCay has stated that it was the flip books of his son Robert that suggested to him the possibility of making animated films.[2] Lightning sketches were an important source of material for the earliest cartoons, and Crafton goes so far as to call them "the birthplace of the animated cartoon" (1984, 48).

The forerunners of clay animation are not so obvious, and several questions arise about its antecedents. The earliest examples of clay animation ask us to explore "the thicket of chronological, social, textual, artistic, psychological, ideological and technological tangles that make up the unexplored underbrush of modern culture" (Crafton 1990, xxi). Specifically, what narrative codes and iconography does early clay animation share with vaudeville, magic shows, cartoon animation, or live-action film from the same period? Did the invention of plasticine around 1900 immediately influence the development of clay animation? What was the state of sculpture in American culture at the turn of the century, and what impact did it have on the development of clay animation?

This chapter will examine the period from 1897 to 1910, a period when plasticine was evolving from a medium for teaching drawing and modeling in schools to a medium for lightning sketches and trick films. The great changes that occurred in the film industry make it difficult to discuss this period. This difficulty is compounded by the fact that very little is known about the artists who created trick films or the specific conditions under which they worked. Nevertheless, trick films do contain the seed of what the medium would ultimately become. This chapter will describe them in sequence and offer some explanations of how their technique and their narrative structure reflected the state of clay animated filmmaking at the time of their production. The aim is to clarify the progression of clay in this earliest period. A short account of the development of plasticine—the raw material of the medium—will lay the groundwork for a closer examination of specific films and filmmakers.

WILLIAM HARBUTT AND THE INVENTION OF PLASTICINE

In the 1890s in Bath, England, William Harbutt perfected a new soft modeling medium, plasticine (see Figure 2.1). It did not dry or harden like ordinary clay. Though plasticine and the Italian *plastillina* vary somewhat in formula, both suspend clay and pigment in a combination of wax and oil. Harbutt's primary innovation was creating a material that was softer and more pliable than its stiffer Italian predecessor. Plastillene is often so hard that it must be carved instead of worked with the hands. It is also very greasy, making it easier to use in mold-making, since it is less likely to stick to plaster. Because it was more pliable, plasticine would become over the next century the basic material for clay animation, a technique that requires the

Figure 2.1 Opening plate from *Harbutt's Plastic Method and the Use of Plasticine in the Arts of Writing, Drawing, and Modelling in Educational Work.*

material to be worked over an extended period of time, usually days or weeks.

Early packages of Harbutt's product made simple claims like, "Plasticine is something new, and hopes to make a friend of you."[3] Soon more ambitious uses were proposed. Harbutt published a book in 1897—*Harbutt's Plastic Method and the Use of Plasticine in the Arts of Writing, Drawing, and Modelling in Educational Work*—laying claim to many innovative uses in English schools. Clearly, Harbutt saw his innovation as twofold: a new material (however closely it resembled earlier nonhardening modeling materials), and new methods, that is, the variety of new uses he envisioned for plasticine that went beyond traditional modeling. The inventor promoted his development as a revolutionary educational tool that could be used in a variety of settings, an approach that recognized the ongoing reforms in nineteenth-century English education. More importantly, the text and photographs of Harbutt's book indirectly suggested how clay might be animated, a point to be examined later.

With 35 to 39 percent of the population under the age of 14 throughout the 1800s, education in Victorian England was driven by population pressure, "by rising expectations for literacy . . . [and a] strong demand for national culture."[4] Harbutt's practical guidebook is squarely in the tradition of Victorian educational reform, showing how the new material could replace ordinary clay in schools. His short text illustrates "a new departure in teaching, entitled the 'PLASTIC METHOD,' by which writing, drawing, and the graphic arts generally, as well as modelling, can be taught in a more expeditious, systematic, and effective manner than hitherto."[5] Admitting that replacing pen and paper with an incising tool and a plasticine tablet was revolutionary, Harbutt nonetheless argued that the occasional use of his material for writing exercises would be beneficial. And throughout, Harbutt's aim was not simply to replace one material with another—to replace *clay* modeling in the schools with *plasticine* modeling—but to institute a new, clear-cut course of study, using plasticine, that was based on broad educational objectives.

Touting the advantages of the medium at every turn, Harbutt describes the three central ones in detail in chapter 2:

> PLASTICINE is a specially prepared composition which possesses the permanent ductility and firmness of wax, and forms a perfect substitute for wet clay and the greasey Plastillinas [*sic*]. It has only been perfected after many experiments. The following are some of its advantages:
>
> 1. Its ductility is permanent, being unaffected by heat, dryness, damp, cold, or time; the longer it is used the greater its utility becomes. These qualities specially recommend it for use in hot climates.
> 2. Its plasticity is greatly superior to that of the best modelling clay, or wax; while it is tenacious in form, it is responsive to the touch.
> 3. It requires no damping or covering with wet cloths, which destroys the finer modelled parts and causes much loss of time. (2)

Though it is difficult to know precisely what the composition of Harbutt's material was, the longevity and popularity of plasticine as a children's toy testifies to the validity of some of his claims.

Not wanting to give students too much freedom with this new material, Harbutt devotes much of his text to describing the "Plastic Method," a highly structured program for using plasticine in the classroom. The basis for the system is a set of relief sculpting exercises presented in two forms: sets of photographs on cards (reproduced as plates in the book), which are given to the child for study and reproduction in the classroom, and one master set of casts of those sculpting exercises, which are kept by the school and inspected occasionally by the student "to strengthen the memory and afford freer scope for the abilities of all, even the most backward" (32). Each plate shows the progressive stages of the construction of a single exercise.

What is interesting about these plates is their sequential presentation of the lesson. Just as the sequential motion studies of the English-born

American photographer Eadweard James Muybridge and the French scientist Etienne-Jules Marey immediately suggested both the development of animation (via single-frame cinematography) and live-action filmmaking (via a continuously running camera), many of Harbutt's card studies are remarkably direct in suggesting techniques for animating clay. It is these lesson plates that carry a strong suggestion of how clay could be animated. One such lesson is given in plate 5, a "how-to" photograph that shows the construction of the basic plasticine "hand tablet"—a piece of cardboard covered with clay—which could be incised for relief drawings (see Figure 2.2). Though the photo is quite explicit, Harbutt adds his description of this process: "Take a pellet about the size of a garden pea, make a roll of it between the finger and thumb, and carry it by a firm pressure in a line as far as it will go; repeat these lines side by side until the card is covered, then smooth with the flat tool and a slight rub of the finger" (47). Latent in this description is a formula for animating a scene by transforming clay "peas" into a flat surface. The photograph foreshadows animation not only by making the process visually concrete

Figure 2.2 Construction of the basic plasticine "hand tablet." Plate 5 from *Harbutt's Plastic Method.*

but by suggesting that such a transformation can be captured photographically.

Similar examples are found throughout the lessons, particularly in plates 25 and 26, which not only depict the construction of a relief pattern when read left to right but display numbers incised into the clay to precisely identify the stages of construction for the final piece (see Figure 2.3). Plate 36 shows the transformation of a simple coil of clay into a snake-like pattern of some complexity (Figure 2.4), while plates 34a, 34b, and 34c show the progressive stages of the construction of a clay fish. Plate 39, which shows three stages of the construction of a flowerlike object, is particularly suggestive of the potential to animate plasticine (see Figure 2.5). In the photograph, two stages are labeled "a" and "b," and the final model of the flower is unlabeled. The photograph suggests a simple animation: we can imagine that the large sphere "rolls into frame" (at "a"), the shape itself suggesting a simple "ball" character (commonly found in later clay films) that frontally addresses the camera lens like a human face. At stage "b," smaller clay beads are surrounding the larger one and two adjacent spheres have been flattened and smeared into petal shapes. Their adjacency, coupled with the Western convention of reading left to right, indicates a counterclockwise movement, a reverse "ticking" like the hands of a clock: we can imagine the beads "popping on" to the flower's center

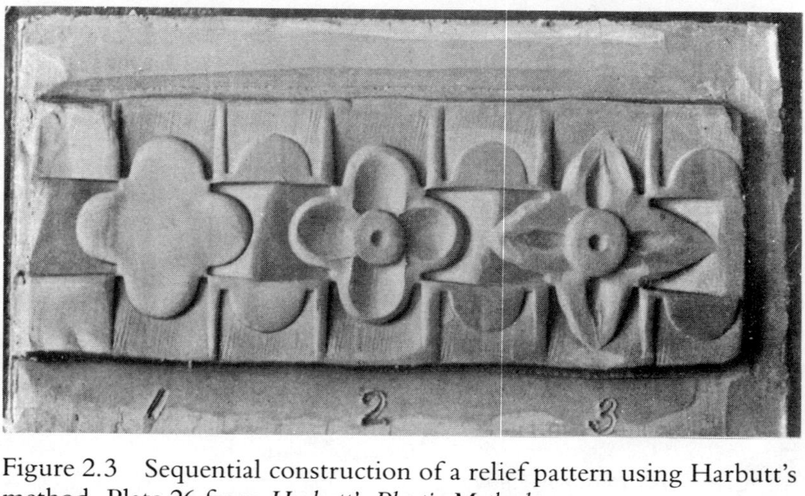

Figure 2.3 Sequential construction of a relief pattern using Harbutt's method. Plate 26 from *Harbutt's Plastic Method*.

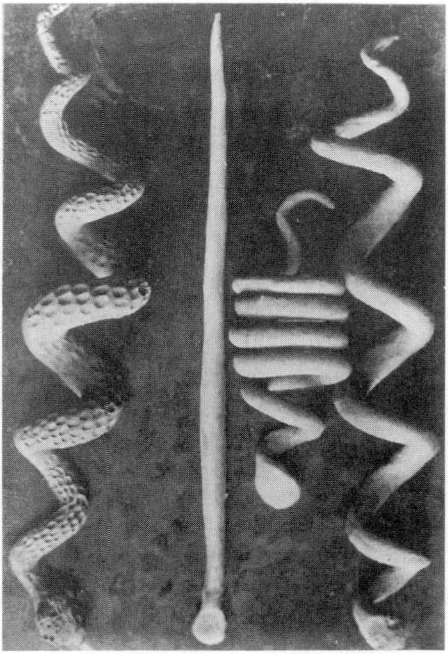

Figure 2.4 Transformation of a simple coil into a snake. Plate 36 from *Harbutt's Plastic Method*.

Figure 2.5 Harbutt's text suggests the stages of a simple clay "animation." Plate 39 from *Harbutt's Plastic Method*.

Figure 2.6 Plate 6 from *Harbutt's Plastic Method.*

and transforming into petals. The largest object in the photo shows the final transformation of beads, coils, and sphere into a flower, resolving and completing stage "b": here, perhaps a zoom or cut-in to the flower would punctuate the ending of our short "animation."

Harbutt's plates also call to mind specific animated films: their technique suggests the relief animation of "Penny Cartoons," and their presentation of animal phyla suggests the metamorphosis of Elliot Noyes's *Clay: Origin of the Species* (see Figures 2.6 and 2.7). An early animator, surveying the plates in Harbutt's book, would be looking at a catalog of relief animation techniques awaiting the sole addition of single-frame cinematography to create clay animation.

The impact of Harbutt's method on the development of clay animation (not to mention in the field of education) is nevertheless unclear. The invention of plasticine was obviously a necessary condition for the evolution of the medium, since plasticine was softer than *plastillina*. Thus plasticine could be worked in front of the camera with ease and offered a wider range of possible movements and alterations than *plastillina*, which often is so stiff that it must be carved. But there is nothing to suggest that it had an immediate effect on animation. The first known American clay animation was produced in 1908,

Figure 2.7 Plate 35 from *Harbutt's Plastic Method.*

eleven years after the publication of Harbutt's book. According to Denis Gifford's *British Animated Films, 1895–1985*, the first clay animation in Harbutt's own country was not produced until even later, when Walter R. Booth directed *Animated Putty* in 1911.[6] In the film, "a lump of putty shapes itself into an eagle's head, a bunch of roses, a windmill, a girl in a hat, a devil, and a boy" (Gifford, 17). The following year brought the production of two clay animated films, but there is no record of further clay animations in Britain until 1981. Apparently, there was no immediate movement of Harbutt's methods into filmmaking.

What follows is a description of four significant uses of clay in motion pictures from 1902 to 1910. After outlining the films and their historical period, I will evaluate their relation to the developing medium at the end of the chapter.

FUN IN A BAKERY SHOP: LIGHTNING SCULPTING

In January 1901, Edison Manufacturing Company completed work on a new studio at 41 East Twenty-first Street in New York. In the new glass-enclosed studio—which replaced Edison's original studio, the tar-papered Black Maria—the filmmakers George S. Fleming and Edwin S. Porter began exerting more creative control over their films, developing longer stories and wrestling with a system of representing spatial and temporal relationships. Edison Manufacturing Company was the key producer of films in the United States during the next three years, but the dismissal of the company's patent suit against

Biograph in March 1902 rendered key Edison patents on motion picture equipment invalid. The return of Biograph and others to production forced Edison immediately to take on even more ambitious projects. The result was a series of longer, more innovative story films, produced by Porter, that joined shots into sequences, including the ten-shot *Jack and the Beanstalk* (June 1902) and the nine-shot *Life of an American Fireman* (November 1902–January 1903).[7] Beginning in the spring of 1902, filmmaking at the Edison studio was in a period of transition as new narrative methods were being developed through trial and error.

Fun in a Bakery Shop was shot by Porter and registered for copyright on 3 April 1902, but it reflects the studio's earlier mode of production. Unlike Porter's longer films, which break the story into a series of shots, *Bakery Shop* is a single long shot, just over a minute in length, that shows a baker constructing a series of humorous faces using a very soft modeling material representing bread dough. Though it lacks any frame-by-frame manipulation of the dough, *Bakery Shop* is nonetheless an important precursor to true animation in clay. Like the filmed lightning sketches that foreshadowed the introduction of drawn animation—offering both a narrative context and an iconography for its development—*Bakery Shop* provides the parallel antecedents for early clay animation (see Figure 2.8).

As the film opens, a baker enters and begins kneading "bread dough" at a table, reaching in his pocket to sprinkle the dough with flour. The baker spies a rat climbing the side of a flour barrel across the room and flings a wad of dough at the vermin. The dough flattens the creature to the side of the barrel. Hurling more dough against the barrel, the baker begins to sculpt the mass into a series of faces, in a kind of three-dimensional lightning sketch. To facilitate the rapid transformation of the face, the camera is undercranked and contains several stop-action substitutions, a technique that had existed at least since Edison's *Mary, Queen of Scots* (1895), and that the French filmmaker Georges Méliès used extensively. The process involves stopping a film camera that is running in real time, making a change or substitution within its view, and then restarting the camera. In *Bakery Shop*, three stop-action substitutions are used to insert new faces into the lightning sculpting routine. An Edison motion picture catalog from 1906 remarks on the speed of the transformations: "It is marvelous to see how quickly a face is formed out of the pliable dough. . . . By one twist of the dough the . . . face is changed from a broad smile to an expression of disgust."[8]

Figure 2.8 Frame enlargement of "Lightning sculpting" in Edison's *Fun in a Bakery Shop*. Reproduced from the collections of the Library of Congress.

A second baker enters, laughs at the smirking sculpture, and is knocked out of the frame when the first baker throws a wad of dough in his face. The first baker returns to sculpting. In rapid succession, he transforms the face into a second series of faces. According to the catalog, these are "busts of different celebrities, such as Buffalo Bill, Admiral Scheley [*sic*], and others. . . . Finally he makes a very comical Irishman with a cocked hat, clay pipe and Donegal whiskers" (*Edison*, G–468).[9] Wiping his hands and stepping back to admire this last piece, the baker is joined by two coworkers—the catalog calls them "Irish bakers"—who laugh derisively at his handiwork. The film ends in slapstick as they promptly dump the baker headfirst into a barrel of flour.

Precedents for the lightning sculpting routine depicted in *Bakery Shop* are found in the stage performances around the turn of the century in which an artist lectured and sculpted clay. Lyman Howe, one of America's leading traveling film exhibitors before 1920, had two such artists—Arthur Lane and Jay P. Kern—in his employ during the 1899 and 1901 exhibition seasons.[10] While its narrative is slight and its physical humor gratuitous, *Bakery Shop* apparently transposes one such stage performance to a bakery.

The filmed performance shares similarities to, but exhibits key differences from lightning sketch films, a related genre popular around 1900. In both, there is a fascination with speed as the artist produces a series of images more rapidly than would be possible in a live performance. In both, the artist begins with a tabula rasa and produces a string of transforming images that often revolve around the human face. But *Bakery Shop* differs from the sketch films in that the lightning sculptor is presented within the narrative premise of the bakery shop. By contrast, lightning sketch films usually present the protagonist as an artist per se, that is, as a painter at his easel. Another difference is that the sketch films often use a closer shot of the easel and show the entire process of transforming drawings. *Bakery Shop* remains in a full shot, and the baker obscures his sculpture by turning his back to the audience and then occasionally revealing the work as it proceeds, in a presentational approach similar to that used by stage magicians and impersonators. Perhaps the most important difference is that, unlike later lightning sketch films that contain true animation—especially Vitagraph's *Humorous Phases of Funny Faces* (1906)—the sculptured faces in *Bakery Shop* neither come to life by themselves nor affirm their independence from the artist. Nevertheless, *Bakery Shop* was a significant precursor to early clay animation.

1908: CLAY ANIMATION EMERGES IN AMERICA

In 1908 two American films were released that contained clay animation: *A Sculptor's Welsh Rarebit Dream* (Edison, February 1908) and *The Sculptor's Nightmare* (Biograph, May 1908). Though the copyright for *Rarebit Dream* was registered as a paper print at the Library of Congress on 13 February 1908, no copy of the film is known to be extant.[11] But a synopsis of that film and a reconstruction of *Sculptor's Nightmare* from the Paper Print Collection makes it clear that the clay usage in both films is remarkably similar. Both establish the narrative premise of a sculptor who, under pressure to deliver commissioned works, falls asleep and dreams of clay that magically builds itself into finished busts. Both draw on the image of a work of art that comes to life, an image popularized by magic shows of the 1890s. Both are trick films that utilize clay to literally animate sculpture, a logical and very basic transformation of a traditionally fine art medium into moving pictures.

The Moving Picture World describes *Rarebit Dream* in its review of 22 February 1908 as a film in four scenes. The film opens in the sculptor's studio as he cooks Welsh rarebit. When the sculptor cannot pay the gas collector at his door demanding payment, the gas is turned off in his studio. Next, an army officer arrives demanding delivery of "three life size busts, which he had ordered some time previous."[12] Without light to work, the sculptor approaches one of his masterworks—"The Lady of the Marble"—in despair and falls asleep on a nearby couch. Then, "[a]rising from the couch, he takes one of his small busts and leaves" (*MPW* [22 February 1908]: 148), an action we later learn signals the start of his dream.

The scene shifts to an antique art store where the sculptor, unable to sell his work, manages to exchange it for an old oil lamp. Returning to his studio, the sculptor begins cleaning the lamp, "when in a cloud of smoke 'The Genii [*sic*] of the Lamp' appears ready to grant any wishes of the sculptor," a magical appearance that may have been achieved through stop-motion substitution accompanied by a flash pot. The genie grants the sculptor's wish for light, his wish to bring his beloved sculpture to life, and finally his wish to have the genie construct the three commissioned busts. "In amazement, [the sculptor] sees the clay slowly mould itself into shape—First Washington, then Lincoln, then Roosevelt, all complete—The genii [*sic*] disappears." When the sculptor begins to kiss "The Lady of the Marble," she overturns the lamp, bringing forth the genie once again, who forces her to return to her pedestal. The sculptor, disconsolate that his lady is once again inanimate, collapses on the floor. "The scene is changed and the sculptor falls off his couch and awakening, realizes it was all a dream—He vows never again to eat a 'Welsh Rabbit'" (*MPW* [22 February 1908]: 148). This closing vow is typical of dream films from 1906 to 1908; according to Russell Merritt, a "persistent undercurrent of ethical and social didacticism [is] implicit within the [dream] vision. . . . [O]verindulgence in food, tobacco, and (especially) alcohol lead to hallucinations so scary or bewildering that the dreamer swears off all further binges."[13]

A Sculptor's Welsh Rarebit Dream combines elements of the classic tale of Aladdin and his Magic Lamp with Winsor McCay's newspaper cartoon strip *Dream of a Rarebit Fiend.* The strip had premiered four years earlier in the *New York Evening Telegram* of 10 September 1904. A mere two years before *Rarebit Dream*, it had inspired the Porter trick film *The Dream of a Rarebit Fiend* (Edison, 1906). The running gag of the McCay strip appears in the last panel, where the dreamer invariably blames his vision from dreamland on the Welsh rarebit (an innocuous dish made from cheese, seasonings, cream, and ale served on toast), a device carried over in both film versions. The central clay image of *Rarebit Dream*—three masses of clay that mold themselves into busts of political leaders—prefigures its use ten weeks later in an American Mutoscope and Biograph Company production, *The Sculptor's Nightmare.*

Subtitled "Vortiginous Aberrations of a Modern Angelo" in the *Biograph Bulletin* of 6 May 1908 (Figure 2.9), *Sculptor's Nightmare* is a clumsy narrative about a group of men who argue over who should replace the Republican incumbent Teddy Roosevelt as the next president.[14] Mack Sennett and D. W. Griffith appeared in the film, with an unknown sculptor as the animator.[15] The film was shot by Billy Bitzer, later Griffith's cinematographer, who at this time was beginning to explore the potential of various camera tricks. Bitzer was the most likely cameraman at Biograph to take up animation since, like other early filmmaker-animators—Georges Méliès, David Devant, Walter Booth, and James Stuart Blackton—he had a longstanding interest in magic. It appears that in the spring of 1908, Bitzer's work at Biograph allowed him to explore the possibilities of trick films.[16]

Like many silent films from this period, the narrative in *Sculptor's Nightmare* remains slow and obscure after repeated viewings, so the

FORM NO. 1309 BULLETIN No. 136. May 6, 1908.

THE SCULPTOR'S NIGHTMARE

Vortiginous Aberrations of a Modern Angelo

LENGTH, 679 FEET. PRICE, 14 CENTS PER FOOT.

Most probable was the assumption of Shakespeare, "Imperial Cæsar, dead, and turned to clay, might stop a hole to keep the wind away;" but, with what scepticism would be received the assertion that a shapeless mass of clay could mould itself unaided into the living, classic features of President Roosevelt. Nevertheless, such is a fact, as shown in this Biograph subject, which is most timely, the nation at present being agog as to the coming presidential possibilities.

A convention is held at the club, with a view to selecting a worthy successor to the present incumbent, and each delegate is steadfastly determined upon his own choice of nominee. The clubroom is graced by a large bust of Roosevelt, and the idea is to replace it by the figure of the coming man. One member insists upon Hughes, another favors Taft, another Fairbanks, and so on, until the assembly is thrown into a tumult of dissension finally bolting, all of them, to have the bust made. Into the sculptor's atelier they burst, each giving the amazed chiseller, who is at the time at work on a statue of Terpsichore, an order for their choice of candidate, paying him in advance. On their departure the sculptor finds himself possessed of more money than he knows what to do with, so taking his model, who has in the melee hidden behind the screen, goes to a neighboring cafe to dine. Having an inordinate capacity for booze, he gets gloriously soused and winds up in the "cooler", whither he is dragged struggling by a couple of stalwart "Bobbies", and is thrown into a cell, where the iron bars prove a serious portcullis in the way of liberty. Throwing himself on the cot, he sleeps, while the wine-induced perturbations conjure most wierd hallucinations. Suddenly there appear three huge masses of clay which slowly, and with invisable aid, form themselves into busts, of Taft, Fairbanks, and Bryan. Then another mass appears and moulds itself into the G. O. P. Elephant, then an animated" Teddy Bear", and finally into a speaking figure of Theodore Roosevelt, whose features relax into a smiling delivery of "De-light-ed". Possibly it might have been this that aroused the sculptor, for he awakes and finds "his pipe is out." It was but a dream. The film as a whole is the most mystifying ever produced, besides one of the most amusing.

A FEATURE FILM

Now that the public is wrought up over the coming Presidential Campaign

THE SCULPTOR'S NIGHTMARE

Comes at a most opportune time, containing as it does, a wealth of comic incidents introducing the Presidential possiblities.

IT IS SURE TO PROVE THE HIT OF ANY MOVING PICTURE BILL

Figure 2.9 *Biograph Bulletin* for *The Sculptor's Nightmare*. Reproduced from the collections of the Library of Congress.

account that follows will draw on both the film and the *Biograph Bulletin*'s more detailed explication of the plot, noting some inconsistencies between the two. Shot 1 (see Appendix for a complete shot list) opens with the men seated around a table in a room with a large bust of Teddy Roosevelt in the background. They gesticulate and argue, indicating in broad gestures their disagreement. When they begin to hold up small signs labeled "Taft," "Hughes," "Fairbanks," and "Bryan" over the bust's face, it becomes apparent that they differ over who should be the next president. These names would have been well known to audiences of the day, because the election of 1908 was a hotly contested one. President Roosevelt had announced his intention not to seek reelection and had designated Secretary of War William Howard Taft as his choice for the GOP nomination. Republican Charles Evans Hughes, who later became chief justice of the Supreme Court, had recently been elected governor of New York and was being widely touted as a contender for the nomination, as was Charles Warren Fairbanks, the current vice president under Roosevelt.

The *Biograph Bulletin* describes this meeting as a "convention . . . held at [a] club," identifies the men as "delegates," and says, "[T]he idea is to replace [the bust] with a figure of the coming man" (Niver, 350). But the film's inclusion of a sign with the name "Bryan" (and later a bust of him) indicates that the scenario is certainly not meant to establish this group as a traditional party convention. The stunning oratory and adept political maneuvering of William Jennings Bryan, a lifelong Democrat, had won him his party's nomination in 1896, and again in 1900. *Sculptor's Nightmare* suggests a "convention" only in the loosest sense, for hanging on the walls are a number of signs: "Our motto: vote early and often," "We are approachable," "We never sell our votes below the market price." Clearly, this is a men's club of some sort, but the film's primary aim is to poke fun at smoky backroom political deal-making.

As the men argue, a ruckus ensues, the men tumble out of the room, and the film cuts to a sculptor's studio (shot 2), where they reenter pointing at their signs and handing the sculptor money. Though the viewer may be more than a little mystified as to their motives, the *Bulletin* explains the underlying narrative: "[T]he assembly is thrown into a tumult of dissension finally bolting, all of them, to have the bust made. Into the sculptor's atelier they burst, each giving the amazed chiseller, who is at the time at work on a statue of Terpsichore, an order for their choice of candidate, paying in advance" (Niver, 350). The scene is chaotic as the men mill about, knocking over the half-made statue and leering at the model who cowers behind a screen. When the screen is knocked down, she chases the men out, grabbing a bucket at the base of the statue and heaving water on them as they exit. Celebrating his newfound wealth, the sculptor and the model embrace and the scene ends with the sculptor miming an invitation to the model to go eat and drink.

The film shifts to a white-tablecloth restaurant (shot 3), where the sculptor's unruly behavior and drunkenness draw the ire of the surrounding patrons. Having swilled three glasses of wine, he orders a bottle and pours a glass for his model. Before she can take a drink, however, she is dragged from the restaurant by a matronly woman (her mother?). The film presents a traditional romantic view of the artist as bohemian—poor yet flamboyantly dressed, prone to strong drink, and operating outside society's behavioral norms. This disparaging view of the artist is emphasized by the indignant reaction of the other customers toward his drinking and boisterous behavior, as well as by the rescue of his model from the restaurant by the outraged older woman, an action that hints of illicit love. This attitude toward the sculptor is reinforced in the *Bulletin* by the use of the double entendre "chiseller," and ultimately by the next scene, in which he is thrown in jail.

As the drunken sculptor falls into a fitful sleep on his jail bed, three pedestals topped with crumpled masses of clay are inserted into the scene in very slow succession, using the stop-action substitution effect. "Popping" these pedestals into the sculptor's cell occupies 17 seconds in the film. Allowing for the fact that early silents were more slowly paced, and that early trick films may have been even more so in order to give their audiences a chance to grasp an apparently magical occurrence, 17 seconds seems remarkably long for this pop-in sequence, suggesting that Bitzer and the clay artist may have been inexperienced with pacing and timing stop-motion events.

Shot 6 cuts into a closer three-shot of the sculpture stands in the jail cell and contains the first animated sequence of *Sculptor's Nightmare*. With the camera framing rigidly fixed to suggest a single continuous shot, shot 6 actually uses a number of takes or "subshots," which appear in the film in the following order (the times given are approximate):

Take 1. After a one-second pause, a reverse take of one minute, 17 seconds, in which the deformed masses of clay appear to magically re-form into finely sculpted busts of Fairbanks, Taft, and Bryan.

Take 2. A 12-second live-action take in which smoke is blown out of Taft's mouth using a mechanical effect. This take is underexposed in the film, perhaps because Bitzer did not correct for the decreased exposure time that cranking the camera at live-action speed would produce.

Take 3. A five-second forward take in which the busts—not yet deformed—are animated. The three figures look around and blink while a wineglass and a cigar magically ascend to the lips of the Fairbanks bust and the Taft bust, respectively. This take contains an apparently inadvertent double exposure.

Describing the specific movements within a backwards take is difficult because the visual impression it gives is a kind of "reverse entropy/decay" and its presentation of events is precisely the reverse of the method of its construction. For obvious reasons, takes 2 and 3 above would have to be shot first, since, once the busts were deformed, they would have to be completely rebuilt to be animated as figures.

As the shot begins, the three clay masses begin to move, with larger clay blobs moving around the base and building up the shoulders and chest of the bust. Next, the large central armature that supports the weight of the head rises up and is covered with clay masses that begin to form into the rough outline of the head. The animator has embedded a number of throwaway "bits" in this building-up segment. A freely constructed swan and lion's head form on the bust of Fairbanks. A small swan "swims," and a monkey face appears on the bust of Taft. Abstract faces appear and disappear on the Bryan bust. Once the general outlines of the busts are formed, smaller clay balls and cylinders "climb up" the chests of the busts to take their places and form eyebrows, lips, and noses. The reverse action ends with the names of the busts appearing on signs below them (see Figure 2.10).

The impact of this take is considerable, even though it is slowly paced. The power of the non-naturalistic transmutations that it shares with traditional metamorphosis segments is increased by the reverse take, a technique that frees us from the constraints of time as we normally experience it. As in other metamorphoses, the destruction of the static, three-dimensional form is apparent, yet the visual impact of a disheveled mass of clay "rising up" into a detailed and coherent form belies one of the most fundamental motifs of human experience—decay and loss of energy.

In a reference to Taft's well-known love of cigars, shot 6 continues with a live-action take of his bust blowing smoke, an effect achieved with a tube and an assistant blowing smoke. This bit is diminished in impact by its underexposure and by the complete stasis of the facial features of all three busts, made all the more apparent by the remarkable forward take that follows it. In take 3 all three busts are animated in a variety of movements. Bryan blinks and "speaks" with broad mouth movements, Taft blinks and looks left and right. Meanwhile, a full wineglass pops onto the sculpture stand and ascends Fairbanks's chest to his lips. Fairbanks empties the glass. It magically descends, is filled, and ascends again. This take is remarkable for its attempt at full facial animation of three figures, with eyeball and lip movements, head turns, and blinks. Though short and containing mistakes typical of a novice animator—such as continuous and rapid movement that lacks appropriate pauses—the take is striking in the rich movements of its detailed figures.

Shot 7 returns to the wider framing of shot 5 as the sculptor awakens in his cell. He rises, stretches, and is surprised to find three busts present, with puffs of smoke coming from Taft's mouth. The sculptor, still unsteady from his bout with wine, removes the goblet from Fairbanks's lips as well as the cigar from Taft's lips. Lifting the goblet to his own lips, the sculptor strikes a pose with his other arm extended and holds that position. His motive for this action is unclear until, responding to offscreen direction, he completes a bit of stage business he had forgotten by pouring what appears to be a small pitcher of milk over the Fairbanks bust. Then he returns to his pose to facilitate the stop-action substitution effect: his goblet, cigar, and all three of the sculptures pop out of the shot. Surprised, the sculptor staggers to his bed and falls into a fitful sleep. A full 15 seconds later, a single deformed bust pops into the frame.

Shot 8 cuts in closer; the *Bulletin* describes its action: "Then another mass appears and moulds itself into the G.O.P. Elephant, then an animated 'Teddy Bear,' and finally into a speaking figure of Theodore Roosevelt [Figure 2.11], whose features relax into a smiling delivery of 'De-light-ed.' Possibly it might have been this that aroused the sculptor, for he awakens and finds 'his pipe is out.' It was but a dream" (Niver, 350). The *Bulletin*'s description is again an embellished version of what actually occurs in shot 8. It takes multiple viewings of the film to identify the figure that the *Bulletin* describes as the "G.O.P. Elephant": it is nothing more than a small, awkwardly formed trunk and eyes that faces downward throughout the brief time it appears in

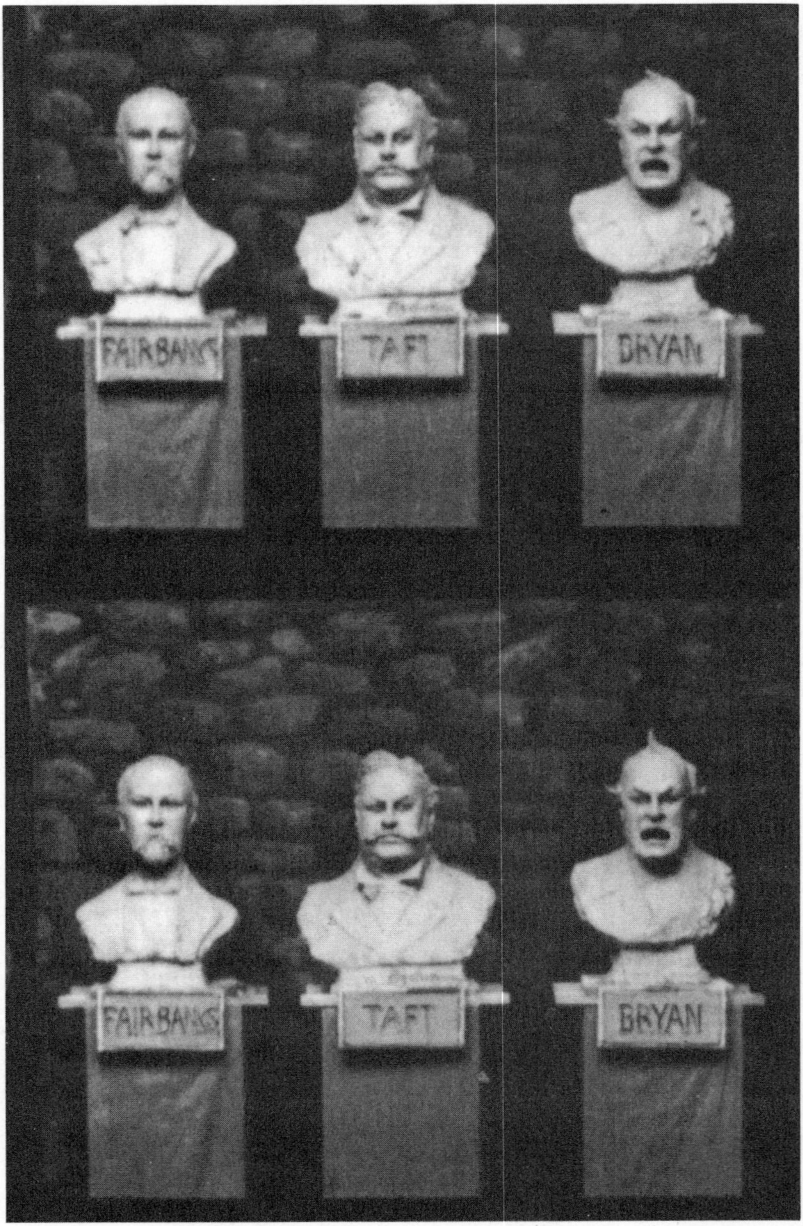

Figure 2.10 Frame enlargement of the busts of Charles Warren Fairbanks, William Howard Taft, and William Jennings Bryan in *The Sculptor's Nightmare*. Reproduced from the collections of the Library of Congress.

Figure 2.11 Frame enlargement of the "speaking" figure of Theodore Roosevelt in *The Sculptor's Nightmare*. Reproduced from the collections of the Library of Congress.

the transformation. In addition, though the figure of Roosevelt is a finely rendered caricature with energetic facial expression, its lip movements bear no clear resemblance to any phoneme but rather move in a continuous, nonspecific way. Though the closing pose of the Roosevelt bust carries a strong sense of his swaggering bluster, the supposed lip sync is expressively but unclearly rendered, no matter what the animator intended the figure to say. This lack of distinctive lip sync may be attributable to the fact that, outside of actors and actresses silently mouthing their words, the technique did not exist in 1908. Regardless, the *Bulletin* apparently takes the liberty of putting words in the figure's mouth in order to set up the play on words, "De-light-ed . . . his pipe is out."

In contrast to these weaker moments, the small teddy bear in this shot, sitting nonchalantly on the mass of clay and swinging his feet in an easy, relaxed movement, provides perhaps the most expressive characterization in the animated segment. There is also a nice throw-away bit earlier on in the segment as a face forms and a series of small clay balls roll into its mouth. The paper print version of the film ends uneventfully in shot 9 as the sculptor stands up, surprised by Roosevelt's bust, only to have it vanish as he goes to embrace it. He falls on the bed and returns to sleep, and the film ends.

Seven months after *The Sculptor's Nightmare* was released, the Motion Picture Patents Company was formed, and its producers assumed their mission was to improve and "uplift" the motion picture and its audience.[17] Thematically, *The Sculptor's Nightmare* anticipated that shift in some respects, if not in others. Its treatment of the drunken artist and the "rescue" of his model underscores traditional moral values, but its references to the current political election are less clearly uplifting. They touch on the issue of civic duty but also poke fun at vote buying. Perhaps the political references to both Democratic and Republican candidates in *Sculptor's Nightmare* were designed to maximize audience involvement with the picture. Doing so would have continued an earlier trend noted by Musser: "A number of Edison films [from 1896] were designed to elicit political reactions from theatrical audiences; the theater was then a site where partisan political opinions could be expressed through shouts of approval or disdain."[18]

The narrative of *Sculptor's Nightmare* is surely indicative of "a crisis in film narrative," which, Bowser says, "had presented itself by 1907–1908, when longer and more complex stories were being attempted with methods that often could not make them clear to the audience" (42). Bowser argues that the refinement of narrative techniques during this period was a natural response to three factors: the diversity of the viewers, who may not have recognized a supposedly classic tale or myth; the uplift movement's demand that films convey a lesson or moral; and the influx of new directors with theatrical backgrounds (54). Recognizing that by 1907 the story film was the key to attracting new audiences to movie houses, producers began to come to grips with new cinematic means to articulate and clarify their narratives. The primary technique they developed over the next few years was editing.

Sculptor's Nightmare, in which the actors were reduced to holding up signs and gesturing at Roosevelt's bust to convey the idea, "I want candidate 'X' to be the next president," demonstrates how sorely needed such methods were. Moreover, as the actors bolt from the club room to the sculptor's studio, there is little motivation suggested for their departure, and even less for their arrival in an atelier. A series of explanatory shots or an intertitle could have clarified their actions to the audience. But lacking either, the cut from club room to studio cannot begin to coherently propel the narrative into the new scene. Once in the artist's studio, the actors are again reduced to pointing to signs--while simultaneously handing money to the sculptor. After brief consultations with the sculptor, the actors wander around like a troupe of slapstick buffoons who seem more interested in leering at the model than striking a deal with the sculptor, who (inexplicably) does not seem baffled for a moment by the whole affair.

More significantly, *Sculptor's Nightmare* lacks even the necessary cinematic language to adequately express a dream state. The *Bulletin* asserts that the artist's "wine-induced perturbations conjure most weird hallucinations" (Niver, 350), but the film language of the day lacks the shot sequence or the cinematic markers to specifically identify the transforming busts as the sculptor's dream. Instead, the film relies on the fitful sleep of the sculptor, the proximity of the busts to him, and their magical appearance—they pop in—to carry the notion that they are his dream visions. (The fact that the "visions" do not immediately disappear as he wakes tends to confuse this reading.) *Sculptor's Nightmare* may simply be another example of "both the difficulties we often experience in deciphering the films of this remote period, and of the 'externality of the narrative instance,' which, as is so often the case, is better articulated in the catalogues than it is on the screen."[19]

Though its convoluted narrative places the film in the mainstream of films from the period, its distributor saw it as out of the ordinary. This was an unusual trick film that could ride the wave of interest in the coming election. The *Bulletin* opens its account with a rambling sentence that explicitly features the clay animation as the central trick in the film and quotes Shakespeare in an unusual rhetorical strategy: "Most probable was the assumption of Shakespeare, 'Imperial Caesar, dead, and turned to clay, might stop a hole to keep the wind away'; but, with what skepticism would be received the assertion that a shapeless mass of clay could mould itself unaided into the living, classic features of President Roosevelt. Nevertheless, such is a fact, as shown in this Biograph subject, which is most timely, the nation at present being agog as to the coming presidential possibilities" (Niver, 350). Here the author hints at animation's apparently magical ability to defy natural law, to transcend the inevitability of death and decay that reduced even Imperial Caesar to wall daub. In this context, the reference to "the living, classic features of President Roosevelt" positions the film's sculpture in the grand humanist tradition: a half-realistic, half-idealized bust that transforms low matter into high art, a timeless rendering of a popular American leader that elevates the film beyond its slapstick narrative. The *Bulletin* closes with the assertion, "The film as a whole is the most mystifying ever produced, besides one of the most amusing" (Niver, 350). As Kemp Niver notes, "AM&B [the American Mutoscope and Biograph Company] was so impressed with the sales potential of their film that their usual manner of informing the trade of the availability of a new picture did not seem elaborate enough. So, for what was probably the only time in their history, they added a flyer, printed in red ink, to the bottom of their standard bulletin, calling it a 'feature film' " (Niver, 350).

According to Bowser, the early usage of the term "feature" meant simply a special film, one "that could be featured in advertising as something out of the ordinary run," and only after 1909 did that usage give way to mean any multireel film (191). For Biograph, that special quality apparently was not so much the animated trickery of *Sculptor's Nightmare* as its topical nature. The flyer closes with this thought: "Now that the public is wrought up over the coming Presidential Campaign THE SCULPTOR'S NIGHTMARE comes at a most opportune time, containing as it does, a wealth of comic incidents introducing the presidential possibilities" (Niver, 350).

The topic of *Sculptor's Nightmare* was current, but the central icon of a statue that comes to life was an enduring image from vaudeville, which popularized the *tableau vivant* or "living sculpture." A tableau vivant was an arrangement of human figures that usually re-created classic works of art. George Odell points out that at least as early as

1837 tableaux vivant consisted of "a number of reproductions of ancient sculpture and paintings, usually by men of athletic mould, who figured in the circus, or between play and farce at the minor theatres."[20] Famous sculptures like the massive, muscular *Farnese Hercules* were frequently used as source material for these exhibitions, though the 1847–48 season saw the production of a number of tableaux that used large numbers of nude women, creating a sensation and a number of arrests (Odell, 5:380). Groups such as the "Living Statues from Cork" were still performing on the vaudeville stage in the late 1860s (Odell, 8:355).

By the 1890s magicians were producing elaborate stage illusions that incorporated the notion of transformation as well as more dramatic context into tableaux vivant. These tricks became the basis for many early films. One such trick, entitled *The Artist's Dream*, was first performed by David Devant on Christmas Day 1893 at Egyptian Hall in London. The "Romance Mystique" involved an artist who, lamenting the death of his lover, takes a potion and passes out. While he sleeps, an angel of mercy transforms the lover's portrait on a nearby easel into a living woman. She speaks tenderly to him and bids him to join her in heaven. But he awakes to find her returned to her place in the painting, and the curtain closes on him standing despondent before the painting.[21] Devant's idea caught on, and "[t]rick films were soon bringing all kinds of portraits to life" (Barnouw, 92).

As early as 1899, a *Biograph Bulletin* described a film in which a poster girl comes to life and kicks a man's hat off the top of his head (Niver, 62). At least two early films incorporated Devant's idea directly into their titles: a Biograph version of *The Artist's Dream* shot around 1899, and an Edison version of 1900 in which Mephisto brings paintings to life. In 1901 Edison produced *The Artist's Dilemma*, in which a sleeping artist is approached by a young woman who emerges from a grandfather clock and asks him to paint her portrait.[22] In *A Statue on a Spree* (Pathe, 1908), a real man rescues his sculptor friend from the anger of the city fathers—who have commissioned a sculpture of a prominent citizen—by standing in for the statue at the dedication ceremony. Later, the sculptor slips some bread and wine to his friend, who becomes intoxicated. As the "statue" staggers through town, the citizens become frightened (*MPW* [7 March 1908], 193). Over the next ten years the protagonist and the premise changed somewhat as American filmmakers produced works with titles like *The Tired Tailor's Dream* (Biograph, 1907), *Marble Heart, or, The Sculptor's Dream* (Vitagraph, 1909); then John Randolph Bray returned to the original title in his version of *The Artist's Dream* in 1913. Meanwhile, working at the Gaumont studio in France, the Spaniard Segundo de Chomon produced *Sculptuer moderne* in 1906 using clay for tiny tableaux vivant that come to life (Crafton 1984, 25). Méliès reused the idea so frequently in films like *A Mysterious Portrait* (1899), *A Spiritualistic Photographer* (1903), and *Living Playing Cards* (1905) that Paul Hammond contends, "Méliès had his favourite, protean images: participants in a game whose driving force is the denial of expectancy and the exploitation of the dynamic instant between the anxiety of dislocation and its release in the ensuing humorous or dreamlike image. The statue that comes to life is such an elected image."[23] There is no evidence that Bitzer or the Biograph staff saw these earlier French films, but taken together, all of these films dealing with a work of art magically endowed with life suggest the lasting attraction that image holds.

Extending this notion, the sculpture that comes to life in *The Sculptor's Nightmare* begins with the dislocating effect of masses of clay that resolve into busts, and then proceeds to thwart our expectations by smoking and literally coming to life, blinking, drinking wine from a goblet, and "speaking." The later appearance of an animated teddy bear that transforms into a highly realistic bust of Roosevelt resolves the dislocation through the humor of the visual pun associating the two. Crafton finds the myth of Pygmalion and Galatea, in which the sculptor-king falls in love with his creation and successfully prays to the gods to bring it to life, retold in "'drawings that come to life'. . . the great theme of all animation" (1979, 414). *The Sculptor's Nightmare* shares the enduring power of that myth while situating its sculpture-come-to-life within a wine-induced dream. The dream here is a framing device [shared] with numerous "dream films" from 1906 to 1908; it both "free[d] filmmakers from the constraints of orthodox storytelling strategies by authorizing the kind of logic that could exploit the mysterious effects of trick photography . . . [and] represented an attempt to ground the film's action and special effects in a subjective point of view" (Merritt, 69).

JAMES STUART BLACKTON AND *CHEW CHEW LAND; OR, THE ADVENTURES OF DOLLIE AND JIM*

James Stuart Blackton is the most significant early developer of animation in the United States, and his contribution to the development of clay animation only recently came to light when his last film containing animation, *Chew Chew Land; or, The Adventures of Dollie and Jim* (Vitagraph, 1910), was screened at the Pordenone Festival in 1987 (Crafton 1990, 328 n. 68). Born in England in 1875 and raised in America, James Stuart Blackton worked when he was a young man as a stringer sketching for the *New York Evening World* and hustled evening jobs performing a number of popular entertainments, including lightning sketching. Sent by the newspaper to the Edison studio in 1896, Blackton was filmed performing his lightning sketch routine in the Black Maria, an encounter that turned his interest toward moving pictures. After cofounding Vitagraph Company with Albert E. Smith, Blackton went on to make one of the earliest truly animated films, *Humorous Phases of Funny Faces*, again based on his lightning sketch routine.

In 1907 Blackton animated *The Haunted Hotel*, one of the most successful early trick films using stop-motion objects. The film showed furniture moving about unassisted and even a knife cutting a loaf of bread by itself. *Haunted Hotel* had an enormous impact in London and Paris, stimulating Emile Cohl and others at Gaumont to investigate the technique and spurring the growth of animation overseas (Crafton 1990, 132). In 1910 Blackton made one of his last films containing animation, *Chew Chew Land.*

The film opens in a schoolroom (see Appendix 2 for a complete shot list): the teacher is absent, and a boy at the blackboard has decided to play a trick on her by placing a piece of chewing gum in her chair. Meanwhile, Jim takes out a pack of gum and shares a stick with his schoolmate Dollie. The teacher returns, sits on the gum, and angrily quizzes several students, trying to uncover the guilty party. Finding Dollie sitting at her desk chewing gum, the teacher assumes she is the culprit. In shot 2, the innocent Jim valiantly stands up to take the blame for her. Jim is kept after school for his gallantry, but he finds Dollie waiting for him at the school door with a bouquet of flowers (shot 5). He walks his new sweetheart home and tries to steal a kiss before returning to his own home.

The Moving Picture World describes the next scene: "Jim, our little hero, tired out by the duties and play of the day, is getting ready for bed. Placing Dolly's [*sic*] bouquet in a glass on a table, sticking his chewing gum on the bedpost, he gets under the covers and goes to sleep" (10 September 1910, 591).[24] The film cuts to a title card that reads, "Jim's dream of Chew Chew land," and then to Jim, in shot 9, sleeping in his bed. "During his slumbers 'Wriggles,' a mischievous imp" (ibid.),[25] enters and beckons Jim to jump out the window with him. A nice match cut shows the imp bounding through the opening and landing on the ground below (shot 10). The sprite conjures Dollie from thin air and again beckons Jim to jump. In the reverse angle shot of Jim at the window, the film reveals for the first time that the window is on the second floor. As Jim climbs out, the film cuts, in another well-executed match cut, to him landing beside the imp (shot 12). Wriggles leads the pair to a garden, where he magically makes a plant recede underground and promptly jumps in to follow it. After the imp lures the children into the hole, the film cuts to a large painted set of an underground cave, and the imp leads them forward into the large cavern (shot 14). Standing before another painted backdrop of the mouth of the cave, Wriggles begins to conjure a magical vision. Shot 16 cuts to an animated take of a plant magically growing as stalks reach upward and leaves unfurl in a backwards take.

Wriggles then conjures a second vision that is achieved in shot 18 by animating what appears to be traditional pottery clay. Grog—prefired, pulverized clay that is used to give strength to the clay body of pottery—is visible in the surface, and the clay actually dries later in the shot. The shot opens with three sticks of gum moving in and out in a kind of magical square dance. A ball of clay rolls into the frame, and one of the sticks of gum is drawn into the ball, which gradually begins to grow. Clay is added until the mound fills the left side of the frame, and then the clay begins to form a hollow-eyed human face. The clay is swept away and smoothed until the eyes, nose, and mouth of a living human head are revealed underneath—a man has inserted his head through a hole in the table at some point in the process. The shot is extended as various balls and wads of clay are animated up and down the man's face and around his neck. The shot ends in live action as the mud-caked eyes and lips open, and the man "stretches" his face muscles, trying to free his visage from the dried clay that remains adhered to it (see Figure 2.12). In shot 19, Jim and Dollie chew gum, laughing and pointing at the man. The dream sequence ends with two flashes of lightning scratched on the film that propel the story back to Jim's bedroom, where he wakes from a fitful sleep and looks around the room, astonished. *The Moving Picture World* describes the film's close: "His mother comes into his room and Jim tells her all about his dream while she is helping him dress, and together they are enjoying all the wonders of 'Chew-Chew Land' [*sic*] as they have been revealed to Jim" (10 September 1910, 591).[26]

Figure 2.12 The "decapitated" head in James Stuart Blackton's *Chew Chew Land*. Courtesy of British Film Institute Stills, Posters, and Designs.

Blackton's clay animation here is done simply as an effect for introducing the live, gum-covered head. The forms are crude, clearly not the work of a trained sculptor and nowhere near the sophistication and polished detail of *The Sculptor's Nightmare*. The movements of the clay masses are ad-libbed, unimaginative, and unexpressive. Yet, this primitive special effect provides a memorable moment. The revelation of the disembodied head embedded in the clay creates the same dislocating effect that earlier stage magicians capitalized on with the decapitation trick, in which a severed head unexpectedly opens its eyes and begins to speak. The pleasure of the macabre image of decapitation is that it both attracts and repels, both suggests death and defies death by coming to life.

The movement of traditional stage decapitation tricks—common in the routines of magicians like Carl Hertz and Harry Kellar—into trick films significantly enlarged the scope of these stage routines via stop-motion substitution. Decapitation tricks were widespread in early American and European films, including Devant's *The Maniac Barber* (1899) and four films made by Méliès between 1898 and 1905 (Barnouw, 94, 96). Stage and film decapitation were probably well known to Blackton. Before his career in film, Blackton had performed with Ronald Reader, a self-described "prestidigitateur," and with Albert Smith, his Vitagraph cofounder, who specialized in mechanical magic tricks.

In *Chew Chew Land*, the dislocation caused by clay "coming to life" is heightened by the fact that it happens so fast—the mound becomes a recognizable face in three seconds—and is so unexpected—no context is established by a sculpted bust or a magic performance. However, in spite of its visual impact, the narrative function of the crude bust remains obscure. The face simply sits and simpers after it is revealed, and the animated clay here seems to be an effect in search of narrative motivation. *Chew Chew Land* shows that Blackton was open to the use of new techniques in trick films, but his choice of clay was probably based on the simple need to provide a dream image loosely associated with the gum sticks that open the sequence. It is precisely this use of an effect for its own sake, this "effects-driven" quality of his early films, that Blackton expressed dissatisfaction with when he later stated, "I have outgrown my joy in lens magic as a thing by itself."[27]

Blackton directed films much less frequently after 1910, but he maintained control of Vitagraph productions through close supervision of projects, from scripting to editing conferences with his directors. He left Vitagraph in 1917 to work independently as a producer in England, where he hoped to produce more stylish films based on literature. Though his English films included experiments with color and innovative lighting, they were not particularly successful, and he returned to Vitagraph in 1923. He stayed for two years until the company was taken over by Warner Brothers, for whom he then produced four independent features. Blackton did not direct films after 1926 but was involved in a number of projects to produce educational shorts and documentaries in the 1930s, including his early archaeology of cinema, *The Film Parade*, a feature that had short runs in New York and Los Angeles. He died in Los Angeles on 13 August 1941, two days after being struck by a car. Though his contributions to the development of motion pictures have yet to be systematically discussed, his death marked the passing of one of the most influential pioneers in filmmaking.[28]

CLAY ANIMATION BEFORE 1910

This chapter has surveyed five key developments in clay animation prior to 1910: Harbutt's invention of plasticine, the lightning sculpting film *Fun in a Bakery Shop*, the emergence of clay animation in two 1908 releases, *A Sculptor's Welsh Rarebit Dream* and *The Sculptor's Nightmare*, and Blackton's *Chew Chew Land* from 1910. Looking at these four early works, the nucleus of the emerging medium is identifiable, but the influence of the antecedent "underbrush of modern culture" was more dominant in shaping these works. Put another way, the progression of these works from 1902 through 1910 suggests that the medium was being used largely as "animated sculpture" and as an extension of existing entertainments within live-action films.

All four films use clay to create realistic forms, though often for dislocating effects. Undefined mounds of clay are used as a starting point from which three-dimensional, life-size, or larger busts or human heads form over time. While the traditional mode of sculpting a bust is followed in all four—smaller clay masses are added and built up to form the larger bust—this process is situated within a dream in *Rarebit Dream*, *Sculptor's Nightmare*, and *Chew Chew Land*. This narrative structure is reinforced by animation techniques. Backwards takes and stop-motion substitution lend a magical, off-kilter flavor as the clay becomes autokinetic.

In *Bakery Shop* and *Sculptor's Nightmare*—and presumably in the traditional portraits found in *Rarebit Dream*—these undefined mounds of clay resolve into realistic, detailed sculptures with finely finished surfaces. The bust in *Chew Chew Land* is more crudely realized. Nevertheless, this penchant for the realistic bust is not surprising since, at the turn of the century, it was a popular domestic sculpture. The bust was used extensively as portraiture for famous historical figures, authors, composers, and artists. Unlike painting, which can easily be exhibited on household walls, the bust remains one of the few forms of sculpture small enough to display on the home tabletop or mantelpiece without the need for a specialized area for display. At the turn of the century, the bust remained central to the realism that still dominated American sculpture. The medium was enjoying a new wave of popularity, invigorated particularly by the epic works of Auguste Rodin.[29] For the sculptor-turned-animator at this time, "Rodinism" may have suggested a new and expressive sense of fluidity and movement, but the impact of the reigning humanist tradition was probably stronger.[30] This tradition prescribed a conventional iconography of busts as the basic premise for clay animated films, from *Fun in a Bakery Shop* to *Modeling* (Fleischer Brothers Studio, 1921). Busts litter the earliest clay animated films, including *The Sculptor's Nightmare*, Willie Hopkins's *Swat the Fly* (Universal, 1917), and facial sculptures are found in *Fun in a Bakery Shop* and *Chew Chew Land*.

But the more immediate stimulus for the animation of clay is not to be found in sculpture but in a number of popular entertainments from the turn of the century. One of clay's earliest uses seems to have been to extend these existing entertainments into live-action films. Like many of the earliest drawn animations, *Fun in a Bakery Shop* is a film that looks backwards to the lightning sketch and to the earliest recording of stage performances in the Black Maria. Similarly, *Rarebit Dream* and *Sculptor's Nightmare* draw on the tableaux vivant and David Devant's stage illusion *The Artist's Dream* for their central image: the bust that comes to life. In *Sculptor's Nightmare*, the bust is treated traditionally, mounted on a stand and shot head-on in a medium shot, a framing that continues, as we shall see, in *Swat the Fly*.

In *Chew Chew Land*, the framing of the human face is lower and closer, a placement that emphasizes the "cut" that the tabletop makes across the figure's neck and calls to mind the earlier magic performances in which decapitated heads come to life. In this and other early clay films, animation is used as an effect embedded in a live-action "narrative," a mélange of slight, disjointed premises that lead to the presentation of various tricks. And though these trick films are by filmmakers trained in stage magic, they center on the dislocating effects created by animated sculpture, effects that are resolved when the protagonist awakes from his dream. These dislocations seem central to both the live action and animation of *Rarebit Dream* and the clay animation of *Sculptor's Nightmare* and *Chew Chew Land*. Like the novice filmmaker who seems to be invariably drawn to the "dream sequence" as the place to not only explore cinema's magical, surreal qualities but to also reassert the primacy of the "real," waking world, early dream films using clay seem the perfect vehicle to explore the notion of a human creation that comes to life, to present a magical spectacle within a comprehensible frame of reference. That modern films like *Closed Mondays*, *Rip Van Winkle*, and *The Potato Hunter* continue to explore this idea testifies to its enduring appeal.

3

Clay Animators in the Early Days of Cel: Willie Hopkins and Helena Smith Dayton

By 1916 cel animation was well on its way to becoming not only an industry but the dominant mode for producing animated films, and new production companies using the cel method were being organized. In cel animation, only the part of the scene that needs to move (usually part or all of the foreground character) is drawn on transparent cel overlays, sandwiched with other elements drawn on cels, and laid over a background drawing. Animating only the moving parts of a scene reduced the amount of labor needed to produce drawn animation.

Of central importance to the new industry were the developments taking place in a company organized by John Randolph Bray and Earl Hurd. Cel animation—a combination of processes patented by the Bray-Hurd Process Company in 1915—was profoundly affected early on by economic factors. Since the cel process could easily be broken into many specialized tasks, animated films could be produced through the development of assembly-line methods to meet the weekly demand for theatrical shorts. Ancillary techniques made cel animation even more efficient. Max Fleischer's rotoscope, a device patented in 1915, made it possible to trace live-action film frames directly onto paper or cels, thus eliminating the need for the animator to conceptualize certain movements. When Fleischer came to work for Bray in 1916, this device gave the company yet another specialized industrial process that could be used to efficiently produce animated films, particularly the training films that the army demanded in increasing numbers when the United States entered World War I in 1917. Also, Raoul Barré's introduction of a peg bar system to hold the layers of cels standardized a method for registering the elements against each other and the background drawing. The rise of the cel animation industry was very rapid: "In a very short time span, from 1913 through 1915, an entire technology developed, flourished, and became standard" (Crafton 1984, 162).

Just as cel animation was becoming an organized industry, clay animation was making something of a comeback: it apparently had not appeared in a film since the 1910 release of *Chew Chew Land*. Producers of cel were so obsessed with bottom-line economics that "[a]ny available shortcut would be taken. . . . While the Bray-Hurd process made possible [the] rapid expansion of production, it severely diluted the quality of the work."[1] Dick Huemer, an animator who started out with Raoul Barré in 1916, recalled that rudimentary scripting, the failure to consider the needs of the audience and establish a context for gags, as well as the failure to analyze motion for a character's movement, led to a general audience aversion to cartoons during this period.[2] The reappearance of three-dimensional techniques, including clay, may have been, in part, a reaction to the poor quality of the new cel animation. Willis O'Brien produced several dinosaur comedies using puppets that were distributed by Edison's Conquest Film Program beginning in May 1917 (*MPW* [12 May 1917]: 978). Chicago's Howard Moss made *The Dream Dolls* (Essanay, 1917), a five-reel animated feature using dolls made of wood and wax.[3] Likewise, in 1917 and 1918, clay animation was more in evidence when Willie Hopkins made a long series of segments for *Universal Screen Magazine*, a weekly reel of topical features, and Helena Smith Dayton made clay animated films that were distributed by Educational Film Corporation of America and featured in an article in *Scientific American*. Though the exact nature of their work is largely unknown, the sheer volume of material Hopkins did for *Universal Screen Magazine* clearly makes him the most significant early clay animator, while the *Scientific American* article places Dayton among the earliest known women animators.

WILLIE HOPKINS AND *UNIVERSAL SCREEN MAGAZINE*

Willie Hopkins produced a series of topical sketches in clay called "Miracles in Mud" for *Universal Screen Magazine*, which began to supplement the three-year-old *Universal Animated Weekly*, a live-action newsreel, in November 1916 (see Figure 3.1). In announcing the new series, *The Moving Picture World* said that the *Universal Screen Magazine* "will treat of new inventions, microscopic and astronomical photography, phases of sociological and civic betterment work and in general of subjects which cannot be strictly classified as 'news' for the [Universal] Animated Weekly. In other words, the Universal Screen Magazine will be a supplement to the Animated Weekly just as the Sunday Magazine section of the daily newspaper supplements and elaborates upon the news of the day" (25 November 1916, 1175).

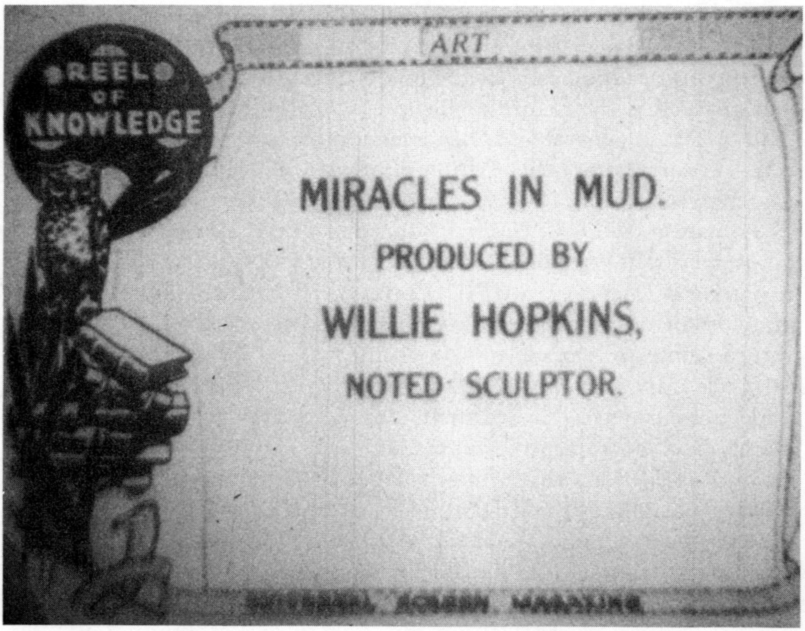

Figure 3.1 Opening title card from Willie Hopkin's *Swat the Fly*. Frame enlargement courtesy of the author.

The Moving Picture World indicates that the first piece made by Hopkins to be included in the series came in the second *Universal Screen Magazine*, released 8 December 1916 (9 December 1916, 1544). Over the next 18 months, Hopkins is known to have produced 52 more segments for the series, covering a wide range of current topics and features. Crafton locates Hopkins's films in a trend that emerged in short films during World War I: the topical caricaturist. In his view, these artists bridged the gap between the emerging series films without protagonists (such as Pathe's "The Boob Weekly") and the continuity series with protagonists—the modern cartoon series that extends from "Ko-Ko," "Felix," and "Betty Boop" to "Looney Tunes," "The Flintstones," and "The Simpsons." When caricaturists such as Henry "Hy" Mayer made the switch from humor magazines to cinema, their personal appearance in weekly shorts served a transitional function. "Slowly, [animation] producers began to make films that reinforced audiences' desires to see the same hero in several films, as in the 'regular' cinema. The topical caricaturists, though not as numerous in the United States as in England, might be regarded as transitional forerunners in that they promoted themselves as 'stars' of continuity series" (Crafton 1984, 266).

In essence, Hopkins began doing in clay what Mayer had been doing for the *Animated Weekly* since 1913. (One of the few Hopkins films known to exist, *Swat the Fly*, is a sketch in this vein, presenting its humor in clay rather than drawings.) Their recurrent work seems to fall somewhere between filming newspaper cartoons as they are drawn and animating simple bits that revolve around narrative situations. Released within newsreels, the humor of these animated sketches was usually topical. The great slaughter taking place in Europe in 1916 and 1917 provided a great deal of controversy for these artists to explore.

Hopkins worked for the *Universal Screen Magazine* from December 1916 until at least May 1918 (after which *The Moving Picture World* no longer reviewed the series in detail). The titles for his films are varied and suggest a number of possible treatments in clay: "What Will Baby Be?" "The Darwin Theory Upset," "Faces U Face," "Mud Pies," "Sad but True," "Nature's Camouflage," "Souls and Soles," and "Barnyard Faces." In his third bit for the series—in issue number 6, released 2 February 1917—Hopkins produced what might have been a long metamorphosis segment: "We see the Evolution of Eve in clay, from the celebrated lady of the Garden of Eden, to the present siren of the beach" (*MPW* [3 February 1917], 740). Other blurbs suggest that Hopkins appeared in some segments, and that their subject matter was probably dictated to promote Universal, including "a few moments with Willie Hopkins, who models a study of Joe Martin, the Universal ape" (*MPW* [31 March 1917], 2158), and "'Bobby,' Universal City's lion actor, poses for Willie Hopkins, world's foremost modeller" (*MPW* [2 June 1917], 1496). *The Moving Picture World* suggests that the war in Europe became the focus for Hopkins in the spring and summer of 1917. Hopkins produced a segment called "Let There Be Peace" in late February 1917, followed by "America, May She Always Be Right," "We Are a United Nation," and "Coming Events Cast Their Shadows Before" in March and April. "The Kaiser's Thermometer" and "Exemption Pleas" from September and November 1917 were followed by "Mother's Liberty Bond" in March 1918.

What is intriguing about Hopkins's work is the amount of material he produced for the series. Just as cel animation was becoming increasingly organized as an assembly-line industry to produce full-length animated shorts, Hopkins was animating short clay segments, more or less on a weekly basis, in a medium that is traditionally worked by a single artist in front of the camera, a method not well suited to division of labor. Of two surviving segments from the *Universal Screen Magazine*, both projected at 16 frames per second, one is 1 minute, 45 seconds long, and the other is 2 minutes, 15 seconds long. If these lengths are typical, then Hopkins produced over 100 minutes of screen material for a regular release schedule over an 18-month period. Of course, what is not known is to what extent frame-by-frame animation was used rather than live-action shooting—that is, to what degree the segments relied on live-action introductions, intertitles, and so forth, to reduce the labor of frame-by-frame production. But Hopkins's work stands as one of the earliest regularly produced clay animations, perhaps the only such "series" prior to the "Gumby" television series almost four decades later. Though cel animation would eventually drive clay and other three-dimensional forms of animation into relative obscurity, Hopkins's work from late 1916 until mid-1918 remains a singular example of regular clay production in a theatrical series.

Swat the Fly, released 14 September 1917, is one of the segments that has survived. The film opens on a title card with a small animated spider descending a spiderweb, then cuts to a medium shot as a mound of clay begins to build in front of a curtain (see Appendix for a complete shot list). Plasticine is added in large handfuls until a flattened orb the size of a large platter has been built. Then the basic outline of a human face begins to take shape, with a narrow, protruding nose, eye sockets, and an ear that grows from the side of the head. The clay is smoothed and refined until the finely chiseled features of a male caricature—a broad face with large ears, a mustache, baggy eyes, jowls, and a slight patch of hair atop his head—are completed (see Figure 3.2). The larger-than-life face is done in deep relief to suggest a profile rather than a full circumference of the head. Once the head is completed, the film cuts to another title card with the same spiderweb motif; it reads, "FRENCHY 'STRIKES OUT,'" a possible reference to the replacement of Sir John French as the head of the British Expeditionary Forces in Europe after the unsuccessful battle at Ypres at the end of 1915, though the figure's resemblance to French is limited and that event had occurred almost two years earlier. In shot

Figure 3.2 "Frenchy" from *Swat the Fly*. Frame enlargement courtesy of the author.

2, a fly walks down the forehead to the tip of the nose, and "Frenchy" becomes more animated, crossing his eyes to follow the movement, wagging his nose in a futile attempt to dislodge the fly, and finally scowling and cursing. His efforts only force the fly to retreat to his eyebrow and then to his ear, both of which go into similar contortions. Though the animation here is expressive, it is limited in movement and displays very little exaggeration. Distortions of the nose, eyebrow, and ear are insufficient to produce the rubbery squash-and-stretch effects that were first systematically explored by Disney in the 1930s.

A second insert title appears, reading, "LORD ALGY ENDEAVORS 'Y'KNOW.'" It is unclear who "Lord Algy" is. The film cuts back (shot 3) to the bust, and we see the face beginning to transform into a smooth, round-faced gentleman with a monocle (see Figure 3.3). To his great surprise, the fly lights on his nose and then on his eyebrow, which he wiggles so hard that his monocle falls out. The

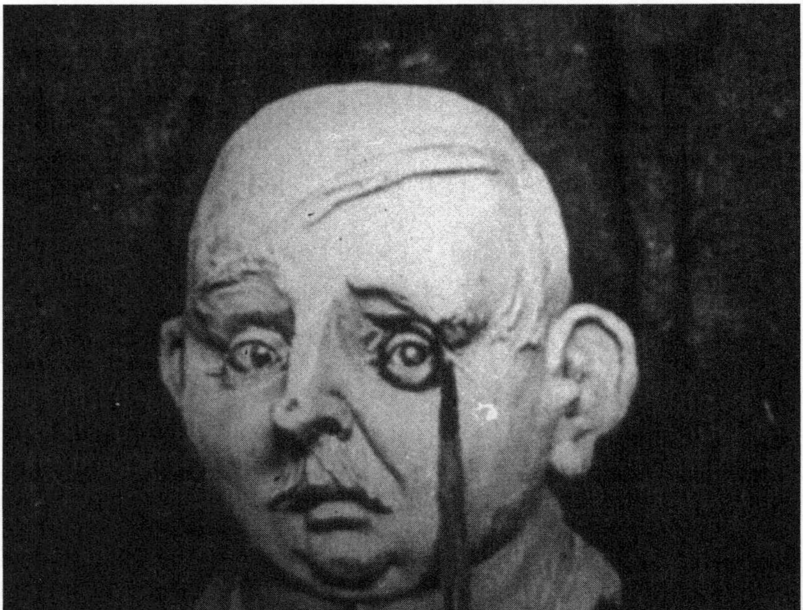

Figure 3.3 "Lord Algy" from *Swat the Fly*. Frame enlargement courtesy of the author.

face quickly transforms into a longer visage, followed by the insert, "O'BRIEN 'SACRIFICES.'" Again, it is unclear whom this title refers to, though "O'Brien" may be Edmund O'Brien, a doctor who gave up his practice to become an actor and ultimately became a contract star for Universal in the 1920s.[4] In shot 4, more cursing and nose and eyebrow wiggling greet the pesky fly until he lights on the tip of O'Brien's nose one final time. The film shifts to live action, and the hand of the artist enters the frame to flatten both fly and nose (see Figure 3.4). The film ends as the artist finally rips the nose entirely from the face.

Interestingly, this closing punctuation of the film is an irreverent, humorous use of the "hand of the artist," an enactment of the enduring iconography of an artist bringing an animated creation into existence, usually in the introduction to the film. Having created the character for the audience, the artist then imbues it with life, thereby position-

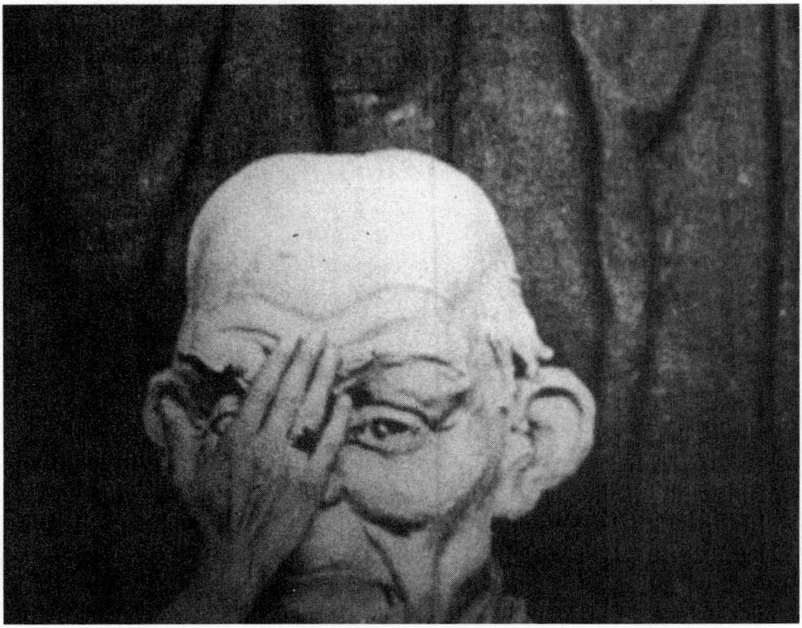

Figure 3.4 O'Brien sculpture flattened by the hand of the artist in *Swat the Fly*. Frame enlargement courtesy of the author.

ing himself as a privileged character between the audience and the animated world (Crafton 1979, 414). Hopkins's reversal of the tradition not only places the iconographic action at the end of the film but emphasizes the return of the clay to its inanimate form through the gesture of ripping clay from the now-static face. Filmed with the live-action camera, the clay is now profoundly inanimate, but the artist lives on—perhaps laughing—beyond the film frame.

Except for the Lord Algy title, the film's titles all contain baseball references. "Strike out" and "sacrifice" are commonplace terms in baseball, but the origin of the phrase "swat the fly" is of particular interest. *The Dickson Dictionary of Baseball* cites the first use of "swat" in the 25 August 1891 issue of the *Chicago Herald*.[5] It goes on to note an item from the July 1948 issue of *American Notes and Queries*: "FLY SWATTER: a term coined by Dr. Samuel J. Crumbine, who in 1904 was appointed head of the Kansas State Board of Health; he was taking a bulletin--on flies as typhoid carriers—to the printer one day, and stopped off to watch a ball game, where he heard 'sacrifice fly!' and 'swat the ball,' etc., and immediately decided to call the bulletin 'Swat the fly.' Only a few months later a man came to him with an instrument that he wanted to call a 'fly bat' and Dr. Crumbine persuaded him to call it a 'fly-swatter.'"[6]

Apparently, "swat" was an emerging slang term of that era. "Swatter" and "swatsmith" were baseball terms coined in 1908. "Swatstick" was first used in 1915 (Dickson, 384). Following Hopkins's release of *Swat the Fly* in September 1917, the term reappeared in other contemporaneous film titles, including *Swat the Fly*, a Katzenjammer Kids cartoon released in May 1918, and *Swat the Spy*, a Fox feature released in September 1918. Given the attraction of the "national pastime," Hopkins's integration of a baseball motif into topical humor, playing off the double entendre in the title, can be seen as an attempt to appeal to the broadest possible audience.

A second "Miracles in Mud" segment believed to be from 1919 survives at the Library of Congress. Preserved in a badly deteriorated print of *Montreal Screen Herald Magazine* 7, the piece is entitled "The Mysterious Fanny" (see Figure 3.5). Playing off the suggestive title, the film presents a number of characters about town who are confused and concerned about "Fanny." Title cards announce, "The Sheriff and Op'ry House Manager (Can't Imagine What's the Matter with Fanny)," and, "The Farmer and Deacon (He's Worried about Fanny)."

Figure 3.5 The hired man from a damaged print of *The Mysterious Fanny* by Willie Hopkins. Reproduced from the collections of the Library of Congress.

Following the titles, each townsperson is presented as a squat tabletop sculpture against a simple white-on-black drawing that provides shorthand reinforcement of his particular profession. Most of the action in the film consists of the figures growing up from mounds of clay and indicating in broad gestures their surprise or confusion. Toward the end of the film, a traveling salesman mugs a confused look with a real cigarette butt in his mouth. The action becomes more elaborate in a bit with "The Hired Man." A clamshell opens to reveal a head, then transforms into a body as the head rises up the chest to form the completed body. The hired man looks left and right and demonstrates his surprise as his neck extends upwards in a Tex Avery–style "take." In the last shot, Fanny's identity is revealed as a blob of clay metamorphosizes into a cow, lying on the ground, who turns and looks at the camera. Unlike in *Swat the Fly*, these sculptures are presented as figures in a drawn setting, and their scale is much smaller as well.

Virtually nothing is known about Hopkins's life, though he is identified as a "Noted Sculptor" in the opening title of *Swat the Fly* and is variously described in *The Moving Picture World* blurbs as "the world renown [*sic*] sculptor," "the Screen Magazine's animated sculpture artist," and even, "the Inventor of the animated clay cartoon." He apparently continued his work in clay over the next few years, since in 1919 he constructed sculptures that were shot with the subtitles for a lavish feature, *Everywoman*, produced by Famous Players-Lasky (the forerunner of Paramount). A trade paper review of the film said, "Many of the scenes are introduced by beautiful fashioned groups of symbolic statuary, something new in filmland and decidedly distinctive."[7] Though his clay animation is substantial in scope, further research is needed to determine the nature of his contribution to the medium.

HELENA SMITH DAYTON: EARLY WOMAN ANIMATOR

Helena Smith was born in 1879. As a young woman, she became a reporter in Hartford, Connecticut, where she met and married Fred Erving Dayton, also a reporter and columnist for a number of newspapers in Hartford. Helena Smith Dayton became interested in sculpture and illustration and began sculpting caricatures in clay that were photographed for magazine illustrations. She began making clay films in 1916 and was working to get them distributed in September 1917. Scarcely one year later, Dayton was in France, her work in film apparently having been cut short by World War I. She was director of a YMCA canteen in Paris (according to her obituary), but the YMCA archives show that from 8 September 1918 to 10 August 1919 she served as a "purchasing agent" and secretary.[8] There is no evidence that she made films after her stint in France. As late as 1933, Dayton was still listed as a member of the Society of Illustrators,[9] an indication that her interest in illustration continued for many years.

In the interim, Dayton coauthored two books with Louise Bascom Barratt for Robert McBride and Company: *The Book of Entertainments and Theatricals* (1923) and *New York in Seven Days* (1925).[10] The 1925 travel book takes the premise of an out-of-towner visiting a New York City resident, who guides the tourist about town for one week, giving a running dialogue of the sights and sounds of the city and in the process learning more about her own hometown.

Later in her life, Helena Smith Dayton began "specializing in clay cartoons [caricatures] of prominent citizens,"[11] though she appears to have focused more effort on painting, presenting shows of her work in New York in 1939 at the Decorators' Club Gallery in the Squibb Building and again in 1943 at the Montross Gallery. Howard Devree reviewed the 1943 show, saying, "Portraits, landscapes, and flower subjects by Helena Smith Dayton make up the current exhibition at the Montross. Her portraits are the most striking part of her work—unflattering and sound, with a mining for individual character in those of Fannie Hurst and Ian Hay Beith."[12] The fact that Dayton moved in circles with Fannie Hurst, the popular and highly paid author, and Sir Ian Hay Beith, a British novelist and playwright, may be explained in part by her husband being the sales manager for Condé Nast Press, from 1924 until he retired in 1950, and "a founder and lifetime historian of the Hartford Yacht Club."[13]

Helena Smith Dayton was 37 when her work as a clay animator was featured in a 16 December 1916 article in *Scientific American* entitled "Motion Picture Comedies in Clay" (see Figure 3.6). This article places her among the early clay animators, and certainly among the earliest known women animators. Dayton's films have not been located, and this short magazine piece is the primary source of information on her work. Like most popular accounts, the article explains the animation process and the labor involved in frame-by-frame production and defines clay by its differences from animated cartoons. Both his interview with Dayton and the magazine's underlying ideology of progress through technology lead the author to position clay animation as "a distinct improvement over its pen-and-ink [cartoon] counterpart . . . [which is] infinitely more laborious" ("Comedies in Clay," 553).[14] At the same time, the writer seems skeptical of claims about the efficiency of producing clay animation: "One would suppose that the photographing process is slow, considering that the sculptor must alter the pose of the figures 16 times to produce one foot. *Yet we are told by Miss* [sic] *Dayton* that 200 feet of film is by no means unusual for a day's work [emphasis added]" ("Comedies in Clay," 553).

Figure 3.6 Helena Smith Dayton sculpting. The original *Scientific American* caption reads: "These droll little figures are remolded sixteen times to produce one foot of animated sculpture film."

In a silent film, normally projected at a speed of roughly 16 frames per second, 200 feet of 35mm film runs just over 3 minutes—high output for one day's work, by any animator's standard. Comparing the amount of labor needed to produce drawn animation versus clay animation is difficult, since the labor involved in the preproduction stage is often not accounted for, as it is not here. However, in his book *Illustrating and Cartooning: Animation*, Winsor McCay says, "When we came to photograph [the] drawings [from *The Sinking of the Lusitania* (1918)] the [camera] operator commented on the fact that he worked an hour photographing one hundred and twenty-nine drawings that go through the machine in eight seconds. These drawings cost me eight weeks of hard labor" (19). Disregarding the labor required by McCay's drawing technique, if the filming of the drawings proceeded at the rate described, a 10-hour day of shooting would produce only

1 minute and 20 seconds of animation. Compared with Dayton's purported 3 minutes of clay shot in one day, it is not surprising that the author qualifies the claim as Dayton's.

The article is quick to point out that, despite its relative ease of production, in certain areas clay animation actually requires greater skill than cartoon animation: "[I]t must not be supposed that the animated sculptures are simpler throughout to produce than the animated cartoons. While the latter can allow of crudeness in certain details of the action, such as the simulation of walking, in the former the walking process must be simulated with almost perfect fidelity" ("Comedies in Clay," 553). Whether or not drawn animation can "allow" more crudely rendered action than clay is an open question, based on the aesthetic value one places on a particular style of animated movement. But here, the writer appears to be restating Dayton's account of the clay process. Given Dayton's experience with figurative animation (described later in the article), she would undoubtedly have been aware of the difficulties involved in creating a believable walk in clay.

According to the article, Dayton's technique was fairly sophisticated, developed by trial and error and close observation of human action. The article reports that the timing of her first efforts was off: "the clay figures went through their antics so fast that the eyes of the spectator could not follow them when projected on the screen." Dayton's early efforts are also described as having had "several characters, each highly animated," which did not work well with audiences; the experience taught her "to limit the main action or point of interest to one figure" ("Comedies in Clay," 553). In photographs accompanying the article, two scrubwomen are shown arguing (see Figure 3.7). The caption indicates that these figures are from a "scene in an animated sculpture playette," suggesting that Dayton's work was sculpted in the style of draped and crudely detailed wooden figurines. According to the article, these 10–12-inch clay figures were finished with clothing and bits of real hair, painted as needed with splashes of color and occasionally supported by wire armatures.

Outside of this account, little is known about Dayton's work. She apparently kept up her work in clay animation at least until the following year, when a blurb in *Motography* said,

Animated sculpture is the latest thing in pictures. The S. S. Film Company is filming Helena Smith Dayton's "cartoons in clay" and they will be released

Figure 3.7 The ascendant mode for clay animation: Helena Smith Dayton's animated clay playettes. The original *Scientific American* caption reads: "With the exception of the scrub pail, these figures are modeled in clay throughout."

through the Educational Film Corporation the early part of September. One of the subjects was run at the Strand Theater of New York and won the admiration of the audience. The subject being made at present is Shakespeare's "Romeo and Juliet," with unusual scenery and costumes.

The film [referent unclear] made by the S. S. Company for the woman suffrage party was shown to Governor Whitman and his staff on August 29.[15]

There are some tantalizing hints here that one of Dayton's films was relevant to the women's suffrage movement (perhaps only because it was made by a woman?), and that the governor of New York, Charles Seymour Whitman, saw these films when he attended a women's suffrage conference in Saratoga Springs, New York, on 29 August 1917. Yet, extensive coverage of the convention in the *New York Times* and the *Saratogian* does not mention a film showing. Since her adaptation of a Shakespeare classic would appeal to a family audience, the distribution of these "playettes" by Educational Film Corporation seems a logical move, bringing the fruits of Dayton's first year of animation into wider theatrical release.[16]

The mention of the Strand Theater seems a conscious effort to give greater significance to her novelties, since it was one of the premier picture palaces in New York, the first to open on Broadway in April 1914. Tying her educational film to the Strand would help move her work into the realm of "uplifting" films, since at the end of 1917 the Strand had initiated an innovative program of daily symphonic concerts and weekly art exhibitions "illustrative of music" for its patrons.[17] The managing director of the Strand, Harold Edel, called the concerts, given by the 40-piece house orchestra, "the ideal form of entertainment, pleasing those who are familiar with symphonic music and cultivating and educating the ones who are not."[18] The willingness of Edel to experiment may also be part of the reason Dayton's films, not yet in regular distribution, were shown there early on.

Later that fall, and nearly a year after the *Scientific American* article appeared, *The Moving Picture World*'s educational reviewer, Margaret I. MacDonald, reported the release of *Romeo and Juliet* in an article entitled "Prominent Sculptor in Film":

> The Educational Film Corporation of America, we understand, is releasing the newest thing in picture production, namely, the animated clay figure production of "Romeo and Juliet," made by the well-known sculptor, Helena Smith Dayton, under the guidance of J. Charles Davis, Jr.
>
> The production is a novelty in one reel. It repeats the pathetic story told centuries ago by William Shakespeare; and while it treats the matter in somewhat of a burlesque style, we can forgive this from the fact that the clay figures are necessary [*sic*] more or less grotesque. All the emotions to which human kind are subject are well portrayed by these queer little figures; and in looking at the picture we are strangely conscious of the union of two of the greatest arts.
>
> Little need be said here of the wonderful talent of Helena Smith Dayton: her work speaks for itself. In the introduction to the picture, we are privileged to watch her deft fingers fashion the form of Juliet from an apparently soulless lump of clay. This mere lump of clay under her magic touch takes on the responsibilities of life, and love, and sorrow which the play requires, and finally grasps in desperation the dagger with which it ends its sorry life, falling in tragic fashion over the already lifeless form of its Romeo.[19]

Once again, the reviewer locates clay animation as an extension of the fine art of sculpture into motion pictures. And though the warped style of Dayton's caricatures apparently contributes to the burlesque quality of the narrative, the reviewer recognizes her talent in making the figures express a range of emotions. Again, Dayton reenacts the "hand of the artist" as she constructs Juliet for the camera.

None of Dayton's films have been found, and copyright records at the Library of Congress offer no clear evidence that her films were ever copyrighted. Whether or not her clay films were widely seen in her day, an account of the medium in a popular magazine for general audiences surely elevated the awareness of clay animation, even for non-moviegoers. Just as Etienne Arnaud had demystified clay animation for French readers in *Lectures Pour Tous* eight years earlier, clay was now documented as an appealing and innovative technique in American animation. In other publications from the period, we find some additional evidence that clay was regarded, even in the context of a demand-driven system of production, as a viable technique. In *Behind the Motion Picture Screen*, a "how-they-do-it" book published by Scientific American Publishing Company in 1919, Austin Lescarboura, describing the works of Helena Smith Dayton, devotes a chapter to "Cartoons That Move and Sculpture That Lives." At some level, that title suggests that the author placed clay animation on an equal footing with cel animation.

After giving a full account of the cel process, Lescarboura follows with a complete discussion of "animated sculpture," as well as "animated doll films" (310).[20] He argues first for their equality: "The appeal [of clay films] is much along the same lines as the animated cartoon film; in fact, the two can be considered twin brothers" (314). Later, he touts the advantages of clay at the production stage: "Compared with the obvious ease with which this work [of manipulating the clay characters] is carried on, the drawing of sixteen separate and finished pen-and-ink sketches seems considerably more laborious" (314). Here, the author of this popular film text sees clay as a technique with its own labor-saving advantages over line animation. This assessment is not surprising, since only one year earlier the work of Willie Hopkins had debuted in a weekly newsreel alongside other cartoon series.

The work of Willie Hopkins indicates that, by 1917, clay animation had moved beyond the isolated trick within a live-action film and was making inroads into newsreel distribution. As Koszarski notes, this move followed trends set by cartoons: "Just as newspaper comic strips arose as adjuncts of expanding urban broadsheets, so animated cartoons would be taken up by newsreel distributors and the press lords who sponsored them" (170). In the regular distribution schedule of one major studio, Universal, which was "well situated . . . with a fine new studio and an aggressive distribution system" (86), clay animation in 1917 was no longer a rarity in theaters. But without a stable of newspaper cartoon characters to draw on, the animation of three-dimensional sculpture—a combination of film and fine art—remained an "art novelty," a technique that had little in common with the print media environment that had made cel cartoons more familiar to audiences.

While finding a new niche in film distribution, clay animation in 1917 "looked backward" by sharing the iconography of earlier animations: the use of the transforming bust in *Swat the Fly* and the "hand of the artist" image that opens *Romeo and Juliet* and closes *Swat the Fly*. But the work of Helena Smith Dayton also "looked forward" to the future of mainstream American clay animation. Based on the photos and captions in *Scientific American*, her use of small clay human figures in "playettes" can be seen as a precursor of clay films, the majority of which are in essence puppet-films-in-clay, films that animate tabletop clay characters in narrative settings. However burlesque their style, Dayton's films must have been ambitious narratives; she did, after all, tackle a well-worn Shakespeare classic that locates human characters in a distant historical setting. In short, Dayton's clay playettes opened the gateway to what would become the ascendant mode for clay.

Perhaps this is what struck the *Scientific American* writer, who locates clay as an innovative, realistic, and improved medium for producing comedies that could compete with the cartoons that had been common in theaters for over two years. "Possessing every feature that goes to make a good comedy on the screen, but having in addition a distinct touch of reality, the animated sculptures about to be introduced should prove most opportune to motion picture audiences which have become quite blasé of late. The initial success and continued popularity of the animated sculptures will meet with universal favor, since the latest innovation is a distinct improvement over its pen-and-ink counterpart" ("Comedies in Clay," 553). Figurative clay narratives, bringing humor and realism to the screen, would be the future of the medium, even though the writer's prediction of "universal favor" for "animated sculpture" would take decades to materialize.

4

Clay Animation in the 1920s

By the 1920s cartoon animation using the cel system was firmly established as the dominant and preferred mode of animation production. Increasingly, three-dimensional forms such as clay had been driven into relative obscurity. Nevertheless, in 1921, clay animation appeared in a film called *Modeling*, an "Out of the Inkwell" release from the newly formed studio headed by Dave Fleischer, a former film editor for Pathé, and his brother Max, a former art editor for *Popular Science* who had worked for the Bray studio. *Modeling* is one of the few known shorts using clay that was released during the 1920s. The film includes animated clay in eight shots, a novel integration of the technique into an immensely popular cartoon series, and one of the rare uses of clay animation in a theatrical short from the 1920s.

A closer examination of this Fleischer film is warranted for two reasons. First, it reveals a number of "Inkwell" traits, particularly the way the studio maintained an element of novelty in the series by integrating different animation techniques to visualize Ko-Ko the Clown's fight for corporeal existence, the unvarying central conflict of the series. This broader look at the "Inkwell" format will show that it embraced a duality of conformity and surprise, of static format and novel technique, of conventional cartoon action set in cartoon space and unconventional animation set in live-action studio space. Indeed, even the central star of the series created humor by incorporating into his established star persona the regular comic routines of a clown and an antagonistic tendency to leave his cartoon world, disrupting the

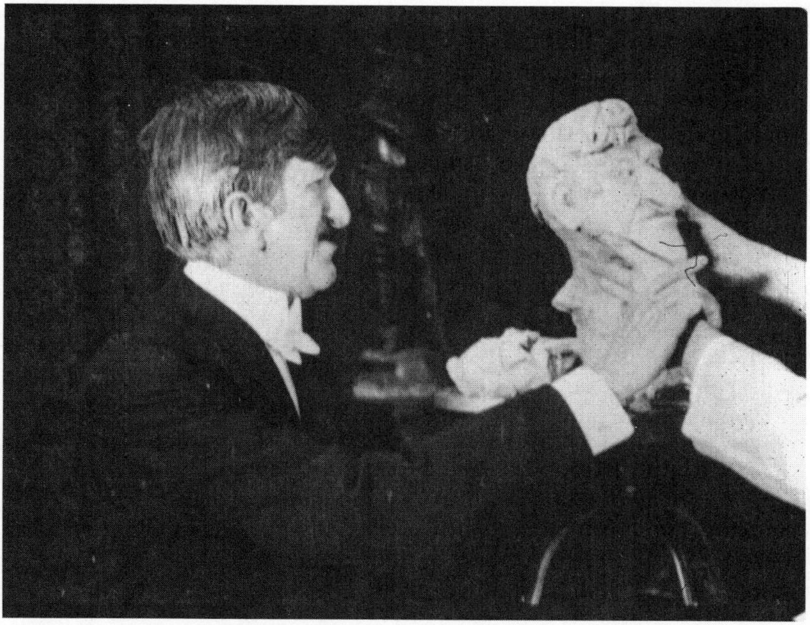

Figure 4.1 *Modeling* shot 15: The Gent disapproves of his bust. Reproduced from the collections of the Library of Congress.

conventions of film narrative and film space. These dualities became central to the audience's enjoyment. Though viewers were comfortable with familiar characters in a familiar format, they came to expect from the Fleischer studio the innovative use of animation techniques to visualize Ko-Ko's ongoing subversion of filmic conventions.

Second, *Modeling* gives some barometer of where the clay technique fit in the East Coast studio production system as it worked to meet regular release schedules. Before turning to a specific examination of the Fleischer studio's use of clay, an overview of the changes occurring in the emerging animation industry will show the broader impact the growing use of flat animation techniques was having on three-dimensional forms of animation like clay.

THE EMERGENCE OF DIVISION OF LABOR IN EAST COAST ANIMATION HOUSES

In the film industry, three-dimensional animation—a technique known from the earliest days of filmmaking—quickly became secondary to flat animation, using either cel overlays or, to a lesser extent, the slash system. As discussed in chapter 3, the cel system involves animating foreground characters in a series of drawings on clear cels that overlay a single background drawing, eliminating the need to redraw the background for each character drawing. The slash system was developed around the same time, in 1914, by Raoul Barré and Bill Nolan, but was never patented. Designed to reduce the amount of labor involved in drawn animation, the slash system involved cutting a hole in a paper background drawing so that, through careful composition, character drawings could be animated underneath. Later, the more common incarnation of the slash system was similar to cel animation. It involved cutting around the foreground character so that the paper drawing could be laid over a single background drawing without obscuring the majority of it, thereby reducing the amount of the background that had to be retraced. Because the slash system was unpatented and used plain paper, it offered the animation producer cost savings on raw materials. Since cels were more costly, they were often washed and reused.

Much of the Fleischer studio's early animation uses the slash system. But because cel eliminated the need to cut out the foreground action, it had an immediate impact on the emerging animation industry. Over the long term, it became the dominant mode of production in Hollywood. The rise and consolidation of the cel technique—which was well suited to division of labor and assembly-line production methods—to fill the demand for theatrical shorts have been well documented by Crafton and others.[1]

By contrast, clay was and continues to be a medium that resists division of labor, since the character movements are created through manipulation in front of the camera, usually by a single animator. And as a practical matter, setting up a studio to produce clay animation in 1914 would have been a difficult business proposition, for despite the rising popularity of sculpture in the early 1900s, the existing pool of sculptors and the existing audience for sculpture were small compared with the pool of draftsmen and the audience for comic strips in the penny press. "Animating sculpture" meant bringing an art form usually confined to museums, expositions, and fine homes to the screen. Drawn animation could easily build on the cultural production that penny press strips had brought to the masses.

From the producer's point of view, the slash system and particularly the cel system were manageable techniques, industrial processes amenable to division of labor. Breaking down the substantial amount of labor involved in the production of an animated short into many specialized tasks presented a viable solution to the producer's problem of delivering enough product on a regular schedule to a marketplace hungry for films. But as cel became the dominant production method, the net effect of this demand-driven system of production was a severe limitation of its boundaries, a trivialization of the technique into the narrow confines of the Hollywood cartoon: "Cel animation originated within the industry of a single country, the USA, and that country was in the process (during World War I) of becoming the leading production force in world cinema. Partly as a result, the cel technique quickly became defined within relatively narrow boundaries. . . . Hollywood defined the cartoon by its difference from live-action films and it has remained a secondary form ever since" (Thompson, 108). The ideology of the cel technique that Thompson outlines—"cartoons are secondary to live action, virtually always comic, and/or fanciful, for children and trivial" (111)—was imposed primarily by the exhibition marketplace it supplied.[2]

From the audience's point of view, early cel animation was very accessible and familiar. Its content was an extension of famous comic strip characters and gags into a new, moving medium that retained many familiar conventions, such as text for dialogue in comic strip "bubbles" and "sight lines" to indicate what a character was looking at. Grounded in the visual humor of penny press cartoons, the mass audience found familiar visual cues and many of the same characters in the weekly cartoon at the movie house. This connection to the penny press probably derives from what Conrad Smith calls "a heritage of newsprint": many early animators, including James Stuart Blackton, Winsor McCay, and Paul Terry, were newspaper cartoonists; others (Sidney Smith, John Randolph Bray, Max Fleischer, Wallace Carlson, Raoul Barré) were employed as illustrators or staff artists at newspapers.[3]

THE FORMAT OF THE "OUT OF THE INKWELL" SERIES

Because it moved beyond the conventions established in early cartoons and produced cartoon "stars" not derived from the strips, "Out of the Inkwell" is crucial to understanding the progression of American animation before the advent of sound.[4] During these years, the "Inkwell" series' adaptation of the slash and cel techniques shows a patterning of content—what we would today call "format"—that was very successful with audiences. The "Inkwell" format was characterized by a recurrent theme—the central conflict of Ko-Ko's struggle for bodily existence and his departure from the drawing board and exploration of the cartoon studio, a journey that inevitably ends when his creators return him to the inkwell—and a recurrent style—whatever novel techniques could be brought to bear to visualize the filmic space where Ko-Ko's struggle occurs.

The "Inkwell" series' central theme was also one of animation's greatest themes. As Crafton notes, "Drawings that 'come to life' may be said to be the great theme of all animation. . . . [T]he narrative content of many animated films, especially in the silent period, may be seen as a heroic struggle by the drawings to retain their unexpected corporeal existence. This is usually expressed pictorially by having the drawings deny their obvious two-dimensionality and enter the world of real objects, with whimsical and spatially confusing results. Usually the artist succeeds in restoring order to the world; Koko [*sic*] must always be recapped in the Inkwell" (Crafton 1979, 414). As early as 22 February 1920, a *New York Times* review touched on this theme as a source of the "Inkwell" series' popularity: "This little Inkwell clown has attracted much favorable attention because of a number of distinguishing characteristics. . . . [H]e has an exciting habit of leaving his own world, that of the rectangular sheet on which he is drawn and climbing all over the surrounding furniture."[5] Throughout the "Inkwell" series Ko-Ko's weekly "habit of leaving his own world" remained a rich source of gags and offered audiences a behind-the-scenes glimpse of the workings of an animation studio.

In many early episodes, the basic "Inkwell" plot could be outlined:

1. The animator's hand brings Ko-Ko out of the inkwell by drawing him in an innovative way (for example, the hand draws a group of ink drops that metamorphose into Ko-Ko).

Figure 4.2 *Modeling* shot 34: Ko-Ko sculpts a snow ball into a bust. Reproduced from the collections of the Library of Congress.

2. Max Fleischer and the animator Roland Crandall are established in the studio.
3. The action cross-cuts between studio and animated scenes.
4. Gags are created that involve the movement of three-dimensional objects from the live-action space into the animated space or vice versa.
5. A visitor enters the studio with an easily identifiable motive.
6. Ko-Ko enters the world of the studio to "dissolve" the situation, creating a string of physical comedy gags that astonish all present.
7. Ko-Ko is ultimately forced to return to the inkwell.

This pattern is repeated in early shorts like *The Ouija Board* (between 1915 and 1920) and *Perpetual Motion* (between 1915 and 1920). As the "Inkwell" cast became established cartoon characters, later shorts relied less on the live-action context and the introduction of visitors to the studio, leaving more time for interaction between live-action and cartoon space and ultimately for longer bits of pure animation. In

Figure 4.3 *Modeling* shot 37: Max hits Ko-Ko with a wad of clay. Reproduced from collections of the Library of Congress.

short, later "Inkwell" films have more Ko-Ko and less Max. But in the early "Inkwell" films, establishing a live-action context for Ko-Ko to exercise his struggle for corporeal existence was a format that was easy to produce, since only a small percentage of the short was truly animated.

The "Inkwell" series probably adopted this format initially because of the economic realities of cartoon production in the early 1920s. It became a successful format because it fulfilled the narrative needs of a five- to seven-minute short and because the Fleischers maintained the novelty of the series by exploring a number of animation techniques, mixing live-action and stop-motion footage with the central drawn character of Ko-Ko. In this regard, Michael Wassenaar's description of the Fleischers' later "Popeye" series fits the "Inkwell" series equally well: "[E]conomy is inscribed in the production process itself through a repetition of plot structures for the utmost effect. . . . What is characteristic of these cartoons is a minimal amount of invention going into plot development and a maximal amount of effort going into the construction of gags within a certain context."[6] Over time, it became a comfortable, repetitive vehicle for audiences.

Working within the "Inkwell" format, the Fleischers could redirect their energies away from narrative construction toward the development of new techniques—rotoscoping, sound, composite imagery, the bouncing ball, setbacks—and toward tinkering with the gadgets that litter their cartoons as props. For the Fleischers, animation was the intersection of their interests in drawing and mechanics. Max's self-described "keen and instinctive sense of mechanics"[7] is evident not only in their methods but in their subject matter in futuristic cartoons like *The First Man to the Moon* (1921), *Perpetual Motion* (between 1915 and 1920), *Ko-Ko in 1999* (1924), and *Ko-Ko's Earth Control* (1928). Within the constraints of the "Inkwell" series' repetitive plots the Fleischers found freedom to experiment with the mechanics of animation. Consequently, the "construction of gags" revolved around film techniques for visualizing the interaction of the live-action world and the cartoon world. As the "Inkwell" series unveiled its new technical tricks week after week, the results were successful enough to help maintain the elevated status of cinema-as-novelty for audiences of the 1920s, audiences no longer fascinated by animated movement alone.

Unlike later character animation done by the Fleischer brothers, the "Inkwell" films tend to rely more heavily on tricks and effects *as effects* for their entertainment. Though sophisticated technical tricks like setbacks were developed for later "Popeye" cartoons, they support stronger characters and narratives. In contrast, the central premise of the "Inkwell" format—Ko-Ko interacts with the live-action world—coupled with the format's scant plots and limited characters forced the Fleischer studio to develop new ways to integrate live-action and cartoon footage. These novel techniques sustain Ko-Ko's "exciting habit of leaving his own world," providing a more complex filmic space and richer layers of visual imagery to decode.

Some of the animated tricks for combining live-action and cartoon footage are quite simple, others more elaborate. In *Bubbles* (1922), a simple still photograph of Max is overlaid with cels of an animated soap bubble, creating the halfhearted suggestion that Max is blowing tremendous bubbles in his living room even though he is frozen in a still. *The Ouija Board* shows Max's surprise by freezing a frame of him with mouth agape and adding an animated overlay of his hair standing on end. More elaborate interaction between Ko-Ko and the live-action world is achieved in *The Clown's Little Brother* (between 1915 and 1922) where Ko-Ko rides and wrestles with a live-action cat. This frame-by-frame composite of cel and live-action background footage—called rotographing—grew naturally out of the Fleischers' development of rotoscoping and was used to combine live action with cel in shorts as late as the 1940s. The use of this kind of technique frequently blurs the line between special effects and animation in "Inkwell" films and underlines their fascination with technique over story.

In *Modeling*, the visitor format described above is closely followed (see Appendix 4 for a complete shot list). Max brings the clown out of the inkwell as a series of ink droplets that metamorphose into Ko-Ko. Max is established at the drawing board, trying to give Ko-Ko some pep, while the animator Roland Crandall works at another easel. An ugly gentleman with a large nose, dressed in top hat and tails, enters to examine a clay likeness that Crandall is sculpting of him in clay (shots 9, 10, and 11). After some disagreement between them—the "Gent" thinks the bust resembles him too closely—Crandall calls for Max's help (see Fig. 4.1). To busy the clown, Max draws ice skates on Ko-Ko and a frozen lake for him to skate on (shot 23). As Max and Crandall try to resculpt the bust, Ko-Ko skates through a series of pratfalls and gags: he chases a bear who has stolen his hat, wrestles in an ice house, rolls the bear up in a huge snowball, and finally, sculpts the snowball into a bust of the Gent (see Fig. 4.2). Angry at Ko-Ko's antics, Max turns to throw a wad of clay at him (see Fig. 4.3). As clay begins to fly back and forth, Ko-Ko escapes into the studio (shot 45), hides in the nostril of the bust, and is chased wiggling across the floor by Max (shots 65, 66, and 67), Crandall, and the Gent, only to return to the safety of the inkwell.

The Role of Ko-Ko in the Inkwell Series: Narrative Function and Spatial Explorations

The Ko-Ko character performs a repetitive narrative function in the "Inkwell" format that fits the historical role of the archetypal clown in Western drama: to "dissolve" the action. In *The Fool: His Social and Literary History* (1935), Enid Welsford states that "the Fool or Clown . . . as a dramatic character. . . usually stands apart from the main action of the play, having a tendency not to focus but to dissolve events, and also to act as an intermediary between the stage and the

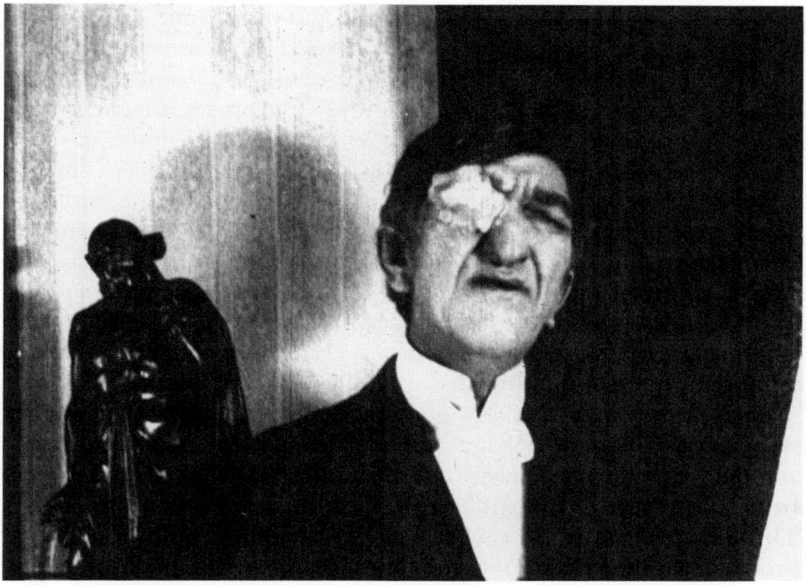

Figure 4.4 *Modeling* shot 40: Ko-Ko hits the Gent with a wad of clay. Reproduced from collections of the Library of Congress.

audience. . . . The Fool, in fact, is an amphibian, equally at home in the world of reality and the world of imagination. The serious hero focuses events, forces issues, and causes catastrophes; but the Fool by his mere presence dissolves events, evades issues, throws doubt on the finality of fact."[8] As an intermediate character between the stage and audience, the clown can comment on the action taking place, giving voice to the audience's thoughts. Though part of the story, the clown is free to defy its conventions.

Welsford's notion of the "fool as amphibian" resonates throughout the "Inkwell" cartoons, since Ko-Ko fulfills many of the archetypal functions she describes. As "amphibian," Ko-Ko exploits the tension between narrative chaos and spatial unity in the "Inkwell" format, and he is also the antagonist in the narratives. In many shorts, he works to destroy the filmic space through a malicious playfulness that exhibits many of what M. W. Disher calls the primary jokes of the clown: falls, blows, surprise, knavery, mimicry, and stupidity.[9] In *Modeling*, for example, we see a rotoscoped Ko-Ko in a traditional knockabout routine attempting to ice-skate (shots 29 and 30), hitting the Gent with a wad of clay (see Fig. 4.4), surprising the Gent right off his stool by hiding in the nostril of the clay bust (shot 59), mimicking the sculpting of Crandall to the exasperation of Max (shots 34 and 35), and stupidly lying upside down on the drawing board with a wad of clay on his head (shot 37). As Ko-Ko foments a confrontation between the Gent, Crandall, and Max, the momentum builds in a series of pratfalls and crude slapstick. Here, as in many of the "Inkwell" films, Ko-Ko tests the live-action characters. And as the film degenerates into a kind of pie fight in clay, the narrative premise of the short—however slight—dissolves.

At the same time, Ko-Ko constantly tests the audience's understanding of the conventions of filmic space in the cartoon. In *Modeling*, and throughout the "Inkwell" series, Ko-Ko frequently ventures forth from his drawing board into the "real" space of the Fleischer studio. This act is, at once, the central act in the struggle for his corporeal presence, a defiance of standard cartoon conventions, and a visual confirmation of his "amphibian" status between the worlds of imagination and reality.

The conventions of filmic space in the "Inkwell" series are reinforced in virtually every episode. At the beginning of most "Inkwell" shorts, we see the artist's hand (or a cutout photograph of a hand) drawing Ko-Ko, a simple act that immediately offers a wealth of clues for decoding spatial relationships in the film. First, it visually differentiates cartoon space—depicted with only black-and-white lines—from live-action space—depicted with a gray scale and realistic photographic detail. Second, it shows these spaces to be "adjacent": Max at the drawing board occupies a space relative to the cartoon space that Noel Burch, in his *Theory of Film Practice* (1981), calls the fifth segment of offscreen space: "behind the camera."[10] Finally, the artist's hand shows the relative scale of the drawn space. These clues, taken together, establish the larger context of the live-action studio space in which a smaller, drawn cartoon space exists. Given the temporal order of their presentation—the artist's hand usually draws Ko-Ko's world, the cartoon world is rarely established first—it seems clear that the Fleischers carefully crafted this reading—not the inverse, in which Ko-Ko's cartoon space is shattered by a kind of Brechtian intrusion of the artist's hand.

Figure 4.5 *Modeling* shot 44: Ko-Ko skis away from his drawing board. Reproduced from collections of the Library of Congress.

This reading of the filmic space in the "Inkwell" series is consistent with the theories articulated by Herbert Zettl in his groundbreaking book on film and television aesthetics, *Sight, Sound, and Motion* (1990). Zettl argues that whenever "graphicated second-order space" (for example, a keyed-in box over the shoulder of a newscaster, or the line world of Ko-Ko) is presented with "first-order space" (the newsroom set, or the Fleischer studio), the audience tends "to perceive the people operating in first-order space as more 'real' than the people appearing in graphicated second-order space" (206). Throughout the "Inkwell" series, the black-and-white line cartoon world of Ko-Ko functions like a video key, repeatedly articulated as smaller, less "real," and adjacent to the photographic, live-action world of the Fleischer studio.

Having established these spatial parameters, the early part of *Modeling* shows us either Max and Crandall in their discrete live-action space, Ko-Ko in his discrete "cartoon space," or the area where the two spaces adjoin, namely, Max's hand interacting with Ko-Ko on the drawing board. Longer animated segments in the middle of the film (shots 28, 30, 32, and 34) in which no live-action elements intrude lull the viewer into accepting Ko-Ko's world, the conventional cartoon space with its drawn, linear perspective and "distant" horizon line. Visual elements that would maintain the viewer's awareness of the "adjacent" studio space—such as registration pegs, the edge of the drawing board, or Max's hand—are beyond the camera's frame. In these longer shots, Ko-Ko inhabits traditional cartoon space, and the audience's focus shifts from curiosity about the studio and the production process to enjoyment of the clown's antics. Each of these shots is a freestanding bit of animation having no direct interaction with the live-action space save for cross-cutting. Shot 34 is almost a whole minute of pure animation, a shot long enough to draw the viewer into the cartoon space without referencing the larger studio context. Though intercut with live-action shots of the studio, these longer animated shots establish the conventional, "transparent" cartoon space the cartoon viewer is accustomed to.

Having established this cartoon space over the preceding few minutes, Ko-Ko's mischievous escape into the live-action space (shots 44 and 45) becomes a more daring transmigration. The escape takes place when the background of the cartoon scene presents a hole in an ice-covered lake. This drawn element in a sense "punctures" the plane of the drawing board, and as Max fishes in the drawn hole for Ko-Ko, the clown moves through it and skates into real space (see Fig. 4.5) from behind the drawing board.[11]

Throughout the "Inkwell" series, the illusion of movement into "real space" is maintained primarily through editing. The cutting in these films suggests the temporal continuity and spatial proximity of the real and animated space: Ko-Ko frequently leaps forward on his drawing board; the film then cuts to Ko-Ko landing overlaid on a photograph of a desktop or a carpeted floor. Using photographic backgrounds that match the live-action studio space and maintaining screen direction aid the illusion. Relying on codes of editing that were firmly entrenched by the 1920s—in particular, the maintenance of motion vectors from shot to shot—the Fleischers were able to convincingly suggest Ko-Ko's movement from the drawing board into the live-action filmic space. For viewers who are technically naive, this suggestion is complete enough to be transparent, and the narrative flows. For viewers who are technically sophisticated, part of the "entertainment"—as it has always been in animation and special-effects films—is to decode how the illusion is being created.

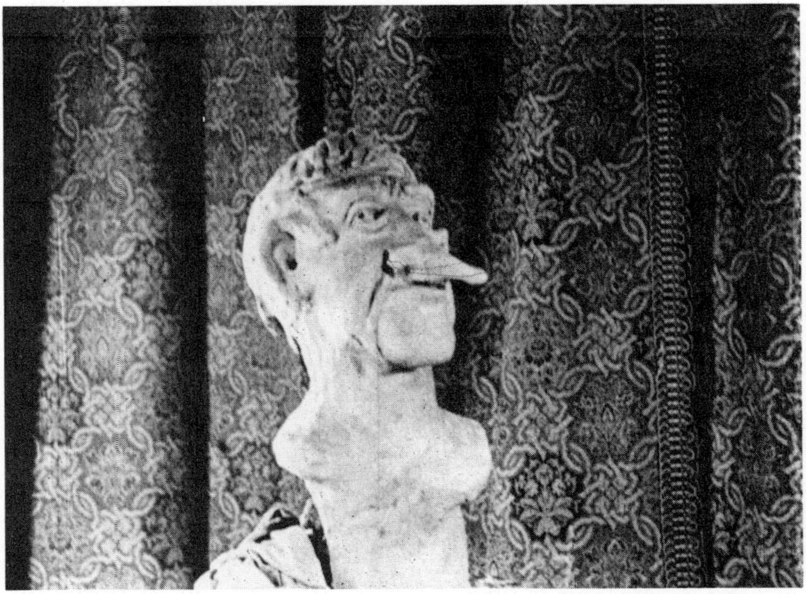

Figure 4.6 *Modeling* shot 55: Nose of the bust wiggles. Reproduced from collections of the Library of Congress.

With live-action space shown in virtually every episode, pixilation of objects is a logical and visually rich method for showing Ko-Ko in that space. Typically, the Fleischers suggest through continuity editing that Ko-Ko climbs under a three-dimensional object in the studio space, and then they pixilate that object. For example, *The Clown's Little Brother* and *Ouija Board* imply that Ko-Ko is inside a pixilated inkwell and a pixilated hat, respectively. These tidy, arresting bits make Ko-Ko's presence in the live-action space more concrete. In *Modeling*, the same pattern is followed, except that the object Ko-Ko climbs under happens to be the nose of a clay bust. The clay is animated first on the bust (see Fig. 4.6), then moves to the floor of the studio. In this context, the use of clay at the Fleischer studio appears to be just another object to pixilate—a different technique used to maintain novelty in the series and, in a larger sense, to maintain cinema as a perpetual novelty.

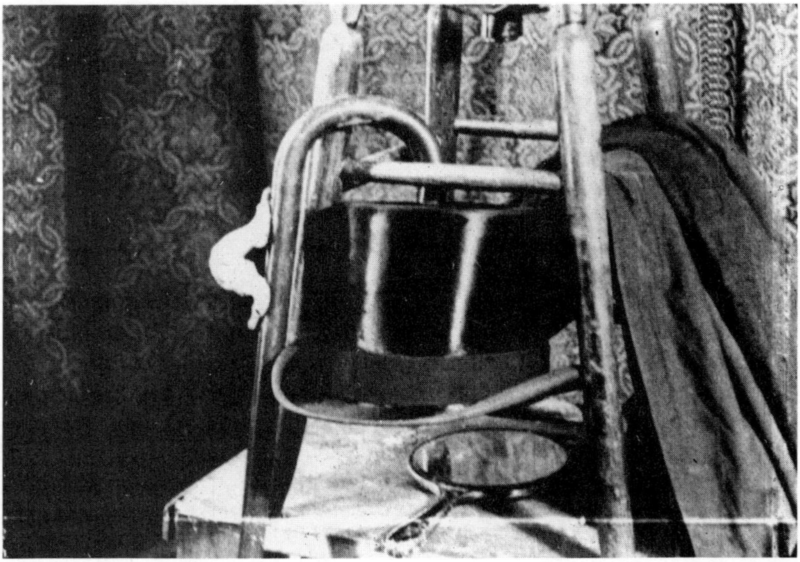

Figure 4.7 *Modeling* shot 62: Clay blob wiggles down the cane. Reproduced from collections of the Library of Congress.

CLAY ANIMATION IN 1921

The clay animation in *Modeling* is primitive in conception but fairly sophisticated in execution. First, the notion that a clay bust must be used to set a context for clay animation is a quaint holdover from earlier works like *The Sculptor's Nightmare* and *Swat the Fly*, but the popular domestic sculpture seems more at home here. In the "Inkwell" series, the Fleischers cultivated an image of their studio as a homey atelier bustling with all manner of artists and tinkerers, often dressed in lab coats. To show Ko-Ko interacting with paints in a cartoon, the Fleischers would no doubt have opted for the simplest narrative premise and set the scene with an artist painting a landscape or still life. Using a literal motivation like a bust to introduce a new technique into the series may be plodding, but it is pure Fleischer brothers. Second, the primary clay form used here is a common coil—the "snake"—often the first object rolled out by a child who plays with clay. Though simple, the form is handled well by the unknown animator, who shows the clay-covered Ko-Ko inching down a real cane (see Fig. 4.7) and along the floor (shot 64). Here, the movement is well paced and suggests the frantic futility of Ko-Ko's flight. Later, the clay inchworm "stands up and looks around" before it is captured (see Fig. 4.8), an expressive touch. Throughout, the accumulated expertise of the Fleischer studio with line animation shines through the simplicity of the inchworm and its movements.

Modeling demonstrates that, in 1921, clay animation remained a simple, accessible, expressive technique, particularly for experienced animators with a knack for experimentation. At the same time, the appearance of clay animation in only one out of six Fleischer films released that year clearly indicates that it had not established much of a foothold in the East Coast animation houses since the burst of clay films from Dayton and Hopkins in 1917. Comparing *Modeling* with the great number of slash and cel films produced in 1921, one could conclude that (1) these flat methods were already seen as the only methods that could realistically meet the huge demand for theatrical shorts, and (2) clay had been written off as an unworkable production method. The overwhelming acceptance by the film industry of flat animation forms—particularly cel—was evident by the early 1920s. But the notion that clay was held in a certain regard (or disregard) by animation houses does not necessarily follow. By 1921 clay was already less popular with producers than it had been when Willie Hopkins produced for Universal only four years earlier. But the fact that clay was used once in the "Inkwell" series says more about a format that invited technical innovation than about the perceived advantages or disadvantages of clay in a demand-driven system of production. At the Fleischer studio, the use of clay animation was more likely just another "off-the-shelf" method that could be plugged into their format, as they did with cutout animation and pixilation.

Sergei Eisenstein described *Merbabies*, a Disney cartoon from 1938, as a "comical liberation from the timelock mechanism of American life. A five minute 'break' for the psyche" (23). In a sense, the "Inkwell" series served a similar function for 1920s audiences. The very format of the series—an animation studio whose work routines are constantly being thwarted by a cartoon character—embodies a comical liberation from the dull drudgery of work, the focus of American life. With its abundance of technical innovations, with its gags based on the magical interaction of live-action and cartoon world, with its central character a knavish amphibian who moves between these two worlds, the "Inkwell" series gave audiences a comfortable format with just the right touch of chaos. As a singular example of clay animation from the early 1920s, the appeal of *Modeling* lies in its destruction of the spatial conventions of its genre, in its combinations of novel animation techniques, and in its central character, who thrives on confounding his creators. These traits support the entire series as well.

THE DINOSAUR, PUBLIC IMAGINATION, AND SILENT MOTION PICTURES

Only two other silent-era films utilizing clay deserve mention here: Buster Keaton's *The Three Ages* (Metro, 1923) and *Monsters of the Past* (*Pathe Review*, 1928). Both of these films use animated clay dinosaurs. *Three Ages* animates a clay brontosaurus for Keaton's entrance in the film; Virginia May presents a traditional version of dinosaurs in a longer educational segment for the *Pathe Review*, a weekly newsmagazine for the screen. Despite the long-standing fascination with prehistoric beasts in the popular mind, dinosaur movies—clay or otherwise—were uncommon in the silent era, and little has been written about the treatment of dinosaurs in the mass media. There have always been obvious difficulties involved in reproducing the animals for the screen, and dinosaurs were seldom seen in American film outside of the work of Willis O'Brien. For example, according to the subject index of *The American Film Institute Catalog of Motion Pictures Produced in the United States: Feature Films 1911–1920*, a text that extensively indexes trade magazines from the period, there were no feature films made during the period dealing with dinosaurs.[12]

Some significant filmic treatments of dinosaurs have loosely coincided with periods of renewed public interest in dinosaurs following major finds in remote areas, particularly McCay's immensely popular *Gertie the Dinosaur* (1914) and O'Brien's *The Lost World* (1925). And while the image of dinosaurs *in animation* has swung between cute and cuddly versions like Winsor McCay's *Gertie* and more vicious treatments, such as that in *Fantasia* (Disney, 1941), the gentle *Gertie* version has influenced animation more, extending into clay animated dinosaurs like Trixie in Art Clokey's "Gumby" series and the Vinton studio's *Dinosaur* (1980). More realistic portrayals of dinosaurs have moved into live-action special-effects films. Our purpose here will be

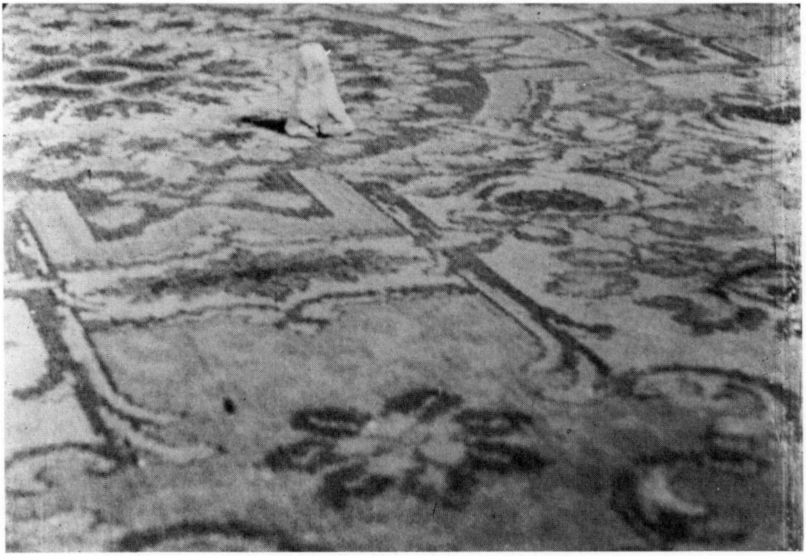

Figure 4.8 *Modeling* shot 66: Clay blob looks around. Reproduced from collections of the Library of Congress.

to trace the interconnections between public interest in the beasts, influential depictions like *Gertie*, and the clay animated treatments from the 1920s mentioned above.

Public awareness of dinosaurs was increased by several digs after 1900. One dig east of Vernal, Utah, sponsored by the Carnegie Museum from 1909 to 1923, captured much public attention through the mass media and a worldwide museum exhibition.[13] During the same period, in 1910, a "dinosaur rush" occurred in western Canada at Red Deer River in Alberta. In 1915 the Utah site was designated by President Woodrow Wilson as the Dinosaur National Monument.[14] This period of public fascination with the dinosaurs spilled over into animated films when *Gertie the Dinosaur* brought Winsor McCay's creation to life in a short initially designed to be used in conjunction with the famous cartoonist's vaudeville stage act. *Gertie* was "an impressive early version of multimedia performance art" (Canemaker 1987, 13). Its popularity was immediate, its impact enduring. One indication of the film's immediate success was the fact that a fake version was produced within a couple of years of the original, probably by the Bray organization. Chuck Jones has said, "The two most important people in animation are Winsor McCay and Walt Disney, and I'm not sure which should go first" (Canemaker 1987, 211).

In all likelihood, the popularity of *Gertie* was noticed by a young man trying to enter the film business in 1915, a man whose lifelong work with stop-motion dinosaurs would ultimately have an enormous impact on the popular conception of dinosaurs: Willis O'Brien. Experimenting with dimensional animation, O'Brien first used clay that year to produce a test film for what would become *The Dinosaur and the Missing Link* (1915). Apparently, O'Brien's test had taught him something about clay's limitations, because *The Dinosaur and the Missing Link* used latex-covered armatures, not clay, for the characters.[15] The five other prehistoric films that O'Brien made for Edison's Conquest Film Program also used latex puppets, the technique that would become the central element in his art as well as the standard method for stop-motion animation in science fiction films.

O'Brien must have recognized early on that latex characters, compared with weighty and malleable clay characters, have the advantages of more expressive movement and unchanging, realistic surface textures. Even in clay films that strive toward realism, there is always a soft, cartoonish crudeness to the characters' features. As the artistry of Willis O'Brien demonstrates, clay simply cannot provide the realism that latex puppets can.

Clay Animated Dinosaurs in *The Three Ages* and the *Pathe Review*

Realism was not the issue in 1923 when Metro distributed *The Three Ages*, a six-reel comedy by Buster Keaton. The film was quite successful, owing perhaps in part to the fact that it coincided with a period of renewed public interest in dinosaurs. From 1922 to 1925, an Asiatic dinosaur rush at the Flaming Cliffs in the heart of Mongolia produced the first find of dinosaur eggs, a discovery that "caught the fancy of the public. . . . [The eggs] became objects of lively interest in the news columns, and dinosaurs, already widely appreciated by people in many lands, became increasingly well established in the public mind" (Clobert, 217).

As the film moves through three different time periods, Keaton must compete with a formidable rival for the affection of a woman. There is no need for exacting realism here, since the clay animation in

Keaton's film is intended, first, as a sight gag, and second, as his homage to *Gertie the Dinosaur.* Keaton's entrance in the prehistoric setting is typically inventive, using selective framing and match cutting for humor in the film.

The scene begins with the "Great Stone Face" reclining wistfully in full caveman attire on an idyllic "rock" that extends beyond the bottom frame line. When Keaton slaps the rock with a stick, the rock begins to carry the impassive Keaton across the countryside; the camera tracks along, creating an extended moment of dislocation for the viewer. The dislocation resolves in the next shot as the film cuts to a long shot of a simply animated clay dinosaur carrying a miniature Keaton across the frame. In typical fashion, Keaton later plays his restrained body movements against the large scale of the beast, climbing to the top of the brontosaurus's "head" and shading his eyes as he peers into the distance. A match cut returns us to animated long shot for the punch line: a tiny Keaton perched like a hood ornament atop the beast's head is "panned" left and right as the beast scans the horizon. On command, the brontosaurus bends down to let the caveman disembark. The clay animation, an appropriate choice here, allows Keaton his usual play against large-scale objects and adds a friendly, cartoonish quality to his trusty carrier.[16]

Following the traditions established in *Gertie* and *Three Ages* of the gentle brontosaurus, Virginia May produced a thematically similar dinosaur short in 1928 for the *Pathe Review*, which contained clay animation. Entitled *Monsters of the Past*, it was packaged in the fifth issue of the series in 1928 (see Figure 4.9). The opening title cards set the scene: "10 million years ago, when the world was young, giant reptiles ruled the earth," and, "These mighty beasts were busy writing their own chapter in the sands of time." Intercut with these two cards is an establishing shot (shots 1 and 2) of a brontosaurus eating leaves and shifting its tail in simple, slow movements, revealing the vegetarian's peaceful, plodding nature (see Appendix 5 for a complete shot list).

The clay animation contributes to the depiction of the brontosaurus's dullness. With the creature in profile and a set—an unimaginative mix of trees—that does not establish much depth in the frame, the shot lacks dynamism in composition as well as movement. This flatly staged, slow-moving style of animation continues throughout the piece and suggests a novice's attempt to avoid rapid jerky movements at the expense of overall pacing. Throughout, the clay models used

Figure 4.9 Title card from Virginia May's *Monsters of the Past*. Courtesy of International Museum of Photograph, George Eastman House.

are bluntly formed with little surface detail to suggest their skin or scales. The next title card announces, "And the sands reveal another chapter," followed by a backwards take of sand moving away to reveal dinosaur bones lying there, then moving together to form a dinosaur skeleton.

Breaking what little setting has been established to this point, the film takes a decidedly educational turn with the next title card: "From these fossils, the sculptor, *Virginia May*, can reconstruct the dinosaurs of the past." The film cuts to May standing in a waist shot at a sculpture stand in what appears to be a study (shot 4). Behind her, a photograph of a ballet dance hangs on a wall that is also covered with an Oriental rug, positioning her work as a feminine pursuit, uplifting and in the tradition of other classical arts. In a backwards take, the film shows May rapidly raising a completed tyrannosaurus from a mound of clay (see Figure 4.10). This backwards take has been carefully

Figure 4.10 In a backwards take, Virginia May "reconstructs the dinosaurs of the past." Courtesy of International Museum of Photography, Geroge Eastman House.

staged so that the action is smooth and seamless, with no extreme movements or technical gaffes that might highlight its technique. This shot at once brings the viewer back to the present, demystifies the scale and composition of the monster models, and shifts the tone of the work to "filmed demonstration." While this shot and the accompanying title card identify May as the character designer of the dinosaurs, the film never addresses the question of who animated the creatures.

After a title card stating that the tyrannosaurus was "many times larger than our modern elephant," a flat two-shot (shot 6) continues the educational tone by simply showing an elephant to scale against the tyrannosaurus (see Figure 4.11). As they face each other, the elephant methodically flaps his ears and swishes his tail. The film continues in the style of an illustrated textbook as title cards announce each

Figure 4.11 Flat staging in *Monsters of the Past*. Courtesy of International Museum of Photography, George Eastman House.

shot: "And he was the greatest flesh eater of all times" precedes a long shot of the tyrannosaurus stepping on a carcass, tearing a leg from it, and, in a closer match cut, eating the flesh (shot 8). The film then pits the evil "T-rex" against a triceratops, the "peaceful vegetarian"—a classic confrontation that calls to mind many Willis O'Brien dinosaur films. In an interesting twist to the staging of this battle, the tyrannosaurus kicks the triceratops and actually hops as he attacks (shot 18), movements that are achieved by extending the monster's tail outside the frame for support. The scene builds to a climax as triceratops impales T-rex, who dies writhing on the ground. The film closes with triceratops inspecting his dead enemy and shifting his tail in restless triumph.

Nothing is known about Virginia May's life, though the restrained style of her animation—an obsessive concern that the action be fluid and not too rapid—marks it as that of a novice. May's animation is flatly staged for the camera, with a predominance of left-right entrances and exits. The sheer weight of her models, combined with the hesitant style, produces plodding action. Overwrought surfaces occasionally crack. These are precisely the disadvantages of clay that O'Brien would avoid with lighter latex puppets.

For all its limitations, *Monsters of the Past* remains one of the few theatrical shorts at the end of the silent film era to use clay. May's work suggests an application of the clay technique in the service of education that was not fully realized until four decades later, when animators like Art Pierson, Elliot Noyes, and Will Vinton produced a substantial body of clay animated educational shorts in the 1970s. The sound era was close at hand, and cel animation quickly demonstrated the power of the intimate synchronization of picture and sound. One year after "Monsters" was released, an era of further consolidation and standardization of American animation would begin with the release of a synchronized sound cartoon from a minor producer about to become a central force in Hollywood, *Steamboat Willie* (Disney, 1928). As the Disney studio began to establish the fluid, richly detailed "full-cel animation" aesthetic in the 1930s, the animation departments of the other studios studied the Disney films closely, taking what they could use from his studio's style. Playing off the conventions of storybook realism the Disney studio had established, newer, sassier versions of the Hollywood cartoon would emerge under the direction of Tex Avery, Bob Clampett, Chuck Jones, and others. The worldwide popularity of Hollywood's cartoon stars and the sheer number of studio cartoons and cel animated features that were produced in the next two decades guaranteed that clay animation would remain a marginal technique.

I have found only two American films between 1928 and 1948 that use clay as a secondary technique. In *Wild Oysters* (Max Fleischer Animated Antic, 1940), Charley Bowers produced a puppet film using some plasticine oysters. Bowers's work was nearly lost until it resurfaced in 1977 at the animation festival in Annecy, France. In 1947 Douglass Crockwell, who had worked in a variety of animation media, included some clay in his compilation film *Glen Fall Sequence* (1946). It was not until the postwar rise of independent filmmaking on the West Coast that clay animation would begin a renaissance of sorts. Leonard Tregillus began animating clay in 1948, making two films in which clay figures are the primary technique. Later, when television created a huge demand for children's programming, Art Clokey would give the medium the kind of widespread visibility it had not enjoyed since Willie Hopkins by bringing forth the first clay star, Gumby. These two independent animators brought new energy to the medium through experimentation, as we shall see in the following chapters.

5

Leonard Tregillus: West Coast Independent

Leonard Tregillus was a chemist who made experimental films, worked for Eastman Kodak, and became one of the leading amateur filmmakers in Rochester, New York, in the 1950s. In 1948 and in 1950, Tregillus gathered around him a group of friends and other filmmakers—principally Ralph Luce[1] and Denver Sutton, with occasional help animating from his wife Connie—to produce two largely abstract clay animated films that use the color, pattern, and form of plasticine objects to create their primary visual impact. These lively films are expressions of the spirit of independent 16mm filmmaking from the so-called underground—the second period of avant-garde filmmaking that flourished, particularly on the West Coast, in the 1940s.

Leonard Tregillus was born in Toronto, Ontario, on 28 September 1921. At the age of five, he moved with his family to the Mill Road estate of the advertising magnate Albert Lasker in Lake Forest, Illinois, where his father, Cyril Alwin Tregillus, took a job as the estate manager. Tregillus attended schools in Libertyville, Illinois, and graduated in 1939 from Lake Forest High School, where he had become engrossed in still photography and experimented with an old movie camera. He went on to Antioch College in Yellow Springs, Ohio, where he majored in chemistry, graduating in 1944. While at Antioch, Tregillus ran the Antioch Motion Picture Advisory Council, which brought a variety of motion pictures to campus. He also began a short animation called *Pop Goes the Weasel* using cels that were used in campus film showings as filler during reel changes. When Tregillus left

Antioch in March 1944, Ed Fischer, who went on to do cartoons for the *New Yorker*, completed the film.[2]

Tregillus moved to Berkeley, California, to enroll in graduate school; with World War II in full swing and the draft looming, he was able to continue his deferment with an assignment to the radiation laboratory at Berkeley until the war ended in April 1945. After the Manhattan Project was wrapped up, Tregillus moved on to the naval ordinance testing station in the Mojave Desert, where his principal activity was photographing test rockets with a high-speed Theodolite camera. Following his marriage to Connie Root on 9 September 1945, Tregillus returned in 1946 to the University of California as a graduate teaching assistant. At Berkeley, he researched the dropping mercury electrode and was awarded his doctorate in chemistry in 1950.[3]

After graduation, Tregillus attained a longtime goal: he moved to Rochester, New York, in September 1950 to take a job with Eastman Kodak as a researcher on photographic film preparation and processing. He remained with Kodak for 33 years, working on a number of different projects, including the Smithsonian Astrophysical Observatory's effort to photograph the Soviet spacecrafts in 1957. His major development for Kodak was Bimat film, which was used in the unmanned Lunar Orbiter to take high-resolution pictures of the moon in the summer of 1966.[4]

While in Rochester, Tregillus continued making home movies and shorts for fun. Though his productions were sporadic, there was a pattern to his output: "Every time I got pregnant," his wife Connie contends, "Leonard would go off and make a film."[5] Working with others at Kodak, Tregillus produced two humorous live-action shorts—*Casey at the Bat* (1955) and *Flashback* (1955)—set in the gardens of the George Eastman House. Tregillus made a number of other avant-garde films and compilations that explored the potential of low-tech effects in 16mm: *Hodge Podge* (1955), *What Your Camera Can Do* (1955), and, with Denver Sutton, *Odd Fellows Hall* (1950). *Odd Fellows Hall* is a farcical romp in the style of Mack Sennett, set in a macabre boardinghouse. In addition to animating dividing clay forms very similar to those Tregillus created in *Proem* (1949), *Hodge Podge* toys with a variety of effects, including stop-motion oil paint on glass, pixilation of the human figure, animated playing cards, and Mondrian-like cardboard squares, inverted camera, and shots made through a metal tube. *What Your Camera Can Do* is a visual textbook that describes simple effects that can be created by the amateur in 16mm.

Tregillus's work in clay animation began while he was a graduate student at Berkeley, a period that marked a revival on the West Coast in experimental filmmaking. In his book *An Introduction to the American Underground Film* (1967), Sheldon Renan argues that, although there was very little experimental film made during the Depression, the growth of 16mm film as a training medium in the armed forces during the Second World War made film more accessible, leading to a regional revival. "It was in 1943, however, on the West Coast that the avant-garde film, then called the experimental film, began its real comeback. The second film avant-garde lasted approximately from 1943 to 1954."[6]

Renan argues that this revival was centered in Los Angeles, with the dominant stylistic force being Maya Deren's *Meshes of the Afternoon* (1943), a film shot in that city. More work followed by three other Los Angeles filmmakers—Kenneth Anger, Curtis Harrington, and Gregory Markopoulis—and spread to other cities. Meanwhile, "San Francisco developed its own film ferment" (Renan, 88). Attending retrospectives of early experimental films at the "Art in Cinema" showings of the San Francisco Museum of Art, Leonard Tregillus was stimulated to experiment in clay, especially after seeing Douglass Crockwell's *Glen Falls Sequence* (1946), a film that ends with a very brief clay animated scene (C. Tregillus letter).

TWO EXPERIMENTAL CLAY FILMS: *NO CREDIT* AND *PROEM*

Heavily reliant on color and transforming shapes for its visual interest, *No Credit* (1948), produced by Tregillus, Ralph Luce, and Jack Chambers, has clay animation remarkably similar to that in Clokey's *Gumbasia*, which would come seven years later. Both films are highly episodic, changing settings and design elements in a series of vignettes that, at times, are well staged and deftly animated. In both films, the camera is sometimes canted to increase index vectors within the frame, and a startling magic effect is created as clay is cut away over successive frames and objects vanish. Though both films convey the pure pleasure of color, editing, and movement, Clokey sticks to more rigidly geometric forms. In *No Credit*, the forms are less geometric, transforming at times into amorphous creations that perform bits of stage business: for example, two spheres struggle to pass through a hole in a clay wall, or clay flowers "consume" clay cylinders.

In spite of some lighting and production problems unique to the amateur—an extension cord falls over the backdrop at one point—*No Credit* is quite sophisticated for beginning filmmakers. The camera is frequently placed low and close to the action, giving the clay figures presence in the film, while set designs articulate the foreground and are deep enough to allow selective focus on the action, heightening depth in the frame. The filmmakers demonstrate their technical virtuosity by animating the film's title in reverse to create an opening gag: "No Credit" is written in clay coils, then animated wads of clay enter and transform the title to read, "This film is . . . no credit . . . to . . . ," followed by a tilt down to the filmmakers' names, "[Ralph] Luce, [Jack] Chambers, and [Leonard] Tregillus." *No Credit*'s combination of visual design and lively animation led to distribution through Cinema 16, which described the film in its catalog as "a charmingly informal and spontaneous film experiment. Smooth animation, wit and artistic imaginativeness combine to create a thoroughly enjoyable cinematic experience that can be enjoyed by both adults and children."[7]

The next year Tregillus and Luce collaborated again, this time on *Proem*, an 11-minute fable that suggests an abstract world of castles and knights, then reveals its point of reference to the real world. Though one of the film's title cards identifies Luce as the copyright holder of this work, according to Connie Tregillus the film was a collaboration. Luce and Tregillus would talk about animating a particular scene, then trade off running the camera and working the figures. Crude in set design and technically unpolished—flicker and exposure problems, for example, are evident—*Proem* is nevertheless capably animated. In copy written to highlight its symbolic overtones, *Proem* is described in one catalog as "a burlesque allegory in eight scenes using modelling clay in semi-abstract forms."[8] Another says, "With gaily-colored modeling clay as their medium, the film-makers have chosen a theme from Lewis Carroll for this witty experimental film. The fluid forms and simple shapes suggest objects and characters. The film is an allegory in eight scenes taken from a game of chess."[9] Viewing the film as a simple allegory, Tregillus himself was somewhat amused by this intellectualized catalog copy (C. Tregillus interview). Its description in *Films on Art 1952* is more apt: "It has the quality of a nightmarish chess game and some highly inventive aspects."[10]

Figure 5.1 Curious clay figure inspects the opening titles for *Proem*. Frame enlargement courtesy of the author.

The opening credit sequence of *Proem* is deftly animated, with simple techniques that imbue the characters with a sense of life (Figure 5.1). A clay ball grows a neck and approaches a box inscribed with the film's title. The creature cranes curiously to read the title, its neck splits into two prongs, then it rolls into a ball and moves to the side of the box. The film cuts to a side view of the box, where the creature reads another credit: "Produced by Tregillus and Luce." The creature bumps into the box and starts it spinning, revealing the final credit: "Music by William Smith." (The film was originally animated to a work by the Hungarian composer Erno Dohnànyi, but at the request of the distributor, the track was changed and Smith, a saxophonist with the Dave Brubeck Quartet, composed an original sound track.) Here, the filmmakers demonstrate a technical command of dimensional animation techniques as the camera smoothly tilts up to reframe the final credit. Simple camera movements throughout the film sug-

Figure 5.2 The guard figure from *Proem*. Courtesy of Connie Tregillus.

gest the animators are quite comfortable with manipulating the camera frame by frame.

The first scene fades in on an imposing castle overlooking a large field/chessboard below. Inside the castle, a group of clay creatures watch as pyramids come together into a pedestal, which is mounted by a circular disc. The characters bow to this object, then literally penetrate its base as the scene fades to black. In the next scene, the camera follows a "guard" emerging from a guard house riding an inchwormlike "horse" (Figure 5.2). In a series of simulated tracking shots, the guard falls off his horse and remounts it, only to fall off again. At one point, the reluctant horse refuses to move and is spurred on by the guard's lance/toothpick. This scene contains some of the most expressive animation in the film, and Connie Tregillus, who witnessed the shooting of parts of the film and assisted in animating some scenes, states that this and the other "good bits" in the film were the work of her husband (C. Tregillus interview).

The third scene of *Proem* opens by intercutting two wholly different kinds of shots: characters shaped like a bishop's miter, who glide about

Figure 5.3 Stylized characters form a ceremonial arrangement in *Proem*. Frame enlargement courtesy of the author.

on an altar in formal, ceremonial arrangements (Figure 5.3), and an abstract "sea" of clay that rises in swells, forming itself into a kind of temple arch. A thief enters the temple/cave, spies a precious jewel lying within a circle, and tries to abscond with it. A guard springs up from the floor, but the thief simply plows over him to grab the jewel and escape. Running through a surreal landscape of pillars and closing doors, the thief is trapped in a cave by the tentacle-like arms of stalactites and drops the jewel into a stream.

The next scene fades in on a queenlike figure moving along a path with her two servants (actually spheres). She crosses through a mountain pass and sees four cylinders dancing and transforming below. As the intricate choreography continues, the figures bow in submission as the king enters, leading the queen and attendants back over the mountain and into the castle. There, the light-colored royal entourage encounters a dark-colored royal entourage, and the queens square off,

Figure 5.4 The opposing armies gather at the close of *Proem*. Frame enlargement courtesy of the author.

indicating their disdain for each other. In rapid succession, the opposing armies gather on the field/chessboard below, the chess motif becoming more apparent as they face off (Figure 5.4). As the armies close in on each other, the film match dissolves to a live-action chess game, an unfortunately blunt resolution of any ambiguity that might remain.

The films of Leonard Tregillus and his collaborators are rooted in the tenets of the 1940s underground, a movement brought on by increased access to 16mm filmmaking materials, as well as by an awareness of the avant-gardists of the 1920s and the explosion of non-Hollywood filmmaking known as Italian Neorealism and French New Wave. The intellectual environment of this era, "[t]he climate of the new man, in which to be new is to be desirable, in which the individual is constantly re-forming his idea of the world, in which a personal point of view is all important, was one of the factors that produced the underground film" (Renan, 46). Producers of these works accepted plasticine on its own terms and were content to let the expressionistic use of color and free-form movement to music augment low-tech mise-en-scènes and crude, nonanthropomorphic figures. As such, these films are playful, personal expressions that speak in broad terms and ask audiences to co-create a loose "narrative" or kinesthetic reading.

Distributed in art houses and classrooms in the early 1950s—Cinema 16 picked up *No Credit* and A. F. Films handled *Proem* and *Odd Fellows Hall*—these films never gained the audience that theatrical releases like *Modeling* or even "Monsters of the Past" did. But, as experimental clay films, they broke new ground that would be more fully cultivated by Art Clokey, Elliot Noyes, and David Daniels when they began to explore clay's potential for creating abstract visuals and free-form films. As we will see in the next chapter, Clokey's dedication to the principles of his filmic and religious gurus—Slavko Vorkapich and Sathya Sai Baba—would enable him to embed the techniques of abstract, underground, non-narrative clay films into a mainstream product for the new medium of television.

6

Clay Animation and the Early Days of Television: The "Gumby" Series

A drastic upheaval in Hollywood during the 1950s had the unlikely effect of returning clay to the mass audience after decades of relative obscurity. The advent of television, which began its first period of sustained growth in 1948, is cited as the chief cause of the decline of the Hollywood studio system. But that explanation is too simplistic:

> In fact a simple tabulation of the decline in box-office takings against the sales of television sets reveals two important facts about the relationship between the film and television industries. Firstly, the decline in cinema audiences had begun well before sufficient receivers had been sold to make television a serious rival. Secondly, that decline continued long after television sets had been bought by most households, which implies that the new medium grew increasingly effective in holding on to its audiences, and that those audiences found new ways of spending their spare cash in the affluent 1950s and 1960s.[1]

A comparison of expenditures between 1946 and 1957 for cinema versus radios, televisions, and records shows that cinema experienced a 13 percent decline while radio/television/records increased 8 percent (Izod, 134). Night baseball and the bowling craze also took their toll on movie attendance. Douglas Gomery points out that the two overriding concerns of returning veterans were purchasing a home and having children, two activities that would have cut movie attendance regardless of the advent of television.[2]

Film studios, panicked by the threat of competition from television, at first tried to buy their way into the medium. Under scrutiny for antitrust violations, and recently ordered to divest themselves of their exhibition outlets by the Supreme Court decision in *United States v. Paramount, et al.* (1948), the major studios were prevented by the Federal Communications Commission (FCC) from making significant inroads into television ownership (though newly divested film *exhibition* companies made exactly those moves). After some unsuccessful experiments with "theater television" between 1949 and 1952, the studios opted for the technological "quick fix" of Cinerama, Cinemascope, Vistavision, 3-D, and an increase in color film production to differentiate their product from television's.

They also searched frantically for budget-cutting measures to take in their operations. With their relatively high production costs per minute, the cartoon production units of Hollywood studios were targets for reduction throughout the 1950s and 1960s. Warner Brothers cartoon production for 1949–52 averaged 30 films a year, but one decade later (1959–62) that number had fallen to 20 films a year. Ultimately, the cartoon units were closed down, Columbia/Screen Gems' in 1949, MGM's in 1967, and Warner Brothers' in 1969.

The studios also began syndicating their animated product to television as part of a package that included feature films. This move ultimately brought cartoons to any local television station in search of program material to fill the dead spots in the local kiddie hour. In 1955, "RKO sold 740 features and 100 shorts outright to General Teleradio, the entertainment subsidiary of General Tire and Rubber—which promptly syndicated them, earning an estimated $25 million from them by 1957." Warner Brothers followed suit in March 1956, selling "outright 850 features and 1,500 shorts for $21 million" (Izod, 165). By 1958 television had access to an estimated 9,500 Hollywood features, accentuating the continuing decline in box-office receipts and leaving exhibitors wondering how anything—from technological innovation to more risqué content—could stop the onslaught of the new medium (ibid.).

THE GROWTH OF CHILDREN'S PROGRAMMING

While theatrical exhibition was declining in the 1950s, television was beginning to exhibit a greater sophistication in its programming strategies, including an emerging understanding of how to program for children. Though "The Howdy Doody Show" which ran from 5:00 PM to 6:00 PM on Saturday evenings on NBC from 1947 to 1960, is generally regarded as the first children's television program, the first children's show to have a profound impact on networks, producers, and advertisers was "The Mickey Mouse Club," an hour-long show, scheduled for 5:00 PM weekdays, that first aired on 10 October 1955.

The show was a remarkably astute move for all the parties involved. ABC-TV, which had emerged from the NBC Blue radio network but lacked the capital to take advantage of the growth of television, had already merged in 1951 with United Paramount Theatres, the newly divested arm of Paramount that was flush with capital and already worried about the decline of moviegoing. Disney, searching for capital and publicity for its new amusement park, Disneyland, saw ABC-Paramount Theatres as the solution on both counts. ABC-Paramount bought roughly a one-third interest in Disneyland, and Disney began to produce "The Mickey Mouse Club" as a break-even proposition that was little more than a vehicle for advertising the new park and the entire Disney product line. ABC gained a broad family audience through the high visibility of the Disney characters and the first television run of Disney theatrical cartoons (Izod, 163).

What was truly remarkable about "The Mickey Mouse Club," however, was the way it transformed children's advertising on television. Cy Schneider, the account executive for Mattel Toys at the Carson/Roberts Agency, points out that "[i]n 1955 there were no recognized brand names in toys. Household names such as Mattel, Hasbro, and Fisher-Price were unknown to the consumer. An adult buying a toy for a child went into a conventional toy store and asked for something appropriate for a six-year-old girl or a nine-year-old boy or perhaps the fad product of the particular season, if there were one. (Imagine doing that today at a Toys-R-Us.) Since children had limited exposure to specific toys, even they hardly knew what to ask for."[3] "The Mickey Mouse Club" changed all that because, "[f]rom 5:00 PM to 6:00 PM on weekdays, the show dominated the airwaves, and every Wednesday from 5:30 to 5:45 when Mattel played their three commercials, 90 percent of the nation's kids were watching the first toy commercials ever put on film" (Schneider, 21). The astounding success of the Mattel "Burp Gun" during Christmas 1955—a product featured in those ads—was testament to the newfound power of television for children. With the Burp Gun, Mattel more than doubled its overall sales volume in one year, and the symbiotic relationship between networks, program producers, and advertisers of children's products was forged (ibid., 22).

As television grew phenomenally in the 1950s and the recycling of studio cartoons became absurdly repetitious, broadcasters looked for new programming sources to fill the lucrative and expanding children's market. The search for cost-efficient program material—cheap shows that delivered large audiences of children to advertisers—gave rise in 1957 to Hanna-Barbera's application of the limited animation techniques that were being rediscovered by the animators of United Productions of America (UPA), an unforgivable crime in the eyes of many animation fans. Television made household names out of Hanna-Barbera characters—Yogi Bear, Huckleberry Hound, Pixie and Dixie—the first cartoon stars born not in movie theaters but in the broadcast medium.

At the same time that Hanna-Barbera began reshaping cel animation (television had none of the major studios' preconceptions about what a cartoon should be), clay had its first chance in many years to reestablish its audience, since television programmers were eager to try out anything on kids as long as the "cost per thousand" (the price advertisers paid to buy 1,000 viewers) was reasonable. In this speculative climate, driven by television's hunger for programming, clay animation brought forth its first television superstar, an offbeat character who represents a convergence of the forces shaping children's television in the mid-1950s: Gumby.

GUMBY, ART CLOKEY, AND HIS MENTORS

Art Clokey is the sculptor-filmmaker behind the blue-green clay star of the 127 "Gumby" episodes produced between 1955 and 1971. (Three more films were produced in the series that did not feature Gumby.) "Behind" is an appropriate word here, because Clokey invested a large measure of his personal philosophy and creative energy in each episode. Transferring the bedtime stories he told his children to film, Clokey presented Gumby and his horse and sidekick, Pokey, in creative six-minute episodes that refrained from indulging in the cynicism and violence Clokey disliked in classic Hollywood cartoons (Figure 6.1).

Television provided Clokey with the opportunity to explore not only a different medium but a message quite different from that of

Figure 6.1 Gumby and Pokey in the original series. Photo courtesy of Art Clokey.

traditional theatrical cartoons. Gumby embodies a simplistic ethic of fair play and kindness toward his fellow animated creatures. He is forever good-natured, open, caring, and happy. With his tiny mitten hands, bell-bottom legs, and whimsical pompadour (suggested by a high school portrait of Clokey's father with a cowlick), Gumby is almost irritating in his utter cuteness (Figure 6.2).

Gumby's unwavering sense of goodness is the logical outgrowth of his creator's lifelong interest in religion. Clokey believes that Gumby is a reflection of the underlying innocence and idealism that have permeated his relatively sheltered life. Clokey was born on October 12, 1921 in Detroit, the son of Arthur Wesley Farrington and Mildred Shelters Cairnes. He was raised a Christian Scientist, lived in a foster home with a woman spiritualist, and was adopted by a devout Episcopalian, Joseph W. Clokey, a composer at Pomona College in Oregon. Clokey studied to become an Episcopal priest before attending film school at the University of Southern California in 1951. In the mid-

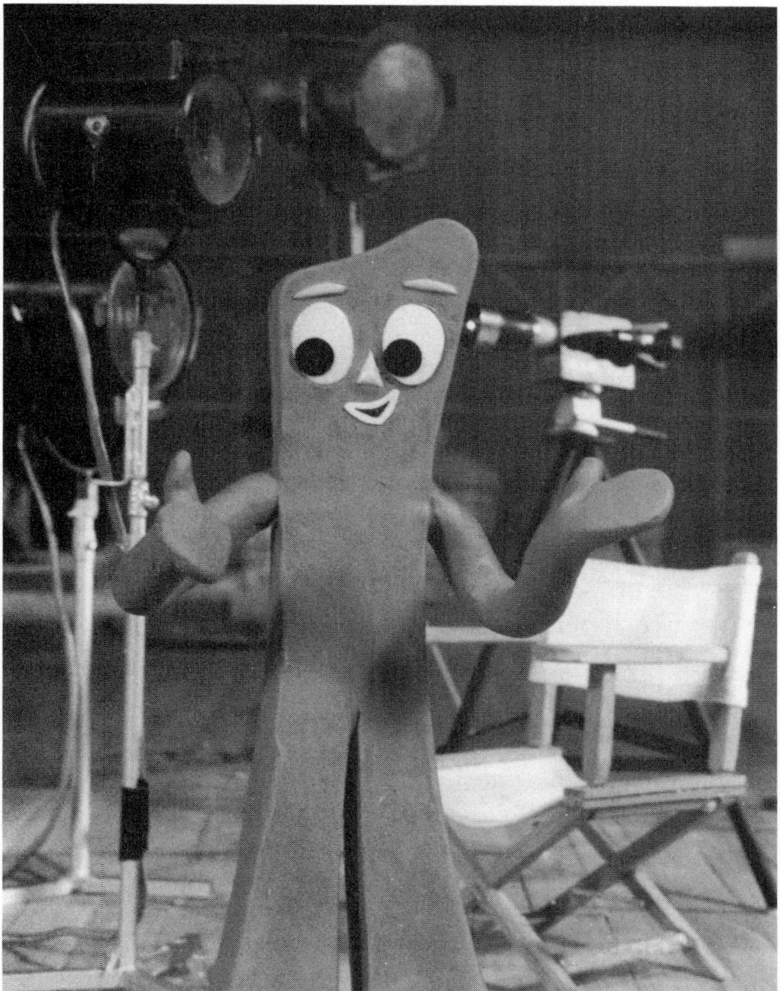

Figure 6.2 The picture of goodness and innocence: Gumby backstage. Photo courtesy of Art Clokey.

1960s, along with the Beatles and a large percentage of the population of southern California, he explored the burgeoning self-awareness movement through a number of groups. "I explored ways to become a better director by getting into all kinds of self-awareness. Encounter groups, psychotherapy, Esalen. You name it, I tried it," he says (1982 Clokey interview). Clokey's continuing interest in Eastern philosophy is evident in his 1975 film *Mandala*, a work with spiritual overtones in which a camera takes a seemingly endless journey through a long series of richly detailed, sculpted clay archways. Clokey says, "I attempted in *Mandala* to suggest a time- and mind-expanding experience, the evolution of consciousness, by orchestrating deep cultural symbols from the collective unconscious." Moreover, Clokey believes that part of Gumby's appeal also comes from our collective past: the appeal of clay is universal, the clay itself being "a symbol of the basic nature of life and human beings. As I've toured the country with Gumby, I've realized that kids pick up on that. Their fascination with Gumby is a gut reaction to clay—not the character—just to the clay itself" (1982 Clokey interview).

Clokey and his wife Gloria journeyed to India to visit the avatar Sathya Sai Baba in 1979 and came away confirmed believers. Clokey claims to have seen the guru materialize objects in his bare hands, and he is convinced that the guru will eventually take control of the world's problems, because he has supernatural powers. Sathya Sai Baba is also credited with Gumby's resurgence: "I stood there with Gumby [before Sai Baba], and he did this circular motion with his arms. I could see the sacred ash . . . coming out of his hand. He plopped it right on Gumby, and when we came home things started to happen across the nation—college and theater tours. The episodes started appearing on TV again, sales of the Gumby toys began to pick up, and then Eddie Murphy did his Gumby skit on 'Saturday Night Live'" (1982 Clokey interview). Later incarnations of the Gumby spin-off toys reflected Clokey's deeply held beliefs: some models had the Sanskrit word for "love" emblazoned on the chest.

While his religious beliefs have shaped the content of Clokey's work, his visual style has been guided by another guru: Slavko Vorkapich, whom he studied under at USC. A Yugoslavian immigrant and a student of painting, Vorkapich came to Hollywood in 1921. Best known for his collaboration with Robert Florey and Gregg Toland on the experimental film *The Life and Death of 9413—A Hollywood Extra* (1928), Vorkapich wrote a few articles outlining his filmmaking theories around 1930. In his application of graphic art principles to filmmaking, Vorkapich parallels Eisenstein's thinking about "conflicts within the shot" (or "montage cell") when he states: "Like lines, colors and sounds, different motions have different emotional values. . . . There are many such fundamental expressive motions and their possibilities of combination are unlimited. To mention briefly only a few: Descending motion: heaviness, danger, crushing power (avalanche, waterfall) Pendulum motion: [m]onotony, relentlessness (monotonous walk, prison scenes, caged animals) Cascading motion, as of a bouncing ball: sprightliness, lightness, elasticity, etc. (Douglas Fairbanks)."[4]

Vorkapich's methods of compressing motion and visual energy into a shot earned him a niche in Hollywood as a montage expert, directing special montage sequences for features, including *Crime without Passion* (1934), *The Good Earth* (1937), *The Last Gangster* (1937), and *Shop Worn Angel* (1938). A 1937 *New York Times* article summarized Vorkapich's methods of montage: "Now, a 'montage,' it might be wise to explain, is a panoramic effect in which the events covering a period of time are boiled down to a succession of rapidly paced interlocking 'flashes.'. . . It is a far different thing from simple continuity cutting and Vorkapich refers to it as 'film ideagraphy.'. . . In preparing a 'montage,' the first task is to ascertain exactly what is to be told. He then writes his own script, listing the central idea involved, with suggestions for expressing them [*sic*] pictorially."[5]

Clokey says with some reverence, "Vorkapich got down to basics. His theory was that motion pictures dealt only with motion and the illusion of three-dimensional objects created by the director's use of shapes, shadows, colors, and motion. He said if you understand how to organize those things through camera angles, camera movement, pace, and so forth, you could make any film more interesting. And it happened to me. I got my first job doing commercials for Coca-Cola and Budweiser because people were fascinated with how I could make the screen come alive in ways that other people couldn't" (1982 Clokey interview). Clokey continued to study under Vorkapich after leaving USC through private seminars that Vorkapich held in his home.

Vorkapich's reliance on fundamental graphic shapes and his concentration of imagery into a kind of visual shorthand is evident in Clokey's abstract animation, particularly in an early work called *Gumbasia* (1955). Clokey notes: "In *Gumbasia*, I filmed geometric and amorphous shapes made from modeling clay of many colors. These shapes moved and transformed to the background rhythm of jazz. I wanted to avoid as much as possible the distraction of recognizable forms in *Gumbasia*. It was an experiment in pure movement, where the whole plane moved out in different shapes this way and that. *Gumbasia* was filled with movements that, when put together, created a feeling."[6]

Vorkapich's tenets, integrated over many years of filmmaking into Clokey's work, are deeply embedded in the "Gumby" series. First, and perhaps most evident, Clokey purposely drew the character designs of Gumby and Pokey from basic geometric shapes, combining simple forms like cylinders, triangles, and circles. This style of character has several advantages for the clay animator. It reduces the time needed to construct a character and simplifies the animation of movements suggested by the narrative. Visually, it offers a cleaner, simplified form for character action and dialogue, regardless of the setting. Moreover, in a medium in which the restraints of simple stories and short running times often require a character's external design to directly objectify its inner state, Vorkapich's "ideagraphy"—making ideas visually concrete and easily identifiable—is clearly useful. For instance, the character designs of Prickle—an erect dinosaur with triangular spines—and Goo—a rounded water droplet with soft locks of hair—visually express what Clokey regards as the two fundamental types of people in the world: "The prickly are the rigid and uptight, and the gooey are easygoing and flowing" (Kaplan and Michaelsen, 4).

Second, Vorkapich's theories of montage are also evident throughout Clokey's work. In many shots in the "Gumby" series, there is careful attention to screen vectors—the angle and direction that a character moves through filmic space. The careful and creative use of these vectors from shot to shot gives the episodes a seamless, flowing style. For example, in the title–theme song sequence that opens most episodes, there are four shots in which Gumby (or his body rolled up into a ball) moves screen left to right along a vector line; the cuts guide the viewer's eye, using very precise matches in screen direction and screen position. In one shot of this sequence, Gumby glides along the established vector line, standing on one foot. The camera tracks along with him effortlessly. In the background, a series of artfully arranged objects break up the screen space, creating a contrasting, syncopated rhythm and providing a visual counterpoint to the flow of Gumby and the camera. At the end of the shot, Gumby collides with an object and appears to tumble into the next shot—a different location—simply through carefully crafted editing. While maintaining continuity of screen vectors is commonplace in film editing, the careful construction of these cuts in "Gumby," reflecting Vorkapich's influence, often approaches true artistry.

Jim Danforth (*When Dinosaurs Ruled the Earth* [1965], *Flesh Gordon* [1975], *Caveman* [1982]), a stop-motion animator who began his career in the Clokey studio after he graduated from high school in 1958, feels that Vorkapich's influence broadened Clokey's filmmaking talents more than it focused his skills as an animator:

> I guess [Clokey] was, and still is, basically a good filmmaker rather than specifically an animator or special-effects person. With his background in film aesthetics and editing, he taught me a lot about editing—much more about editing, in fact, than about animation. Art introduced me to this kinetic, arabesque style of cutting that he'd picked up from Vorkapich.
>
> But once he'd taught me all these wonderful things about editing, the paradox was that, if I started applying them, he'd get real upset. I remember one scene where I had a character fall backwards into the camera lens, block the image completely, then roll away from the camera and stand up in the next shot. I remember Art got annoyed at that—it smacked of some kind of editing, and we were supposed to be animators. Art would still rather be making art films. So he'd toss in some of Vorkapich's philosophy into these little puppet films when he could, but somehow it wasn't okay for us to do it.[7]

After leaving USC and Vorkapich's tutelage, Clokey struggled to find work wherever he could. At a prep school in Studio City, California, Clokey taught everything from art to chemistry and tutored a child whose father happened to be Sam Engel, the powerful producer from Twentieth Century-Fox and head of the Motion Picture Producers' Association. "Sam was fascinated with *Gumbasia*, the art film I'd made under Vorkapich," Clokey recalls. "He said it was the most exciting he had ever seen and suggested I animate clay characters in films for children. He financed the first *Gumby* pilot film, so he's sort of the Godfather of Gumby" (1982 Clokey interview).

"Gumby" went into production in 1955 and aired on NBC in the summer of 1956. The first five episodes were aired in rotation on "The Howdy Doody Show," beginning 16 June 1956 and continuing through 20 October 1956. Five new episodes premiered between 3 November 1956 and 2 February 1957.[8] Gumby soon got his own network show, which ran Saturday mornings from 10:30 to 11:00 on NBC from 23 March to 16 November 1957.[9] The show was set in Mr. McKee's Fun Shop, with Bob Nicholson, formerly of "Howdy Doody," hosting as Scotty McKee. Clokey's production budget for the clay animated segments was $650 per minute, roughly half what Hanna-Barbera was spending at the time for a minute of limited cel animation. By contrast, Clokey prided himself on producing full animation—in three dimensions—that capitalized on the inherent advantages of the medium: the movement in space of objects that create their own shadows and perspective; a high level of surface detail, found naturally in clay and in the children's toys used for props and set pieces; and the screen "presence" a three-dimensional character has when photographed at eye level.

Though NBC gave Clokey complete artistic freedom in his animations, the technical simplicity of many episodes reflects the limited budgets and short production schedules under which he worked. Colored gobo patterns thrown on cycloramas were frequently the only backdrop for an obvious tabletop set. Mistakes were often not rephotographed. Flying objects whose wires are visible, objects that lose registration, and clay that sags over a number of frames were commonly left in the final cut. The pacing of the action is much slower than in the classic Hollywood cartoon. Clokey's rejection of the studio aesthetic of gags, takes, and violence and his reliance on slower pacing did, however, provide one benefit: longer screen time for any given shot. Special effects were usually simple and occasionally obvious to the point of shattering illusions. In "The Small Planets," the filmmaker resorts to the most basic low-tech special effects: scratching the emulsion off the film to suggest retrorockets firing, and using cotton to suggest smoke. Throughout Clokey's mise-en-scène, miniature objects, doll house furniture, small plastic plants, and children's trains, trucks, tractors, and spaceships are prominent. These objects provided simple solutions to the problem of set design.

But, more importantly, the toys and miniatures reflect Clokey's fascination with creating narratives set in a "pretend world," a childlike approach that has obvious appeal for children. For adults and older children, the inclusion of real objects prompts a continuous decoding of the image, a constant comparison of scales and surface features to determine the nature of each object, a search of the frame for identifiable objects. An unconscious set of questions runs through a "Gumby" episode: Is this object clay or not? What material is it made of? How big is it really? Frequently, a mass-produced object of popular culture, or an object of known size and composition, provides the Rosetta stone to decode these questions: Gumby stands on a 45rpm record; Gumby gets entangled in a toy gumball machine; Gumby stands near an egg that has smashed a toy car; the Blockheads hide behind real toy building blocks. Compared with the early work of Will Vinton, whose mise-en-scène is richly detailed and almost entirely made of clay or clay-covered objects, this style looks quaint and unsophisticated, a pastiche that serves only as a backdrop for the narrative. Clokey argues, "Using only clay and clay-covered set pieces gives Vinton's work a certain sophisticated appeal to the intellect, to the artist and adults. Vinton's work is good art. But I'd go crazy, I wouldn't have the patience to do the fabulous things he does. Our stuff has a mass appeal, particularly to kids, because we included real toys and used other materials to dress our sets. We used a mix of media simply to get across a narrative" (1982 Clokey interview).

Gumby ran only one year on the network. When a management dispute prompted the NBC board of directors to fire the network president, Pat Weaver, in 1957, the ax fell on "Gumby," too, since the series was a pet project of Weaver's. Clokey scraped together the money to buy the rights to the episodes NBC had financed and, rather than paying a distributor 40 percent of the gross, traveled the country himself syndicating the program in major cities. Clokey was struggling now with two full-time jobs: both producing and marketing "Gumby." While he was trying to continue production on new episodes, Lakeside Toy Company of Minneapolis, Minnesota, impressed with the show's performance in major cities, approached Clokey with a licensing agreement to manufacture Gumby toys. Relying on a strategy as old as Felix the Cat, Clokey hoped spin-off merchandise would increase the profitability of the animated series and simultaneously increase the popularity of the show.

Gumby toys were a smashing success. Given the immense new marketing power of television to reach into the American home, it was not surprising to find a set of Mickey Mouse ears, a Davey Crockett coonskin cap, and a Gumby doll in most television homes. Lakeside representatives now roamed the country, buying and bartering local spots for their toy line (including Gumby) and using those purchases as a bargaining chip in syndication deals with local stations for the "Gumby" series. The stations received good children's programming at a reasonable rate, and Lakeside cultivated the profitable symbiosis between broadcasting and toy manufacturers that Mattel's Burp Gun had pioneered. With Lakeside handling most of the syndication chores, Clokey was free to concentrate on production.

After "Gumby" had become successful, Clokey was approached by the Lutheran Church in 1959 to produce a series of puppet films illustrating Christian ethics for children. Using articulated puppets,

Clokey created the "Davey and Goliath" series from 1959 until 1972. Each episode ran 15 minutes, over twice the length of "Gumby." With two series in production, Clokey employed almost 20 people in his growing operation: 4 storyboard artists, 6 to 8 animators, a camera technician, 3 people building sets, as well as a battery of people in the front office. Clokey also produced 6 television half-hour specials for the Lutheran Church using Davey and Goliath: "Christmas Lost and Found" (1965), "Happy Easter" (1967), "New Year Promise" (1967), "School . . . Who Needs It" (1971), "To the Rescue" (1975), and "Halloween Who-Dun-It?" (1977).[10]

GUMBY RESURRECTED

The revival of Gumby in the 1980s had its roots in the growth of filmmaking courses on college campuses nationwide, the heightened awareness of animation created by the rise of independent animators during the 1970s, the 1974 Academy Award for *Closed Mondays*, and a nostalgia for almost any television show from the 1950s. A low-technology medium, clay has for years shown growing popularity with the independent, low-budget student filmmaker. Riding this initial wave of interest in clay, Clokey made some personal appearances around Los Angeles and toured college campuses in the early 1980s. He was astonished at the enthusiastic response that greeted him. College audiences packed auditoriums and sang the "Gumby" theme song that television had etched into their childhood memories over 20 years earlier.

About the same time, Eddie Murphy brought forth on NBC's "Saturday Night Live" his stand-up foam-rubber version of the green clay hero and the now-famous refrain, "I'm Gumby dammit!" Television's power to highlight, to glamorize, hit full force when it returned a fading animated figure to a high place in the nation's consciousness. Clokey's reaction to the ensuing hoopla was typically low-key. He saw Murphy's act as part of the renewed interest in the lost innocence of the 1950s, and characteristically, he viewed that interest in religious terms: "I never minded the whole Eddie Murphy thing. I've got a good sense of humor, and I think it's a reflection of his true response to the series. We're always being put down today. People tell us, 'You're a lousy person. You're an inferior person.' But

Figure 6.3 More elaborate mise-en-scéne from the new "Gumby" series. Photo courtesy of Art Clokey.

now people are responding, saying, as Eddie Murphy says, 'I'm Gumby dammit!' That means, 'I'm what Gumby represents: an innocent, good, pure person'" (1982 Clokey interview). Spurred by the free network publicity, sales of "Gumby" episodes on videocassettes and of Gumby paraphernalia revived, and have remained steady.

In 1987, with the Gumby revival in full swing, Clokey signed a deal with Lorimar Telepictures to produce a new series of episodes for national syndication. The $8 million budget was to fund the production of 99 new six-minute episodes. These episodes were combined with some of the older existing episodes to make a syndication package of 65 shows, three episodes per show (Figure 6.3). With Lorimar's backing, Clokey was able to produce animation with "better sets, large crowd scenes, finely crafted soundtracks, complex computer-controlled camera movements, and other luxuries that were not available when the original series was produced some 21 years ago."[11] Thematically, the new shows parallel the old ones by "stressing positive attitudes and values including consideration, cooperation and the ability to resolve problems without resorting to violence" (Cohen, 8). The

Figure 6.4 Gumby rocking in his first feature film, *Gumby 1*. Photo courtesy of Art Clokey.

package was syndicated in 92 markets around the United States, representing 79 percent of the viewing audience.[12]

From 1989 to 1992, the studio produced a feature-length film called *Gumby 1* (Figure 6.4). Working independently, Clokey took the profits, existing sets, and many of the animators from the new series to ensure that he retained complete control of his original script. The crew of 18 animators for the series was pared down to 5, and the 87-minute feature took $3.2 million and 30 months to shoot. The story is "authentic Gumby, through and through," according to Clokey, and revolves around the evil Blockhead's attempts to foreclose on Gumby's barn-studio. Gumby organizes a miniature version of Farm-Aid with his new rock band to benefit the locals. Before the film ends, Gumby has journeyed into the Middle Ages, flown into outer space, and made a music video with his girlfriend. The film is expected to open in the fall of 1993 (1993 Clokey interview).

Art Clokey, the man who revived clay animation by exploiting its potential in the new electronic medium of television, has clearly played a crucial role in the medium's coming of age. A spiritual person, Clokey brought forth a nontraditional character in a nontraditional medium and managed to survive under the economic demands imposed by television. The durability of the "Gumby" series stands as the best evidence that clay animation is viable and appealing filmmaking, and Clokey's perseverance in finding a niche for his series paved the way for the new generation of clay animators.

7

Claymation®: The Vinton Studio Style

Will Vinton is now known as the producer of the California Raisins and as the driving force behind an elaborate style of clay animation called Claymation®.[1] But Vinton was unknown in 1974 when he and Bob Gardiner made a clay animated film called *Closed Mondays*. The film went on to win the Academy Award for animation that year, in a category whose name had recently been changed from "Best Short Subject—Cartoon" to "Best Short Subject—Animated Film." The change was significant, for it acknowledged both the decline of the Hollywood cartoon and the explosion of independent animation in the United States and Canada during the late 1960s and early 1970s. According to John Canemaker, these independents were "part of a new generation of independent animators. . . . They work in places far from the Hollywood/New York film industry and they reject studio aesthetics, large staffs, and assembly-line production methods, particularly the studio preference for the 'cel' method."[2] For clay animation, the Academy Award also marked a coming of age and a recognition of the power of the medium in talented hands.[3]

THE EMERGING ANIMATOR

Will Vinton was born in McMinnville, Oregon, a suburb of Portland, on 17 November 1947 to Gale Vinton, a businessman, and Saima Vinton, a bookkeeper. He began making films while studying architecture at the University of California at Berkeley, where he was interested in the fluid clay sketches created by the sculptural architect Antonio Gaudi. He says:

I got started independently making films in 1966 when I was at Berkeley. There wasn't really a film program there at the time, so I learned filmmaking by trying to make it as much a part of the architecture program as I could.

I . . . enjoyed learning filmmaking the way I did, which was to bend anybody's ear that would talk to me about it. It was much more hands-on, practical experience. . . . I've always just tinkered with stuff. I've always had this fascination with physics and mechanics and physical contraptions. And it wasn't until after I graduated that I learned some of the more traditional filmmaking information.

I did mostly live-action films, some documentaries on architecture history, some experimental stuff, and some films where we'd move an animation camera through miniatures and models.[4]

Vinton met Bob Gardiner at Berkeley, where Gardiner was studying art. Their first collaboration was *Culture Shock*, a rough compilation of home movies and experiments in clay. The film won a first prize at the Berkeley Film Festival in the early 1970s, hinting at the potential appeal of clay for audiences. After graduating, Vinton spent a summer working for Northwestern, a film production house in San Francisco, then went to work for Odyssey Productions in Portland. He had made a dozen or so short films by the time he made an 86-minute documentary, *Gone for a Better Deal*, in 1970: "It was all about the sixties and the youth counterculture. It was a documentary that tried to be entertaining and fun but also told some inside information about what the lifestyle of the sixties was and was not" (1979 Vinton interview). When Vinton was not working at Odyssey, he and Gardiner shot *Closed Mondays* in Vinton's basement over a 14-month period.

Closed Mondays has the free, unrestrained feeling of a first work, an appealing crudeness and lack of polish. The story is simple. The fantasy elements are simple. Clay is used in the film as the natural, unrefined substance that it is. Close shots of the wino's face show fingerprints and texture, and the shots done on glass, portraying one of the wino's fantastic visions, show clay smudges and streaks. Compared with later works from the Vinton studio, the sculpted figures are unsophisticated. As a result, *Closed Mondays* exudes the warm, free, human look of a film animated primarily with the hands.

Closed Mondays does not exhibit any extraordinary sculpting techniques, but one of the virtues of clay is that it does not demand refinement to be successful. Clay forms have a presence that is striking, no matter how crude the form, because they naturally cast shadows, exhibit surface detail, and create perspective. These traits make clay an easy medium for the novice to exploit. *Closed Mondays* demonstrates this accessibility and also foreshadows Vinton's later commitment to the narrative and to the technological advancement of the technique.

Closed Mondays won the Academy Award, first, because of its engaging story, and second, because it applied several new clay techniques to that story. Like classic works by Disney, the film establishes a naturalistic setting from which the central character departs into a fantasy world, a narrative structure well suited to animation and one the Vinton studio used repeatedly. The original version of the film opened with the wino entering the gallery past a sign announcing the week's exhibit, "the usual crap," suggesting from the outset the film's skeptical view of art. (The line was later matted out at the request of the distributor.) The film goes on to explore a range of responses to various styles of art. As the wino peruses the gallery's sculpture and paintings, fantastic visions take over as the works come to life and draw him into their world. The wino's gallery tour shows how art can unlock personal visions and personal responses in the viewer. His muddled reactions range from tearful empathy toward a painting of a washerwoman, reminiscent of a Rembrandt, to confused disgust toward a modernist, geometric work ("What was that guy thinking of?"), to openly hostile outbursts toward a computer sculpture ("Blabbermouth computer!") (Figure 7.1). In an ironic twist, the wino himself is frozen and gilded into a standing sculpture in the film's final shot, suggesting the ability of art to become all-encompassing, to capture all aspects of life.

Closed Mondays is a remarkable synthesis of simple story and fresh technique, and perhaps the most remarkable technique introduced was precise lip-sync dialogue using a life-size clay bust. Though earlier characters like Gumby had approximated lip-sync dialogue with simple, broad mouth movements, Vinton and Gardiner actually shot live-action footage of the actors reading their lines to be used as a frame-by-frame reference for the pacing and sculpting of clay mouth positions (as well as body movements). This "clay rotoscoping" of reference film—particularly in close-up—brought the full impact of this lip-sync technique to the screen for the first time.

In *Closed Mondays*, Vinton and Gardiner also orchestrated camera movements—tracking, panning, and dolly shots created one frame at a time—just as earlier, more expensive dimensional shorts like George

Figure 7.1 The wino and the blabbermouth computer from *Closed Mondays*. Courtesy of Will Vinton Productions Archive.

Pal's "Puppetoons" had done. Adapting techniques he had developed in college for moving cameras through architectural models, Vinton constructed low-tech, plywood camera rigs for producing animated camera moves. As the wino wanders through the gallery, an extended point-of-view shot careens through the gallery toward a painting. The additional effort involved in creating this camera movement gives a dynamic suggestion of his drunken exploration and positions the audience with the wino. Applying this technique to further the narrative is typical of the production values that Gardiner and Vinton struggled to bring to the medium.

The uniqueness of Vinton's stylistic innovations became even more apparent in *Mountain Music* (1975). Ostensibly an animated rock concert set in a mountainous forest, the animated musicians are not well developed as designs or as characters. However, the real star of the film is the set itself, an entire forest of miniature clay trees, clay streams, and clay animals.[5] The sheer scale and level of detail involved in constructing this set showed a strong commitment to creating a complete clay world. As the Vinton character designer and animator Barry Bruce notes, the actions of a clay character tend to appear more convincing in a clay world. "It really bothers me to see a clay character with an obviously wood tree next to him because all of a sudden your audience starts trying to figure out how you did the animation. . . . That's a distraction when you're making plot-oriented films" (Bruce workshop). Maintaining the illusion of a complete clay world has produced a mise-en-scène in the longer Vinton films that includes few nonclay objects, bringing a consistency and aesthetic wholeness to his studio's style.

ADAPTATIONS: VINTON'S LONGER CLAY NARRATIVES

Three longer films followed *Mountain Music*. Each runs 27 minutes, a long form in animation, nearly half the length of the first feature-length animation, the 58-minute *Snow White* (Disney Studio, 1938). By adhering fairly closely to the original narratives in these longer films, Vinton established his studio as the preeminent storyteller in clay with *Martin the Cobbler* (1976), *Rip Van Winkle* (1978), and *The Little Prince* (1979). As adaptations of narratives of substantial length, they present human action within a specific setting and develop dramatic conflict and in-depth characterization. These dramas marked a significant break with the existing body of clay shorts—trick films, humorous clay films, and even the short clay adventures of Art Clokey's Gumby—and foreshadowed Vinton's interest in bringing a clay feature to the screen.

Martin the Cobbler follows the plot of Leo Tolstoy's short story, "Where Love Is, God Is" (1885), almost to the letter. In the original work, Martin, a cobbler who has lost faith in God because of the death of his family, is left a Bible by a passing pilgrim. One night while reading it, Martin falls asleep and hears a voice announcing, "I am coming to you tomorrow." The next day, as he periodically glances out the window in expectation of the Lord's visit, he has the opportunity to be charitable to several passersby: a street sweeper, a mother and her infant, a small boy, and an old woman. As the day ends, Martin is left wondering why the Lord has not come. As he reads his Bible that night, the passersby reappear to him in a vision, each saying, "It is I, Martin." Reading his Bible again, Martin realizes that the

Lord *has* visited him: "In as much as you did this to the least of my brethren, so you did it to me."

The Vinton version duplicates the action of Tolstoy's tale by including the three encounters with the passersby. Indeed, smaller details have been meticulously re-created in the film, such as the description of Martin's basement residence with one ground-level window through which he recognizes the passing townspeople by their shoes. This strict adherence to the original short story imparts to *Martin* a strong dramatic structure and a clear resolution of Martin's inner conflict, which is the basis of the film's realistic tone. Vinton did take the liberty of adding one character: the mouse who resides in Martin's house. The addition of this little creature to the story follows the Disney tradition of offering comic relief through often diminutive sidekick characters, such as Thumper in *Bambi* (1942), Jiminy Cricket in *Pinocchio* (1940), and particularly Timothy the Mouse in *Dumbo* (1941).

Although the original version of Washington Irving's "Rip Van Winkle" (1819) has a romantic setting and some character development of Rip and his wife, Dame Van Winkle, unlike Tolstoy's tale it lacks action and dramatic conflict. In fact, the entire plot consists of Rip being drugged by a mysterious group of gnomes he encounters deep in the Catskills during one of the hunting trips he takes to escape his nagging wife. Awakening 20 years later, he returns to town and slowly comes to realize what has happened to him. To supplement Irving's meager plot, Susan Shadburne's adaptation superimposes on the story a conflict between Mr. Vanderdonk and Rip.

Although Vanderdonk appears briefly in the Irving version, in the film he is given a prominent role as a landlord intent on collecting his rent from Rip. Owing to his laziness, Rip has fallen into arrears. In the film, a needy neighbor interrupts Rip's journey into town to sell his crop. Rip generously gives the neighbor some of his harvest and loses most of the remainder off the back of his wagon as it rumbles into town, ensuring once again his default on the rent. Although none of this action occurs in the book, it sets the stage for a final confrontation between the miserly Vanderdonk and Van Winkle when he arises from his 20-year sleep.

Shadburne's sentimental stock plot of wicked landlord versus kind-hearted tenant is not enhanced by an equally sentimental musical number, "Here Am I," which unfortunately is heard twice during the film. The second rendition comes as Vanderdonk picks up where he left off 20 years earlier, berating Rip to pay up his rent. The song's introduction, as awkward as any in a bad Hollywood musical, occurs when Rip interrupts Vanderdonk's tirade to say, "Mr. Vanderdonk, I don't have any money. I've never had any money. But I do have a new song I'd like to share with you." Vanderdonk accepts Rip's song as payment in full; one can only surmise that the rent Rip owed did not amount to much. The film's resolution has Vanderdonk taking Rip into his home, contrary to the story, which has Rip's daughter taking him in.

Regardless of the merits of the musical additions to the script, the addition of some conflict was surely necessary given the lackluster nature of the original. And even though the landlord subplot appears superimposed on the film, it is offset by Vinton's capitalization on the story's setting and on the opportunity for fantasy that Rip's encounter with the gnomes presents.

REALISM AND FANTASY IN VINTON'S WORK

Rip Van Winkle is typical of the Vinton studio's longer narrative films in its inclusion of a dream or vision sequence. Vinton argues that the inclusion of non-natural, visual entertainment through dream sequences enhances the overall impact of these films:

> For anything to be exciting in terms of its visual effect, you have to play it against something else. You just can't play it and play it. It wears out. So what we've tried to do in our films is to create a world that you go into that you accept as reality. And then we play with that world either through dreams or visions, which makes those visions, I think, a little more powerful. To me, films—even live-action films—that are just nonstop abstractions are harder to relate to than films which set a stage, which set a context and then take you off on a journey and then back into that context. (1979 Vinton interview)

In *Rip Van Winkle*, Rip's journey begins with a drink of grog offered by the mountain gnomes. As Rip falls into a deep sleep, his 20-year slumber is visualized with an elaborate segment of relief animation—flat slabs of clay animated on a rostrum camera. The foreground movements of an incredible array of clay forms are closely synchronized to the sound track—it descends in an ominous crescendo—and the forms are matted over a continually moving background of time-

Figure 7.2 Storybook realism in *Rip Van Winkle*. Courtesy of Will Vinton Productions Archive. © Will Vinton Productions, Inc. All rights reserved. Claymation® is a registered trademark of Will Vinton Productions.

lapse clouds.[6] Thus, in direct opposition to the storybook realism of Vinton films, elaborate clay relief animation is used here to sweep the audience into Rip's phantasmagoria, a detour that ultimately returns the audience to the story's more tangible setting in the clay Catskills. As in animated films from *The Sculptor's Nightmare* to Disney's *Dumbo*, the visions produced by strong drink are an opportunity for escape from the narrative into a land of fantasy.

Nevertheless, grounding *Martin* and *Rip* in naturalistic narratives not only simplifies script development but also offers some very practical advantages, according to Barry Bruce: "In order to avoid fistfights, we tend to move toward realism. Everybody can agree on that. If we say, 'What does a birch tree look like?' and we get in a fight, we go to the library and look it up" (Bruce workshop).

Given their storybook realism, the early Vinton films dictate very detailed, naturalistic character designs (Figure 7.2). The Claymation® figures are broadly rendered so the audience can quickly identify their gross character traits: for example, the angular features and long, hooked nose of Vanderdonk in *Rip Van Winkle* suggests the archetypal miser. *Rip* in particular demonstrates the rising influence of the character designer Barry Bruce, who first joined the staff on *Martin the Cobbler*. *Rip* marked the beginning of cleaner, more expressive faces based on a traditional style of caricature known as the *portrait-charge*, a "loaded likeness" in which a large head with slightly exaggerated features is placed on a small but detailed body. This style of caricature was popularized in America during the 1870s in the pages of *Vanity Fair*. In his sophisticated sculpting of Rip's head, Bruce used large coils to suggest hair and meticulously smooth surfaces for skin and clothing, while exaggerating the nose and mouth of his oversized head in the manner of the portrait-charge. This style of figure became a trademark of the Vinton studio and is most evident in the Mark Twain figure from *Adventures of Mark Twain* and the Ray Charles and Michael Jackson caricatures in the Raisin commercials for the California Raisin Advisory Board. In short, Bruce's artistic influence in the studio as a character designer has been considerable from the beginning.

After the figures are built, they are "costumed" during the design process to fit the various settings of the script. Authentic touches, such as Rip's rusting musket and ragged clothes, are instrumental in fleshing out a scene. And given that the characters must present a range of emotions in these tales, a significant area of directorial control at the Vinton studio is the use of live-action reference film to work out characterization, gesture, and action. The net result of careful character design and artful use of reference film is a style of animation that conveys naturalistic human movement in shorthand; though it limits body movements and is slightly stiff, this style is rich in the range of gross facial gestures that can be written on oversized heads.

The storybook realism of *Martin* and *Rip* gave way to a more lyrical, impressionistic production, a clay animated rendition of Antoine de Saint-Exupery's ethereal fable *The Little Prince* (1943), a delicate allegory of a child from outer space moving in a grown-up's world. Many critics have seen in *The Little Prince* overtones of Saint-Exupéry's own life, and his wife once stated that the book was an allegory on their love.[7] Though addressed to children, its philosophical ramifications are more apparent to adults. The story's appeal to both children and grown-ups springs from "its poetic charm . . . its freshness of imagery, its whimsical fantasy, delicate irony and warm tenderness," all of which place it among a "select company of books like La Fontaine's *Fables*, Swift's *Gulliver's Travels*, Carroll's *Alice in Wonderland* and Maeterlinck's *Blue Bird* which also have a dual appeal" (Smith, 200).

Vinton says the imaginative nature of the story forced the studio to break new ground:

> In *The Little Prince*, we shifted away from realism, the realism that's in everything from *Closed Mondays* to *Rip Van Winkle*. We toy with realism in those films by using clay lip sync, facial expression, and so forth. But in *The Little Prince*, we tried to avoid dealing with reality. We tried to use visuals that were more symbolic of the *meaning* of the story, rather than a straight, literal visualization. So as a result, we changed the Claymation® technique itself.
>
> I think the story was crying out for something more than a literal interpretation. I personally hated the Lerner and Lowe musical that Paramount did of *The Little Prince* [1974]. All the lines come out just as literal as they could possibly be, and they added these song-and-dance numbers. They're running across the desert and singing and dancing and kicking up sand. The whole thing is just preposterous. So we were reacting to that as much as anything.[8]

The resulting film compresses sophisticated optical effects (primarily slit scans), the movements of kabuki theater, stark camera work, and clay painting into an elegant story. The animation follows the order of the original work and uses the Little Prince's lines verbatim but eliminates some scenes, like the planet of the tippler, in order to fit the 27-minute format.

Outside of the optical techniques used, the film's stylization centers on kabuki-like movements and nontraditional camera usage. In an early desert scene, this stylization is announced as the Little Prince gestures to the pilot with his arms, which rapidly grow into a kind of "wing-shaped trail" as they move up, then return to normal as the "wings" are progressively cut away from the bottom (Figure 7.3). The effect mimics in clay the stagger frame printing techniques of Norman McLaren's film *Pas de deux* (1972) and is intended to add a magical quality to the Little Prince's movements, though its effect tends to be more dislocating by focusing the audience's attention on the technique itself.

The visual stylization continues in the next scene as the Little Prince—speculating that a sheep on his planet may jeopardize his precious rose—annoys the pilot, who is trying to focus his attention on repairing his engine. As the dialogue continues, the film shuns tradi-

Figure 7.3: Stylized movement in *The Little Prince.* Courtesy of Will Vinton Productions Archive.

tional over-the-shoulder shots for a cutaway of the pilot's hand working on the engine in close-up. As the Little Prince's musings about his planet compete for the pilot's attention, the engine is literally overrun by clay roses. The pilot battles to maintain his focus on repairing the engine, and the roses are cut away only to regrow as the Little Prince intrudes once more, a transformation of their competing concerns into an economical though somewhat clumsy visual metaphor.

Later, avoiding an anthropomorphic rendering of the Little Prince's rose, the film presents instead a faceless blossom that uses her leaves as arms and stem as a body. The rose emotes simply through body language animated in a long sequence of pauses, movements, gestures, and dissolves. These movements were suggested by shooting reference film of mime artists. Vinton notes:

> We did shoot reference film for *The Little Prince*. We used mime artists and people who knew Japanese dance. It was not so much filming action as filming interpretive movement. It was more for particular gestures, because you can't rely on it exactly, you want to select those things in it that are best. . . . We would have the mime artist listen to the track and say, 'This is what the character wants to say. How would you do that with your body?' It was only marginally successful because they would get into movements that were too esoteric to read well for the average person by the time you transfer them into clay. (1980 Vinton interview)

Clay painting provided the final and perhaps most significant element of stylization for *The Little Prince*. Adapting the clay relief and clay matting techniques pioneered in *Rip Van Winkle*, the studio explored the possibilities of animating foregrounds and backgrounds independently by matting clay animated foregrounds over clay painted backgrounds. Where *Rip* uses live-action, time-lapse techniques for background skies, *The Little Prince*'s moving *clay* skies were created by animating smeared and blended mixtures of clay and oil paint with a pallet knife on glass and marrying it to the foreground action in the optical printer. Joan Gratz, an animator who joined the Vinton studio during the production of *Rip* and went on to win the 1992 Academy Award for *Mona Lisa Descending a Staircase*, created a fluid "waterfall" of clay in subtly changing colors to stylize the desert sky in the initial meeting of the pilot and the prince. Through the artful use of this technique, Gratz was able to animate not only clay skies but a striking sequence that depicts a swirling, impressionistic waltz of the Little

Prince and his rose. Vinton says clay painting complements the stark use of camera in the film:

> In the desert scene, normally you would go in and do over-the-shoulder shots, two shots, and so forth. I'm very comfortable with that because I come from live-action commercial film production. But with this film, we wanted to do it a bit differently, we wanted to say something else. We see the pilot and the Little Prince as tiny specks on the horizon of this flat, empty desert. There's hardly anything going on. But perhaps we've done something else in the shot instead—brought the sky to life and had it mean something in terms of the dialogue. (1980 Vinton interview)

THE FIRST CLAY FEATURE: THE ADVENTURES OF MARK TWAIN

The Vinton studio continued to expand in the early 1980s and even produced a few commercials. But shorts such as *Dinosaur* (1980), *A Christmas Gift* (1980), *Creation* (1981), and *The Great Cognito* (1982), as well as a clay animated trailer for Bette Midler's performance feature *Divine Madness* (1980), continued to dominate the studio's production. By 1983, less than a decade after *Closed Mondays*, the Vinton studio's filmography included 12 films and 9 commercials—almost 250 minutes of animation—and the studio had grown to around a dozen full- and part-time staffers.[9] About the same time, the studio had embarked on the production of a feature film that would be over three years in production and was ultimately released in 1985: *The Adventures of Mark Twain* (Figure 7.4).

In his book *Traveling in Mark Twain* (1987), Richard Bridgman comments on how travel writing such as *The Innocents Abroad* (1869) and *Roughing It* (1872) gave the author both freedom and structure:

> Travel writing not only encouraged Mark Twain to comment on striking aspects of the world . . . but it also permitted him to use his special literary gifts, which displayed themselves best in the short bursts of pointed observations, anecdotes, episodes and tales. . . . Still, while the journey produced variety, it also conferred an elemental order on the random experiences. . . . However arbitrary or disproportionate the stages of the journey might be, they still lay along a central organizational spine that started somewhere, moved linearly, and ended somewhere.[10]

Figure 7.4: The first clay animated feature: *The Adventures of Mark Twain*. Courtesy of Will Vinton Productions Archive.

In an attempt to capitalize on these qualities of Twain's writing—small episodes structured by an overarching journey—the Vinton feature is loosely based on the transatlantic balloon journey of *Tom Sawyer Abroad* (1894). Shadburne's script places Twain himself in a Jules Verne–style paddlewheel balloon, traveling to meet Halley's comet on its return to earth in 1910, an event that Twain correctly believed would coincide with his death. Within the larger journey, the film is free to explore fragments from Twain's fiction: "The Celebrated Jumping Frog of Calaveras County" (1867), "The Mysterious Stranger" (1916), and *Mark Twain's Notebooks and Journals* (1975). The film easily draws on episodes from "Adam's Diary" (1893), "Eve's Diary" (1905), and "Captain Stormfield's Visit to Heaven" (1907), all of which Twain originally constructed in extract form as diaries.

In the film, Huck Finn and Tom Sawyer stow away on the balloon trip with Becky Thatcher. Replacing Jim from the original work with Becky Thatcher obviates the need to deal with the messy underlying issue of slavery at any level. Through the magical "Index-O-Vator," an elevatorlike device on board, these squeaky-clean characters are transported to the different "decks" holding Twain's fictional worlds. As a narrative device, the "Index-O-Vator" is a bit clumsy, but the film's larger journey to meet Halley's "celestial schooner" allows a grander sweep than had any of the studio's earlier work: the balloon navigates the Atlantic skyway like a riverboat, passes through London, anchors for a while on a sphinx, and ultimately rendezvouses with the comet in space.

Similarly, Shadburne mines a deeper thematic vein via the Twain character's cynical and sarcastic bent, exploring the duality of his light and dark sides. Lighthearted tales from Twain's fiction, notably "Jumping Frog" and "Adam and Eve," are balanced with darker, more troubling ones. The possibilities of this darker vision are apparent as the stowaways encounter an evil incarnation of Satan in a stylized Noh theater mask in "The Mysterious Stranger" (Figure 7.5). But ultimately these possibilities are frittered away by the clumsy treatment of a dark and mysterious Twain alter ego lurking about on the ship who literally fuses with the lighter protagonist before being transported into Halley's comet. Despite this literalness in resolving the author's dual nature, it is the Vinton studio's technique that continues to energize this longer work.

The film runs 72 minutes; in the longer format, Vinton enjoys some simple luxuries: he is able to hold shots longer for dramatic impact, offer differing points of view on events through character asides, and drop in a line of Twain's acerbic wit wherever possible. Like Disney's first feature, the longer format not only brought an expansion at the Vinton studio but forced changes in the Claymation® process. Since characters would be needed to play many longer scenes, shot months apart, molds were developed for casting multiple copies of the key characters' heads, which were cast, retouched, embellished, and substituted as needed during the production. New armatures using nylon ball-and-socket joints and lead wire were perfected, as well as a method of animating Twain's lip sync using substitute clay mustaches. Moreover, traditional feature film techniques—like the use of a Foley artist to create a fully realized sound-effects track—complement the Vinton mise-en-scène of elaborate settings in international locales and

Figure 7.5: Character sketch for the "Mysterious Stranger" segment of *The Adventures of Mark Twain*. Courtesy of Will Vinton Productions Archive.

lavish clay painted sky backgrounds. Taken as a whole, these modifications produce a clay film with the scope and tone of a traditional feature.

Critical response to *The Adventures of Mark Twain* was mixed. Vincent Canby praised the "Mysterious Stranger" sequence but dismissed the rest of the film, saying, "It's a G-rated fantasy designed, I would think, for young children. Yet it's so unusually literate that, I suspect, only adults and maybe only adults who are Mark Twain scholars, might fully understand what's going on. . . . The odd nature of the film isn't helped by the Claymation process, for which, of course, it was specifically designed. The clay figures and backgrounds, including a clay waterfall, are ingenious but not particularly interesting. Everything looks soft, squashy and sort of ugly . . . like watching a shelf of animated knickknacks."[11]

Stanley Kauffman in the *New Republic* praised the Vinton technique but likewise puzzled over its intended audience:

> Vinton's difference is that he has found a way to make movement, especially changes in facial expression, much more refined than any such work I've seen. . . . A small problem. Obviously the film is intended for children. But which children? Will those who are old enough to read Mark Twain relish the condensations and appreciate being treated as children? Will those too young to have read him be interested? I don't know. But because of the skills and the amiability of the enterprise, it's worth taking a chance with any children you know. . . . [E]ven if your junior companions don't respond, you'll likely have an enjoyable time.[12]

Both critics, noting the prominence of technique over story and questioning the film's intended audience, echo the lukewarm response the film met with nationwide. Nevertheless, it had some impact. Given the difficulty of distributing non-Hollywood animation theatrically, the nationwide showings—however limited—and the serious critical attention this picture received showed its significance in the field. And in the larger canon of animation, the production of a medium's first feature is a milestone marking the maturation of a technique, a rite of passage from the bush leagues to the big leagues, from trivial entertainment to full-scale narrative. Does clay animation's first feature mark the medium's full flowering in the same way that cel's first feature, *Snow White*, did in 1937?

If nothing else, *Mark Twain*, coming a mere 11 years after Vinton began his work in clay, confirmed his status as the preeminent producer of narrative clay. Like the Disney studio, the Vinton studio has been one of the leading innovators in the field, committed to advancing the technological sophistication, creative possibilities, and viability of the medium. From the beginning, Vinton's vision for clay has been nothing less than the creation of an entire clay animation industry, as he said in 1979: "People who saw *Closed Mondays* or *Mountain Music* said, 'That's nice, but what else can you do with it?' That's so narrow-minded. I'm sure people said to Disney, '*Steamboat Willie* is nice, but what else can you do with it?' Well, obviously cel has become an enormous industry. I really believe there's no reason why clay could not be as big a phenomenon. It's a cottage industry now, but it has real potential" (1979 Vinton interview).

The scale of Vinton's vision for the medium, his production of the first clay animated feature, and the development of a spin-off industry of clay figures, T-shirts, and a Saturday morning television show based on his Raisin commercials (though he did not share in the royalties for these ventures) prompts immediate comparisons with Disney. Without question, Disney's influence has been greater, and the Disney empire's production, control, and marketing of an array of popular culture merchandise is unrivaled and widely discussed.[13] Disney's impact has been pervasive worldwide for over 60 years, but one of the first places that impact was felt was within the cel animation industry itself, where his films were studied by other studios to unlock the developing principles of the Disney style, a style that became synonymous with the term "full-cel" animation. In a much smaller arena, the Vinton films have defined the modern style of clay animation, and like Disney films of the 1930s, the Vinton "full-clay" style became a carefully imitated standard in the 1980s. Recognizing that comparisons across the media of cel and clay animation may be difficult at times, a closer look at the two producers may clarify Vinton's contribution to clay animation, as well as some of the fundamental aesthetic differences in "full" animation between the two media.

VINTON AND DISNEY

A succinct description of the Disney style is given in the title of a book by Frank Thomas and Ollie Johnston, two former Disney animators: *Disney Animation: The Illusion of Life* (1981). Disney animation *suggests* the world we know, but it is not mimetic art in the way that the sculpture of Frederic Remington or the painting of Andrew Wyeth is; rather, it is an extended, stylized illusion, a highly constructed world that resonates with real world order but actually establishes its own order, an order dictated by Disney's worldview and the tenets of the full-cel style.[14] Thomas and Johnston spend over 500 pages deconstructing how each element of the "illusion of life" is created, what the "special ingredient" of Disney animation is. What emerges repeatedly is just how far you must move away from the real world to create Disney animation, to hold up Disney's "magic mirror" to the world. Disney character animation may be lifelike, but it has a *stylized* life of its own based on 12 principles, as articulated by Thomas and Johnston, that are commonly grouped under the rubric "squash and stretch" (47–69). While these tenets can be separately articulated, in the course of watching a Disney animation they are reduced to mere forces within an ever-changing "field" (to borrow terms from Gestalt psychology), a field that is so complex that it may defy a complete description.

The oeuvre of the Disney studio is extensive, but many broad characteristics come immediately to mind. As Disney animation is primarily character animation, many of the most prominent traits reside there: animation of animal characters differentiated by species and style of movement; extensive use of secondary movement within the character; exaggeration; overlapping action; squash-and-stretch techniques to produce a very wide range of fluid and sophisticated character movements; use of large numbers of characters within a single shot through the use of "crossovers"; cycles; and so forth.[15]

By contrast, the Vinton films under discussion here—the early shorts produced from 1974 to 1979 and the feature-length *Twain*—exhibit a much narrower range of characters, most of whom are humans. What is common to these works is the reliance on strong, closed narratives, with a central human character. In fact, for an animation studio with a relatively large output of shorts, there is a remarkable lack of traditional fable, fairy tale, or fantasy material in Vinton's work, versus that of Disney, "the modern Aesop."[16] Vinton enjoys varying degrees of success in dramatizing these narratives for the screen; little in his oeuvre has the emotional power of a *Pinocchio* or the tragic resonance of a *Bambi*. *Martin the Cobbler*, the first and most satisfying longer work from the Vinton studio, began a series of less successful adaptations of human stories that culminated in *The Adventures of Mark Twain*, a looser narrative that settles for more saccharine characters. Though the central characters in these works range from a Russian cobbler to a Catskills hunter, from an interplanetary child to an aging skeptic, breathing life into them simply does not present the kinetic opportunities of animating a Goofy, a Donald Duck, a Pluto, a Dumbo, or a Belew. Perhaps any character animation would seem stiff and tight in comparison with those of Disney, whose early, unrestrained explorations of movement and synchronized sound earned him more respect than any previous animator had gained. Grounded in naturalistic human narratives, Vinton films have characters whose movements are more uniform and limited than those found in Disney, and they suffer a kind of sameness—they are evenly told human stories that feature evenly animated human characters. In spite of its numerous technical innovations and the refinement of clay lip sync, Claymation® simply has not broken much new ground in the area of expressive character movement. Early Vinton animation seems unadventurous compared with the rubbery, bouncy, kinetic 1930s animation of Disney, and at worst, it can even be stiff and unnatural. Scenes of Martin the Cobbler trying to dance with Vladimir, or of a rigid formation of birds flying over Rip Van Winkle's head, or of the pilot gazing at the stars in *The Little Prince*, make apparent the technical limitations that occasionally ossify Vinton animation.

Much Vinton animation consists of human characters walking, talking, and gesturing. But even in works featuring nonhuman characters—like the Raisin commercials and specials—the mode of movement references a highly recognizable style of *human* movement that was the trademark of Motown singers. Even these Raisin movements—more stylized and energetic than most—do not exhibit the extremes or exaggeration common in Disney, since the animator is ordinarily working with a single figure rather than a number of models in substitution, limiting the amount of clay that can be moved around.

Later Vinton works—for example, the "Angels We Have Heard on High" segment from *A Claymation® Christmas Celebration* (1987), "Casual T. Cat" (1989), a public service announcement for the American Academy of Pediatric Physicians and "Cecille" (1990) segments for "Sesame Street"—are bolder in the design and execution of movement. One technique that is systematically used in *Claymation® Christmas* is a simple rocking of one of the host characters, Rex, forward/upward, then backward/downward, to suggest he is rising on his toes for emphasis as he speaks and gestures. This simple innovation removes a certain "deadness" and static feeling from the character's dialogue, compared with earlier characters who merely stand flat-footed and speak. The "Angels We Have Heard on High" segment from *Claymation® Christmas* exhibits a much looser, bouncier style of movement as a couple of lovesick walrus figures skate to the

Figure 7.6: The lovesick walruses from *A Claymation® Christmas Celebration*. Courtesy of Will Vinton Productions Archive.

traditional Christmas carol, generating a remarkable range of pratfalls and slapstick humor (Figure 7.6). Here, Claymation® rises to the challenge of a simple premise set to music, as the couple pirouette, fly, and fall on figure skates. In "Casual T. Cat," Avery-like "takes," point-of-view shots, and extreme stretching are used as the cat flies through the air. Similarly, in "Cecille" (1990) segments that appear on "Sesame Street," we see rubbery ball characters with lips squashing and stretching into a number of extremes that mimic the conventions of Hollywood cartoons. Both the pace of the action and the range of expressive movement in these pieces give some indication of just how far the limits of the medium can be stretched to mimic the classic cartoon.

The evolution of Claymation® through experience and the inclusion of substitution animation may account for the broader range of movements in these works. This factor, coupled with the influx of new animation directors into the studio, has expanded the range of designs and animated movement found in Vinton films considerably.

In these respects, perhaps the maturing Vinton studio of the 1980s paralleled the maturing Disney studio of the 1930s.

Another primary innovation of the Disney studio was the exploration of color as a formal element in film art. Lewis Jacobs describes Disney's development of "the mobility of color," an elastic and expressive application of color that showed producers of live-action films how expressive the new medium of color film could be: "As Disney's animals flew, danced, ran, and changed shapes, so *the film's color became animated* [emphasis added], changing hues with each of the dramatic developments—becoming gay, sinister, cold, warm, or extravagantly varicolored in an unswerving disregard for reality and a delightful flair for mobility that matched the unbroken rhythm of the sound."[17]

Disney's oeuvre was fertile ground for applying color in a new way. Maintaining color continuity from scene to scene may be a fundamental rule for Hollywood films, but color mobility makes sense in a world that establishes its own unnatural order. Color mobility is simply one more way for the animator to make a character's emotional states explicit: when Donald Duck is mad, his whole body turning scarlet red is no stranger than the smoke coming from his ears.

The studio's exploration of the new technology of Technicolor extended beyond its characters into background drawings, which create an evocative, atmospheric, storybook world to foreground the characters' actions. Though Thomas and Johnston catalog a surprising range of background styles in Disney animation, the settings created are mostly balanced, romanticized, and detailed outside the action areas.[18] Background colors became a key determinant of a scene's mood in Disney films; however broad the range of colors used, they are almost always used harmoniously. Disney's development of an effects department would support and standardize the atmospheric look of key scenes involving clouds, lightning, smoke, haze, rain, shadows, water, and so forth.

When Claymation® presents three-dimensional forms of children's stories, it echoes the storybook color schemes found in Disney. In spite of the limitations clay presents for designing with color, Claymation® uses saturated colors in a broad range of hues, a use of color that is usually rich, harmonious, and high in energy. A range of color schemes is found in *Rip Van Winkle*, for example, as Vinton re-creates the Catskill Mountains in an inviting palette of vibrant blues, greens, and white birch trees. Vinton darkens the palette as Rip enters the den of the mountain gnomes, expands it in a profusion of colors during Rip's drunken reverie, and finally shifts to a warmer, lower energy scheme to resolve the film as Vanderdonk and Van Winkle live out their final years together. Similarly, *The Adventures of Mark Twain* is somber in its overall tone as the despondent Twain journeys on his paddlewheel balloon to join Halley's comet. Twain broods in a darkly paneled Victorian study outfitted with Tiffany lamps and Oriental rugs in maroons, browns, and golds. This melancholy color scheme is punctuated by more brightly colored excursions into Twain's fictive worlds: Captain Stormfield's journey to the neon gates of an alien heaven, and Adam and Eve's battle of the sexes set against a vibrant, cartoonish landscape. Like Disney, the Vinton films tap the potency of color to enliven a scene or intensify mood.

One may not find a truly mobile color scheme in Vinton films, but the sensuous chromatic transformations of the sky in *The Little Prince*, and the metamorphosizing animals in *Creation* draw on clay painting's brighter palette, derived from the addition of oil paint to the clay and its ability to blur and smear the boundaries between shades. Sequences that closely synchronize movement and color are found in Vinton's work as early as the "pulsing blob" sequence from *Closed Mondays*, though more vivid, imaginative color usage can be seen in the optically enhanced "dance" of the fox and the Little Prince and in the drunken dream of Rip Van Winkle.

Color usage in the background of a Vinton film is often crucial to establishing a palette for a given scene, for influencing mood and emotionally heightening the drama. Yet, Vinton sets—particularly those of the set designer Don Merkt in *Rip* and Joan Gratz's in *Mark Twain*—have a sensuous, physical presence that Disney backgrounds do not. How can this be explained? Obviously, clay renders the background dimensionally, versus cel animation's flat renditions. And the gingerbread quality of Claymation® architecture, with clay surfaces and sculpted details made of coils and slabs, creates a tactility that simply cannot be achieved in two dimensions. But more importantly, while a Disney background drawing "may be dramatic, startling, powerful, or thrilling," given Disney's overriding interest in character animation, the background will "still be only a background for the action" (Thomas and Johnston, 248). Vinton films achieve the same result through selective focus, deemphasizing the background to support the action. But often sets are foregrounded through the use of subjective shots or unusual camera placements, and in many instances the set pieces literally transform into characters. Some striking moments result from these techniques: a mouse's point-of-view shot and a camera pushing through a window in *Martin the Cobbler*; the talking mountains and subjective camera usage in *Rip Van Winkle*; the faces on the organ pipes moaning and singing as Mark Twain plays a dirge. As sets are explored in the films, the audience experiences a kind of magical "doll house tour." The fascination that these films share with other forms of miniatures is brought to life through the camera's shifting perspective.

Thus, the full-clay style as practiced by Vinton (and now perhaps a score of other producers) is more detailed than sparse, more colorful than subdued, more smooth than textured, more evenly animated than kinetic, more interested in caricature than character, more realistic than experimental. Perhaps full-clay animation is only now beginning to explore some of the traditional turf of full-cel animation: the use of squash-and-stretch techniques and the broad treatment of nonhuman characters.

VINTON AND THE RAISIN PHENOMENON

After releasing *The Great Cognito* in 1982, the Vinton studio produced no other shorts for the nontheatrical market. Creating the *Twain* feature, the special effects for *Return to Oz* (1985), and the "Vanz Kant Danz" music video for John Fogerty tied up much of the studio's capacity from 1983 to 1985. Vinton had made nine television spots between 1978 and 1984, but in 1985 alone the studio produced ten television spots—including six for Kentucky Fried Chicken—marking a substantial shift toward commercial production. This increase in production for television was part of a larger trend in the 1980s, as animation permeated MTV and Nickelodeon, littered network promos for broadcast and cable networks, and made a comeback in television series like "Pee Wee's Playhouse" and "The Simpsons."

Though the studio won Emmy Awards for the "Come Back, Little Shiksa" (1987) segment in ABC's "Moonlighting" series, *A Claymation® Christmas Celebration*, and *A Claymation® Easter* (1992), its most conspicuous success in television was the California Raisins, a series of five spots produced for the California Raisin Advisory Board (CALRAB) from 1986 to 1989: "Late Show" (1986), "Lunchbox" (1987), "Playing with Your Food" (1987), "Raisin Ray" (1988), and

Figure 7.7: The California Raisins. Courtesy of Will Vinton Productions Archive. © Will Vinton Productions, Inc. All rights reserved.

"Michael Raisin" (1988) (Figure 7.7). Other commercials used the Raisins by piggybacking on the CALRAB campaign for specific markets or by licensing the Raisins for specific products: CALRAB'S "Locker Room," "Intermission," and "Zun!" (1989) for Japanese television; Sun-Maid Raisins' "Late Show" (1987)—which added a tag for Sun-Maid to the original Raisin commercial for distribution in the United Kingdom[19]—and "My Girl" (1988); and Post Raisin Bran's "Big Stars" (1988), "Honeymooners" (1988), and "Raisin Search I, II, and III," (1989). The origin of the campaign was CALRAB's desire to convince young adults that raisins were a "hip" snack, thereby expanding the market beyond the one traditionally targeted: mothers with young children. It was hoped that, for anyone aged 25–55 who viewed raisins as nutritional but uninteresting, the Marvin Gaye Motown classic used in the spots, "I Heard It through the Grapevine," would rouse some positive memories. Moreover, sponsorship by a respected industry board added credibility to the commercials. Later spots continued the "hip" associations, using Ray Charles and Michael Jackson.

The primary energy for these spots derives from the musical variations on "I Heard It through the Grapevine," but the musical energy is matched in the staging and cutting. Resembling performance videos, the spots cut to follow guitar riffs and punctuate lines with close-ups of lead singers or longer shots of backup singers in tightly synchronized dance steps. The spots are intriguing because they caricature the stars, conventions, and iconography of rock-and-roll video, a potent and pervasive form. As the commercials unfold, the audience engages in an informed reading of the imagery, a playful decoding of references to classic gestures and stereotypes that have been built over the 40-year association of television and rock and roll.

Sculpted in the broad caricature of the portrait-charge, the Claymation® models of the stars Ray Charles and Michael Jackson are instantly recognizable, stripped-down versions of the real people. Coming to understand over successive viewings how the essential features are distilled in the spots becomes a kind of game for the audience. Even the less individualized raisin-types, such as the "Motown backup singer," the "funk guitarist," and the "rapper," are instantly readable in the fast-paced spots, though it may take several viewings to notice the long eyelashes and gleaming teeth of the backup singer, the headband, granny glasses, and mustache of the funk guitarist, or the baseball cap and medallions of the rapper. Beyond the energy of the music, what appeals to audiences is the amusing reading of exaggerated features and gestures sculpted in these figures.

As William Feaver states in *Masters of Caricature: From Hogarth and Gillray to Scarfe and Levine* (1981): "[T]he [printed] *portrait-charge* was a focusing of attention, a means of peering at a man, scrutinizing him with a fortune-teller's deliberation, noting every crease and wrinkle. The caricaturist could go further than the photographer. Not only could he provide a meticulous account of the subject's appearance . . . but he could also accentuate the significant characteristics. . . . In a sense the *portrait-charge* is the ripest form of caricature. It brings out the force of personality rather than the whole man."[20]

In a television spot, the "account of the subject's appearance" is evident, but the caricaturist's scrutiny of the subject, his distillation of the "significant characteristics," may take several viewings to appreciate. Using reference film to *animate* these portrait-charges, the "force of personality," the essential energy of performers like Charles and Jackson, is made explicit. Charles's dark glasses, goatee, and signature side-to-side rocking of his torso and cocking of his head are interwoven with a rocking piano version of "Grapevine" in the "Raisin Ray" spot, while the pelvic thrusts and dramatic posturing of Jackson are fleshed out in the single white glove, black concho belt, porkpie hat, and single jheri curl dangling over his forehead in "Michael Raisin." The Jackson spot is by far the most energetic, rendering the dramatic frenzy of a Michael Jackson concert with follow spots, optically printed star dust that ripples through virtually every shot, and twinkling butane lighters and flashcubes from an arena. "Rapper" grapes materialize, and the arena "security guards" in their yellow T-shirts stand firm at the edge of the stage as an audience of "vegetable heads" howl and faint at Jackson's performance.

The commercials were effective: raisin sales, following a long period of flat or declining growth, rose 1.5 percent during 1987.[21] Veronica Buxton of Foote, Cone, and Belding, the San Francisco agency that created the campaign, says: "Over the five years the campaign has been underway, sales have increased in general. This is a commodity campaign, as opposed to a product campaign. Factors that influence commodity consumption are complex, including weather and price structures. These ads brought the products to 'top-of-mind' for the consumer and enabled the individual brands to get support at the retail level—where the sales are made—for things like store displays. In that way, they were very effective."[22]

Whatever their impact on raisin sales, the spots created a national craze for California Raisin paraphernalia, as $500 million worth of retail toys, bedsheets, T-shirts, and other products bearing their likeness were sold in 1988.[23] Though Vinton did not share in the royalties from the spin-off merchandise, he did purchase the rights to produce two prime-time specials featuring the Raisins for CBS, "Meet the Raisins" (1988), a wry "rockumentary" directed by Barry Bruce, and "The Raisins Sold Out" (1990).

Raisin mania had died down a bit by 1990, but the advertising campaign is ongoing. Though Vinton lost the California Raisin account in 1990 to Sculptoons, a San Francisco–based company made up of ex-Vinton employees, the ad agency has returned to Vinton to produce "Raisin Robots," the latest Raisin spot (released on 24 October 1991) (Buxton interview).

With their sneakers, snapping fingers, cool attitudes, and cooler moves, the Raisins represent the power of clay animation to captivate the consciousness of the mass audience on the same scale as Mickey

Mouse or Bugs Bunny. The Raisins marked the first time since Gumby attracted a children's television audience in the 1950s that the typical television viewer recognized clay characters and bought the spin-off merchandise. Behind-the-scenes stories on "Entertainment Tonight" and CBS News' "48 Hours" gave a broad television audience a look at clay production techniques.

Will Vinton's significance in the field of clay animation extends far beyond his best-known creations. The sources of his influence are many: the Academy Award he shared with Bob Gardiner for *Closed Mondays*; the relatively wide distribution of his early films, particularly *Martin the Cobbler*; his development of the full-clay style; his studio's substantial output of films produced frame by frame, including the first feature film in clay; the immense popularity and wide range of the studio's non-Raisin television commercials and television specials; his studio's forays into film trailers, special effects, and prime-time sitcoms; and even some of the special effects for the 3-D *Captain Eo* (1986) film for Disneyland.

According to the studio's releases, "The nineties marks a new era of expansion and diversification for Will Vinton Productions. Keeping its solid production base, the company is expanding into associated creative fields such as publishing, licensing, and international co-productions and film distribution." Vinton has even answered the numerous requests of fans for art from the studio and capitalized on the trend of collecting original cel art by producing "an exclusive Claymation Art Line consisting of handmade original and limited edition sculptures of popular claymation characters . . . the first collectables in the history of clay animation."[24]

The work of the Vinton studio has been the subject of retrospectives at Annecy and Hiroshima, been nominated for numerous Academy Awards, and won three Emmy Awards, two Clio Awards, and many international awards in film festivals from Ottawa to Moscow, giving some indication of the breadth of the contribution Vinton films have made to the medium. More than any other producer, Will Vinton has worked to make the clay medium as big a phenomenon as cel animation, to make it as widely seen and accepted as the classic cartoon. Vinton sees no limits to the medium of clay and wonders why its popularity has been so late in coming: "I've often said that if Walt Disney had been a sculptor instead of a graphic artist, maybe things would have flip flopped" (Barrier, 58).

8

Bruce Bickford and David Daniels: New Visionaries in Clay

After Bob Gardiner and Will Vinton's *Closed Mondays* won the Academy Award in 1974, clay animation not only grew exponentially in the number of films produced but spread geographically, starting with Vinton's studio in Portland, Oregon. Since clay animation had never been ensconced in Hollywood—unlike cel animation—it was geographically free of the West Coast studios.

Many artists from all over the world have worked in the medium since 1974. The New York animator Elliot Noyes, an old hand at clay animation, made a clay relief film called *The Fable of He and She* that same year, foreshadowing the emergence of the "Penny Cartoon" series on "Pee Wee's Playhouse" years later. In Brooklyn, Jimmy Picker and Robert Grossman collaborated on *Jimmy the C* (1978), and Picker won an Academy Award in 1984 for *Sundae in New York*, in which an all-star cast of caricatures lip-sync the song "New York, New York." Grossman went on to make an award-winning commercial for Carrier Air Conditioning. In Bloomington, Indiana, the independent filmmaker Tim Hittle created his series of Jay Clay films, which were shown in film festivals and on "Saturday Night Live." After the success of Vinton's California Raisins, clay became a ubiquitous medium in educational programming by the Children's Television Workshop, in prime-time specials, and particularly in television commercials, where it has sold everything from pizza to door locks. Clay animation studios sprang up to produce clay commercials in places as distant as San Francisco (Sculptoons) and Charlotte, North Carolina (John Lemmon Films), while in England, Aardman Animations produced clay films like *Creature Comforts* (Nick Park, 1989), which won the Academy Award in 1990 for "Best Animated Short Film." I am told that in 1992 the C-span broadcasts of the nightly Russian newscast show a clay animated commercial for the new Russian stock exchange.

Though all of these artists—particularly Tim Hittle—have demonstrated considerable vision and command of the medium, to my mind only two artists have produced unique styles of clay animation since the Vinton studio began its rise to dominance. Laying the foundation of realistic narratives in clay, the Vinton studio has provided a base of expectations that other clay artists can play off, in much the same way that Tex Avery, Chuck Jones, et al. played off the conventions of storybook realism that the Disney studio created. And two artists have gone far beyond the Vinton studio's aesthetic, exploring techniques in clay that push the limits of the medium and pursuing themes on the fringes of mainstream clay animation. Through an obsessive pursuit of technique, through a visual strategy of profusion, pastiche, and eclecticism, Bruce Bickford and David Daniels have produced work that rises above the flood of clay animation that Gardiner and Vinton unleashed, creating highly original and personal visions in clay.

Though Bickford's work has tended to be less commercially viable than Daniels's, the work of both artists in feature films, music videos, television segments, and commercials has a signature style that separates it from the mainstream, from the slick, refined clay animation fashioned by the Vinton studio and its offspring. One indication of their natural talent, their precociousness in clay, is that both artists began their lifelong pursuits in animation before *Closed Mondays* captured popular attention for the medium in 1974.

BRUCE BICKFORD

Bruce Bickford was born in Seattle on 11 February 1947 to George Bickford, an architectural engineer, and his wife, Audrey Bickford, both graduates of the University of Iowa (Figure 8.1). Like many young animators of his era, Bickford was intrigued by the animation process in *King Kong* (1933) and in the films of Ray Harryhausen, particularly *The Seventh Voyage of Sinbad* (1958). It was the ubiquitous Norelco shaver television spot, however, in which Santa Claus rides

Figure 8.1 Bruce Bickford. Courtesy of William Cayton/Christy Atkinson.

a set of floating shaver heads over snow-covered hills, that gave Bickford a simple image with which to experiment.

He tried his first object animation in 1964: a regular 8mm movie of cars shot in the rough terrain he found in the shadow of Interstate 5, which was being constructed near his home. Though the film demonstrates an intuitive grasp of cinematic principles ("it got me started"), Bickford was somewhat disappointed that he did not achieve the "floating heads" effect of his original inspiration. The film evidenced some of the usual problems of first-time filmmakers: Bickford's footprints, for instance, were seen to move erratically on the ground in some of the shots, an unintended effect that nevertheless caused one of his high school teachers to comment, "The footprints are the best part."[1]

As his experiments continued, Bickford drifted more toward clay animation. "I started animating model cars, but I put little clay people in them. And after a while I started animating the clay figures in the cars. And then pretty soon I just went to clay figures" (Bickford interview). Surprisingly, television's Gumby did not influence Bickford, who says, "I had been animating for some time when I saw my first 'Gumby.' In fact, when I finally did see one, I was slightly aghast. This old owl character had feathers rolling up and down on his head as he talked—a kind of misplaced surrealism. And they used real water in one scene—a novel idea but distracting. Bits of debris were floating around randomly. So 'Gumby' was never a real inspiration" (Bickford interview).

Bickford lived with his family on the west rim of the Kent Valley near Seattle until he joined the Marines in April 1966. He spent three years in Vietnam at Quang Tri, 15 miles south of the demilitarized zone, but "I didn't get off base much, so I don't feel like I had much of an experience." Bickford shot some more animation experiments while out on leave in 1967, but he became more engaged with the medium when he returned from service in 1969 with a 16mm camera. In the summer of 1971, he made a series of animated scenes—including a giant crane attacking a tree and a four-minute battle scene—that was dubbed *Last Battle on Flat Earth*,[2] a title Bickford himself admits "doesn't mean a whole lot" (Bickford interview). Beginning in the fall of 1971, and for much of 1972, he worked in his parents' basement on a barroom scene. Bickford did his first work in line animation in 1974 while living in the university district of Seattle with Carl Krogstaad—an experimental filmmaker—and completed another film, entitled *The Start of the Quest* (1973–74). Much of this work ended up in compilation films assembled by the rock iconoclast Frank Zappa: *Baby Snakes* (1979), *The Amazing Mr. Bickford* (1987), and *Dubroom Special* (1984). Bickford's collaboration with Frank Zappa, though an arduous and ultimately disappointing chapter in his life, remains one of his formative professional experiences.

When Bickford journeyed to Los Angeles in 1973, looking for work and interviewing for various jobs, he met Zappa through the animation house that had done work on Zappa's *200 Motels* (1973). Bickford had long admired Zappa's music and showed his early films to the guitarist, hoping for some sort of collaboration. After Bickford had returned to Seattle, Zappa finally called him back and asked him to come down to work for him. In June 1974—the same year Bob Gardiner and Will Vinton were releasing *Closed Mondays*—Bickford finally made the move, bringing all of his early films with him. The terms of his employment with Zappa specified that he turn over all the rights to his pre-1974 films to Zappa, so that they could be in-

Figure 8.2 The basic principle of strata-cut animation: achieving motion by slicing blocks of clay with embedded imagery. The camera is mounted above the block. Photo courtesy of David Daniels.

cluded in a feature film that Zappa was planning. For the next six years, Bickford would work on a series of scenes for that evolving, ill-fated project before leaving Zappa to return to Seattle.

In retrospect, Bickford believes that his first task in Los Angeles should have been determining how this early material could be integrated into a coherent feature. But he did not worry much about the larger structure of the project at the time. Zappa was either touring or in the studio, so "there was no—almost zero—organization. And then there was less organization as the years passed. I should have been pushing for a single film, but Frank had his own ideas for films to make. He would come up with an idea, but there would never be any follow-up. I was trying to work on these films, but I made a lot of mistakes. I made a lot of figures that never got used, and that was time I should have spent animating. I got sidetracked a few times, probably a few times by him and mostly by myself" (Bickford interview).

Bickford made several scenes for *Greggery Peccery*—whose many adventures were chronicled on Zappa's 1978 album *Studio Tan*—and for *Billy the Mountain*, a rock theater piece from Zappa's 1972 album *Just Another Band from L.A.* In 1975 and 1976, Bickford began working more in transformation animation, a method that would become his characteristic style. Unclear on how this material would ultimately hang together, Bickford continued to animate and to build characters. "I was so out of the loop," he says, "that I didn't even think about it. I started doing the stuff like this one extended sequence where you're going through some guy's eye socket and it turns into a room, and then you're going up stairs and through different spaces. I was just experimenting with different modes—like set size changes by enlarging the set every frame, adding more on to it and building it up" (Bickford interview).

About this time, Zappa parted ways with his manager who took all of Zappa's film and tape archives with him when he left, including Bickford's pre-1974 animation. The legal impasse between Zappa and Cohen continued until 1982. Since *Baby Snakes* was released in 1979, none of the early material was included, an omission that, according to Bickford, seriously weakened the film. "*Baby Snakes* could have been a different film," he says, "if that pre-1974 stuff could have gone into it. At least it could have made a feature film, whether or not it would have fit together well" (Bickford interview).

By 1978, Bickford was "trying to get his work scene together" (Bickford interview) when Zappa came to Bickford's studio in Santa Monica to film him animating; these scenes appear in the opening to *Baby Snakes*. When Bickford took Zappa aside and told him he could no longer handle the Los Angeles scene and was returning to Seattle to work, Zappa rented a house for him in Topanga Canyon outside of Los Angeles, a "solution" that turned out to have its own problems.

Isolated from the city, Bickford now worked essentially alone. He first tried to convert part of the house into a studio, with shelves and workspaces. Then he set about animating a cel sequence for *Baby Snakes*, an arduous task for someone working alone for the first time in cel animation.

> It took about five weeks to draw 1,000 frames, which amounts to about 40 seconds. Then we got all that xeroxed onto cels. Then it took about another six months to paint this stuff, because it was very detailed. I had to go over it—all 1,000 frames—many, many times because you can only do one color at a time.

> I made a shelf thing for these things to dry, and sometimes I'd be doing several colors at once if I could. I was doing in-between stuff, where there weren't even any lines to follow. I was putting pattern work into the toes of the Billy the Mountain character, to enhance the pattern of the drawing, things like that. I had to study the previous frame on each of these things to see that I'm doing things just right frame by frame. It was time-consuming. (Bickford interview)

In fact, this 40-second scene took seven months to animate.

After five years of collaboration and no film in release, it began to look like Bickford and Zappa would part ways. When *Baby Snakes* finally opened in December 1979, it was a 166-minute mishmash of concert footage, animation, and interviews. Janet Maslin opened her review in the *New York Times* by saying, "'Baby Snakes' is a shapeless, inexcusably long concert film made of, by and about Frank Zappa, whose particular blend of avant-garde pretension and sophomoric glee doesn't do much to make the time fly by." Maslin said Bickford's work was "deftly executed . . . but with an exhausting emphasis on maggoty shapes and putrefaction."[3] *Variety* said that, technically, the clay segments "were scrupulously done, but overkill makes them as boring as everything else here."[4] Returning to Seattle after the film opened, Bickford found himself without a résumé reel: he had access neither to material he had worked on for five years nor to virtually all of his pre-1974 films. Over the next few years, as the animation he had done for Zappa was released on home video in various compilations like *The Amazing Mr. Bickford* and *Dubroom Special*, Bickford would buy a copy so he could show his work around.

After toying with more line animation in Seattle, Bickford began animating what would eventually become the 29-minute *Prometheus' Garden* (1988). The animation proceeded over seven years, finally coming together around the dual notions in the title: the figure in Greek mythology, who created men from clay, and a setting in which to express the environmental concerns that had been building in Bickford's mind since high school. He says the film "is not really a serious story. . . . Most people would probably carve it down some." But "in Prometheus' garden, anyone can be a Prometheus, because the clay in the ground there is alive. I see these [figures as] little nature spirits [who] materialize to oppose the guys who want to cut down the forests, destroy the garden" (Bickford interview). With the help of the film editor Janice Findley and a grant from the Washington Arts

Figure 8.3 David Daniels animating the metamorphosizing announcer's head for Honda's "Metamorphosis." The clay animation is matted into existing live action footage. Photo courtesy of David Daniels.

Council, Bickford was able to finish the film and return to a long-standing, evolving project called "Tales from the Green River."

Bickford's Grotesqueries: Contradicting the Norm

The work of Bruce Bickford has no real parallel in other three-dimensional forms of animation. The originality of his vision—what captured Frank Zappa's attention in the first place—is remarkable, as is his ability to animate that vision in a profusion of minutely detailed clay creatures and line drawings. By working small—entire sets are frequently no more than a clay space the size of a grapefruit—and by single-framing rather than double-framing, Bickford maintains a high level of technical control over his figures while exploiting the myriad surface imperfections that naturally arise in clay figures that small. Tactile detail and melting fluidity, coupled with the embedded iconography, make Bickford's clay arresting; it suspends the viewer in a kind of trance. Once engaged, you have to shake yourself free from a

Bickford film, and the first questions you ask are, "What is this?" and, "How long is this going to go on?" Bickford offers us a visionary landscape, a hallucinogenic retreat into magical settings where figure and ground may transform into the other at any moment, enchanted settings in which modern technocrats are easy villains and nature is under siege.

In the process, Bickford's animation calls to mind "grotesque art," a term from the Italian *grottesca*, literally, "cave painting." When Roman baths were excavated during the Renaissance, they were mistakenly identified as ancient artificial grottoes, and the paintings on their walls, combining architectural, floral, animal, and human elements in a chaotic and heterogeneous whole, were seen as outside the classical norms of harmony and balance. Hence, things exotic, things that go beyond the cultural norm, became identified as "grotesque." Like grotesque art, Bickford's profuse, continuously irrupting, metamorphic, plasticine stream of consciousness combines foliage and fantastic human and animal forms into a distorted and bizarre hybrid that destroys regularity and order, that questions beauty and goodness.

As a result of Bickford's fecund imagination, films like *Baby Snakes* and *Prometheus' Garden* contain some of the most singular fantasies ever animated in clay. When these clay fantasies are grafted onto Zappa's concert and backstage footage, the structural and conceptual problems that result are evident. In *Baby Snakes*, the opening clay excerpts are presented repeatedly in a series of behind-the-scenes vignettes that layer the image through rephotographing the film on a flatbed editor or on a video screen shown playing in the background. Clay segments are intercut with concert footage, only to reappear later shot off the flatbed editor. The film moves in and out of the self-referential mode: at one point, as some of Bickford's imagery unfolds on the flatbed, a tiny clay Zappa figure walks out onto the ledge of the viewing screen, watches for a moment, then turns to the audience and shrugs his shoulders. Later sequences demystify the clay process by showing Bickford in time-lapse sculpting a scene and playing with a small clay set.

In *Baby Snakes*, the discursive nature of Bickford's world is further muddled by this continual layering and replay of his imagery by Zappa. Two examples will suffice. As Bickford speaks his opening voice-over, the film shows a variety of footage: time-lapse of Bickford sculpting (footage we identify as emanating from the camera we have just witnessed Zappa single-framing); a tiny, animated clay Zappa sit-

Figure 8.4 Clay image from *Buzz Box*. Photo courtesy of David Daniels.

ting on a flatbed editor with the real Zappa sitting out of focus across the room; an animated editing glove climbing Bickford's leg. All this footage is clearly behind-the-scenes material for the documentary. When the animation is finally seen full-screen, unmediated by flatbed or video screen, it races through an iconography of "Castl Disco," reclining female figures who caress their own breasts, cars, and architectural spaces. A single face metamorphosizes into a multitiered architectural space with eleven portals, a balcony with a rail, and a miniature staircase with eight tiny steps. The camera dollies in through the railing, and a figure with a trident emerges from a clay wall. The figure transforms into a reclining female, and then into the huge head of a peccary that recedes and shrinks. Over all of this, Zappa weaves a nightmarish, childlike track of heavily synthesized toy pianos, munchkin voices, screams, cymbal crashes, and wheeling percussion as Bickford muses in voice-over: "Neither the torture chamber nor the disco knows about the existence of each other. But there is psychic contact between the two. The evil doings on the disco floor have their counterpart in the dungeon below. The more you get

Figure 8.5 Strata-cut eyes on the television viewer suffering "retina rot" in *Buzz Box*. Photo courtesy of David Daniels.

engrossed in modern-day . . . modern-day notions about talisman or any kind of psychic art, the manipulation of psychic objects, pretty soon you realize that anything goes. Some guy could pick up a piece of dog shit and say, 'Look, you hold this and the force field around this will flow into you.' "[5]

Bickford's rambling monologue, his eclectic progression from disco/torture chamber to the manipulation of psychic objects, is echoed in the desultory visual onslaught of fluid, metamorphosizing object/spaces, replete with the cracking, crumbling surfaces of his obsessively detailed miniatures. The visual assault of this segment is increased by intimate camera placement and simulated camera movement through these object/spaces. Frequently, the camera moves through the iris of a character's eye. As these spaces enlarge for the camera to "move through," they begin to take on sexual and symbolic overtones, in the manner of Georgia O'Keeffe's enlarged flower forms. Zappa's music and layering of the imagery merely multiplies the elements in Bickford's filmic irruption.

Later in *Baby Snakes*, more unrelated episodes of Bickford's animation, exploring a range of characters and settings, are strung together. The camera moves through the nostril of a face and the animation shifts to an orgy of bodies, which metamorphosize into a sailing ship, which passes a rock, which transforms into a literal "skull rock." The ship rocks on a flexing clay sea and sails into a grotto, which metamorphosizes into a cave wall covered with faces, which change into myriad intertwined feet. The animation moves to a movie theater, where the film playing shows a massive face with seven eyes, three mouths, three noses, and eight ears attacking a group of people. As two men watch the film, one man's head transforms into a hamburger, which turns and bites off the other man's face. The animation shifts to an urban streetscape with a single red car careening down the road, driven by Greggery Peccery. The car pulls into a grotto, and Peccery goes into a large office full of secretaries. In short order, the film moves through a string of recurring icons: the flatbed editor, Zappa editing film, a woman caressing her breast, and a face/foot that menaces the camera. The scene then becomes more nightmarish and sexually explicit, calling to mind the unreal landscape of Hieronymus Bosch's *Garden of Earthly Delights*. The profusion of fluid, metamorphosizing, intertwined creatures produces a naked man whose penis ejaculates a gargoyle, which lands on a copulating couple. The fantasy landscape brings forth the pyramid and eyeball from the great seal of the United States (found on the one-dollar bill) and ultimately moves into a film camera with Bickford seated behind it, animating.

Baby Snakes is typical of the uses to which Bickford's animation from the Zappa era has been put. In *The Amazing Mr. Bickford*, his compelling visuals are also simply strung together like beads to accompany music, and the pastiche of music and metamorphosizing figures and grounds precludes any sustained reading of these works as films. Frank Zappa controlled the editing of Bickford's work, which was intended originally for a variety of music video projects. Zappa's habit of reworking and rereleasing various music projects carries over to his cutting of Bickford's animation, which has been repackaged as needed for these films.

But even in Bickford's most comprehensive vision, *Prometheus' Garden*, a seven-year effort that Bickford directed himself, the viewer continually struggles to make sense of the film. Bickford creates an exotic land of artifice, enchantment, and bloodshed, and his film opens with the most compelling profusion of clay characters ever seen in the medium. Drawing from the myth, clay figures are brought forth by an artist, only to proliferate in the magic soil, entire fields sprouting up with tiny clay people. For each clay person, Bickford substituted tiny figures over successive single frames, creating a spurt of growing clay "sprouts," a burst of kinetic energy that feels like enchanted time-lapse. Though the film shifts to a wooden structure and ultimately moves underground—where barbarians with swords and axes threaten the peace of the garden—a profusion of characters continues to fill a grotesque landscape. The film apparently follows its own logic. In Bickford's words, *Prometheus* "is sort of continuous. It wasn't just random scenes. I tried to keep a loose line of action from scene to scene. I made storyboards for some of the *Prometheus* stuff, but quite often I'd get completely diverted from the storyboard. And the last five minutes is pretty random, just one thing following another" (Bickford interview).

Bickford's signature style is evident in the discursive and detailed vision of *Prometheus*. Whether the work is for hire or for personal expression, his vision is remarkably consistent from film to film. Bickford often presents scenes with overt but incomprehensible narratives. But if you ask him about a typical scene, one in which a single character may stand out from the other 50 within the scene, he can recite a detailed account of what that character is doing, what his motivations are, though that reading is completely obscured from the viewer. Periodically, one is frustrated by the visual overload of Bickford's clay world, as details pile on top of more details, as characters and symbols spring forth. And often Bickford's world turns inexplicably violent, characters literally ripping the insides out of other characters.

Cognition is challenged in a Bickford film. Though we struggle to comprehend his obscurities, Bickford himself has already warned us in *Baby Snakes* that what we think is a psychic object may be dog shit. Nevertheless, the fluid, melting details of Bickford's clay suspend the viewer in a detached state as bizarre space liquefies into bizarre space, like the relentless unfolding of some monstrous Busby Berkeley set. At the center of these layers lies a profound dissatisfaction with the modern world, a desire to ridicule, upset, and overthrow the norm, a frustration that bubbles underneath obscure narratives. Bickford says, "I hardly feel like living in this world where it's legal for people to destroy rain forests or wipe out species of animals. I don't know what else to do about it, except to try to make a film." In the same vein,

Bickford calls his production company "Leisure Class Productions" because "that's my hope for the world, actually. That leisure could be a lifestyle that would replace competitiveness, the blind destructive competitiveness we have now. Not just for rich people that can afford leisure. Middle-class people should be doing something because they want to, [they should] quit trying to just make money and start working for the betterment of the world, even if it's just making entertainment, making movies" (Bickford interview).

DAVID DANIELS

David Daniels was born on 31 October 1958 in San Diego, the son of Morris Jetson Daniels, a sociologist at San Diego State University, and Doris Irene Taylor Daniels, an elementary school teacher who had also taught children's music and art. Daniels's mother encouraged creativity in the family, and at age five, with the help of his older sister Shelley, he built "Claytown," a miniature clay village set up in an area that their mother let them dedicate to playing with clay. Here, Daniels and his sister explored the medium over a period of years, building and destroying in their own clay kingdom, making clay modeling an everyday part of their childhood. Daniels says that "Shelley was really my first art teacher with Claytown. She was very precocious art-wise, very delicate. She had an excellent sculptural touch, and she taught me a lot when I was young."[6]

At age eight, Daniels recalls, his sister built a small but highly detailed birthday cake, alternating layers of clay "icing" and "fluff." "I'll never forget the spark of wonder it gave me," Daniels says, "when she cut the cake into little one-eighth-inch slices, and the layers buried within reappeared clear and crisp as ever. I knew intuitively that something magical could be done with this stuff." Though he had yet to film the process, Daniels had discovered the basic principle of strata-cut animation: achieving motion by slicing multicolored blocks of clay. "Strata-cut in its simplest form is this: if you take a cone and cut it away with the camera looking down from the top, a dot becomes a larger and larger circle," says the artist. "That is the first principle, and everything else follows from that. It's really the controlled use of shapes as opposed to animating shapes" (see Figure 8.2). Unaware of the wax-slicing experiments of Oskar Fischinger in the 1920s, or of Douglass Crockwell's *The Long Bodies* (1946–47), Daniels was excited by his discovery from the outset; he now says, "I'll never know why it took me 14 years to return to cutting clay" (Daniels interview). His sister Shelley is now working as a sculptor on Tim Burton's animated feature *Nightmare before Christmas* (1993).

In 1972, at age 14, Daniels animated in super-eight a clay short called *The Duchy of Frog*, which went on to win first prize in the Kodak Young Filmmakers' Festival in 1973. As a communications major at the University of California at San Diego, Daniels made experimental films like *Consume and Flesh* (1978), "a film which showed the onslaught and repetition of consumer images as a form of consumption itself" (Daniels interview). After dropping out for a year, Daniels graduated in the film program at San Francisco State in 1981, working in animation as well as experimental live action and documentary. In *Disco Proletariat* (1978), Daniels cut silent images of derelicts and "beautiful people" living flamboyant lifestyles to a structured, rhythmic beat. At each screening of the film, Daniels would tune in a live radio station to supply the disco track, making the film different for each viewing.

During the summer before graduate school, Daniels took a month to experiment with clay, working to come to "a structured understanding of time and motion and animation principles that could be achieved with a lump of clay cut sideways. I would try one approach and then another, to see what resulted. Going into Cal Arts, I had a clear understanding of the strata-cut technique, even though I hadn't animated anything with it" (Daniels interview). Pursuing a graduate degree in motion graphics, Daniels finally did return to clay slicing for a series of animation experiments that resulted in his master's thesis, *Buzz Box* (1986). The film took 14 months in 1983 and 1984 to animate and two years of raising money, editing, and scoring to bring to completion.

During the same period, Daniels worked on some horror films in Los Angeles, but not on anything "very steady, or very lucrative, or very interesting." When Daniels married Colombe Jodar, a Chicago-based flight attendant, in 1986, he could fly anywhere, so he "took a chance going to New York and finally crashed Broadcast Arts, the production company for the first season of 'Pee Wee's Playhouse.'" The company, owned by Steven Oakes and Peter Rosenthal, had just moved to New York and landed the "Playhouse" show. Working under tight deadlines, in crowded conditions, with low pay, Broadcast Arts was a springboard for hungry new artists fresh out of school.

Daniels recalls, "They gave me a job as a cameraman, based on *Buzz Box*, and eventually they ran out of animators. So in the first year I animated the bunny rabbits hopping on the hill for the opening of 'Pee Wee' and three episodes of the 'Penny Cartoon' series ['My Room,' 'Kids' Rights,' and 'Allen']." The style of clay relief animation in the "Penny Cartoons" was already fully developed by the English animators from Aardman Animations, so his input was limited. "They had their own style, and I just followed through and made my own little mark on it. I sort of Americanized it by adding speed blurs and more graphic zip. I tried to make it snappier, more kinetic" (Daniels interview).

When Paul "Pee Wee Herman" Reubens moved the show to Los Angeles for the second season, Daniels moved, too, and produced two remarkable strata-cut segments in 1987: "The Declaration of Independence" and "Christopher Columbus." Each segment was shot in six weeks with the help of only one production assistant; Daniels himself constructed the artwork, lighted the set, and programmed the motion control camera. He says, "I'll never do that again. It was completely insane. But I worked hard for them because they gave me a chance to do my own type of work. And it turns out that I was the only animator who worked on all five years of the show, mostly on things that didn't fit into any category—an animated Jhambi head, a clay Picasso painting that comes to life" (Daniels interview).

After "Pee Wee" ended, Daniels's next project was the Peter Gabriel video "Big Time" (1987), which includes strata-cut segments as well as a scene in which vegetation-covered hills grow faces and begin to sing. Daniels moved toward commercials with a series of spots for the California lottery (1990) and a commercial for Honda called "Metamorphosis" (1990), the first project that he worked on as an independent director represented by the Los Angeles–based production company Limelight. In the spot, an average-looking television announcer extols the virtues of Honda scooters. Suddenly, his head begins to transform into a series of hideous, colored faces that grow giant blue ears, bulging eyes, rainbow skin, and a huge gaping mouth. The transformation reverts to the normal announcer just as suddenly, and he apologizes to the audience, saying, "Sorry about that." The process involved shooting the clay faces on glass (see Figure 8.3), alternately front-lit and back-lit to produce a traveling matte, as well as rotoscoping to produce a three-dimensional match of the clay face to the announcer's face as it reverts to normal. As the clay face reverted to the human face, Daniels used makeup and glass eyeballs to bring the model as close as possible to the human face.

David Daniels has continued to demonstrate his command of mainstream figurative techniques in several advertising projects, including a series of spots for the California lottery. His bouncy and technically sophisticated style is evident in spots like the lottery's "Pot 'o' Gold" (1990), in which a "loser" is smashed by a huge falling lottery ticket. The clay figure for this spot makes the term "loser" visually concrete with his potbelly, hawk-bill nose, and slick ducktail hairdo, disco dancing in a blue polyester, bell-bottomed leisure suit and platform shoes. As the giant ticket begins to fall, Daniels creates a Tex Avery–style "take" as the loser anticipates the crash, his mouth open like a cash register drawer and his eyes bulging out like traffic cones. But with all their polish and deft characterization, these mainstream works do not have the energy or visual punch of Daniels's more offbeat works.

In 1992 Daniels left Limelight and Los Angeles with Colombe and their newborn son Oliver to move to Portland, Oregon. The Will Vinton studio had agreed to represent Daniels as part of an overall company strategy to diversify the studio's look. In Portland, Daniels has worked on a number of projects using a mixture of three-dimensional and two-dimensional techniques, trying to enlarge the Vinton style beyond the mainstream clay animation that it has made so popular. Daniels says, "I'm trying to mix strata-cut with other forms of animation now—with photo cutouts, rotoscope, impressionism, computer texture mapping, and other techniques. I think it's healthier to use clay in combustion and contrast to other styles and looks. Within the same piece, each can be woven together to show how different the other is. Other animators seem to be going to this. Even figurative clay animators are going to foam bodies and clay heads so that the expressiveness of clay and its sculptability are in the areas where you need expression, and the sturdiness of foam in the body where you need stability" (Daniels interview). None of his current projects has involved strata-cut, but given the impact of the technique, Daniels will likely return to it in the future.

Strata-cut and the Films of David Daniels

Because strata-cut builds a patterned block that is sliced to reveal the cross-section, the technique calls to mind the ancient glassworking technique called *millefiori*, or "thousand flowers," by the Venetian glass artists who revived it. Millefiori glass is made by arranging long, colored glass rods into patterns and heating them until they fuse together. The larger fused rod is then cut into slices, which can be reheated to produce surface decoration on glassware, or pressed into molds, which are heated to produce bowls, plates, and other moldware. The concept is also used in the manufacture of some hard candy and taffy.

Daniels describes the strata-cut aesthetic as kinetic yet highly efficient at the shooting stage:

> The stratified layers of rock and sediment buried inside the earth itself—like swirls inside a marble cake—find expression and metaphor in this technique I invented called strata-cut. Just like a bulldozer is used to reveal the lines of color and shape beneath the surface of the planet, a knife is used to reveal the latent animation boiling inside a block of layered clay.
>
> The magical thing about it is that time and space are woven together, each one affecting the other. And as you cut it up, you release the images embedded inside. They come sprawling out in a burst of kinetic energy. It's very primitive and very high-tech at the same time. There is a fluid metamorphosis that competes well with computer animation. It is a slow-moving molten medium that does some things like explosions and liquids very well.
>
> Another advantage of strata-cut is that it can be very time-efficient for the number of "pixels per inch." Unlike 3-D or figurative animation, it may take a week or more to build an image or "block," but only a day or so to animate it. Because the animation is latent inside the block, at the shooting stage, it is a pretty fast process. In many instances, all you have to do is cut it away and follow focus.
>
> Strata-cut can also fill the frame with continuous, seamless, changing images without the need for figuring out in-betweens. If you've ever had your mind severely bent from not sleeping for three days, your eyes begin to see everything "crawling" and "shimmering." This psychological effect is mimicked very well by strata-cut.[7]

Daniels's thesis film *Buzz Box* offers an early glimpse of some of his most compelling techniques, even though it is ultimately unsatisfying as a film (see Figure 8.4). A series of strata-cut and three-dimensional experiments structured around an imagined television "week" that assaults and ultimately destroys a viewer, *Buzz Box* opens with an intensity that leaves it no headroom; there is nothing left to build toward. The problem is accentuated by a sound track built from highly processed bits of sampled television audio. The most common effect used in the track is an extended reverb technique that calls to mind top 40 radio, producing a series of diminishing echoes of the last line of a phrase: for example, "Buzz box . . . box . . . box . . . box." The effect is overused throughout, and the track as a whole is overwrought, suffering from a sameness that de-energizes rather than energizes the work.

In the film, each day of the week brings a new show—"Retina Rot," "Scanline Fever," "Marilyn Stein," "Twilight Circus"—building toward Friday's "War Gazzam" and Saturday's "Re Runz." A parade of television iconography—the stand-up announcer, the newscaster with keyed graphic—as well as bits of text like "special," "mega," "ultra," "it's the new you!" and "news update," are animated using a range of techniques. At points in the film, Daniels demystifies strata-cut by changing the end-on, tight framing of a loaf of clay being sliced to a wider, high-angle shot. This framing shows a series of loaves—containing a car, an airplane, a tank—on a tabletop being cut, the cross-sections falling away like slices of bread. A loaf embedded with a mushroom cloud pattern flips and spins on the tabletop, "dealing out" slices of clay like playing cards. Later in the film, the slices are used like clay cutouts to form a variety of pop-art patterns, including faces beneath hair made of mushroom clouds or airplanes.

As the television viewer is reduced to a baggy-eyed insomniac who begins to disintegrate, his gaping mouth fills with the images pouring out of the screen (see Figure 8.5). In *Buzz Box*, Daniels explores how television's proliferation of consumer images, its fragmentation of news—"the machine-gun–like recitation of numerous unrelated items"[8]—and its immediacy—"the false sense of urgency . . . that tends to inflate, and subsequently deflate, the importance of all subject matter" (Schiller, 28)—ultimately leaves the television viewer confused and powerless. Daniels returns to a similar theme in a remarkable 30-second opening he created for the MTV show "Idiot Box" (1990). The opening climaxes as a television cracks open to reveal a hideous jack-in-the-box, whose face is animated with strata-cut to reveal a tin can embedded inside his brain. The tin can opens, the brain emerges, and the corpse of the jack-in-the-box rocks on a spring in a tangle of wires as the television closes like a vault, revealing the title, "Idiot Box." Though the notion that television corrupts is not new, the theme is well expressed in those moments of *Buzz Box* when Daniels pushes the molten, kinetic quality of strata-cut to its limits, or when he uses it as a single element in a frenetic mélange like "Idiot Box."

Two strata-cut works made for "Pee Wee's Playhouse" demonstrate how the technique can be combined with traditional figurative clay animation. In "Christopher Columbus," Daniels uses objects buried in a very large clay loaf to establish the setting for a dialogue scene between clay models of Pee Wee Herman and Columbus aboard one of the explorer's ships. As Pee Wee tells the story of the voyage in voice-over, the camera tracks with the slicing. The strata-cutting of the loaf reveals a rotating globe that falls away to reveal a series of three ships. Since Daniels sculpted the three ships into the clay loaf as curves—or more accurately, as a series of three curved "waves"—the ships "sail" right to left in succession as the loaf is cut away; these moves synchronize with Pee Wee's voice-over: ". . . the Nina, the Pinta, and the Santa Maria." Here, the strata-cut animation is used emblematically: visual interest centers on the transforming loaf—clearly seen here as a loaf on a tabletop covered with a map—and the revelation of images connected with Columbus's voyage. In this non-traditional "scene setting," the strata-cut process is foregrounded as the traveling camera follows the incremental cuts unearthing the embedded icons. This movement brings the audience into the next scene of Columbus and Pee Wee on a boat. Daniels deftly animates the rocking of the boat and some fairly close lip sync without trying for the precision of movement or smooth surfaces of Vinton-style animation. He also uses strata-cut slices laid on the end of Columbus's telescope to depict a reflection of the sun setting.

His "Declaration of Independence" segment is similar; strata-cut is used to reveal emblems that establish a scene. Here, the camera moves in as the loaf brings forth a patriot winking, hands waving flags, the barber-pole rotation of color stripes on the words "4th of July," and fireworks exploding as the exterior of Independence Hall "wipes" into view. To cover the transition from strata-cut exterior to a traditional, 3-D, clay animated interior of the hall, Daniels creates a long rectangular loaf—small on one end, larger on the other—that depicts a window springing up into view as it is sliced in increments. The film match wipes to an interior shot pulling away from a window as Benjamin Franklin and the founding fathers prepare to sign the Declaration of Independence. Asked for a quill, Pee Wee produces a ballpoint pen for the occasion and scolds John Hancock, "Think you wrote it big enough, John?" The film closes in a close-up, as "Your Pal Pee Wee" is inscribed on the document.

Daniels is at his best when he integrates the potential of strata-cut into simple narratives like the "Pee Wee" episodes. By contrast, when he uses the technique in *Buzz Box* to slice out clay cutouts to produce a proliferation of similar images, one wonders why color photocopies would not work just as well. Strata-cut is more compelling when the image embedded within the loaf is uncovered, when the layers fall away and the transforming strata is revealed.

Integrated into the three-dimensional figurative clay that Daniels has already mastered, strata-cut adds variety to the clay world and a visual interest that blends effortlessly with traditional clay in the same way that clay painting does. Thinking of movement as a continuous solid form that embodies time is no doubt a difficult skill to master. Daniels's short career has demonstrated the basic methods and the potential of the technique. In an age hungry for unique imagery, strata-cut will remain a fruitful area for clay artists to explore for some time.

9

Clay Animation in the 1990s

Animation in the 1990s appears to be poised for a revival, particularly cel animation. The increase in cel production became a broad trend in the 1980s and early 1990s as new animation series were widely distributed on both cable ("Rugrats," "Doug," "Ren and Stimpy") and broadcast television ("Tiny Toon Adventures," "Duck Tales," "The Simpsons"). Cel films particularly made an impact in the feature film market, with high-grossing features like *Beauty and the Beast* (Buena Vista, 1991) and *Who Framed Roger Rabbit?* (Buena Vista, 1988). Cel features became more abundant and more varied than ever with the release of films like *Fern Gully . . . The Last Rain Forest* (Fox, 1992), *Rover Dangerfield* (Warner Brothers, 1992), *Cool World* (Paramount, 1992), *Bebe's Kids* (Paramount, 1992), *An American Tail: Fievel Goes West* (Universal, 1991), *The Little Mermaid* (Buena Vista, 1990), *All Dogs Go to Heaven* (United Artists, 1989), *Oliver and Company* (Buena Vista, 1988), and *The Fox and Hound* (Buena Vista, 1981).

In particular, *Beauty and the Beast* gained the attention of Hollywood studios: it quickly grossed over $150 million, was nominated by the Academy of Motion Picture Arts and Sciences for "Best Picture" (not simply "Best Animated Film"), and has unlimited potential in re-release well into the future. The film seems destined to break all sales records for Disney: in its first six days of release on home video, *Beauty and the Beast* sold seven million copies, four times higher than the same six-day total for the previously all-time best-selling home video, Disney's *Fantasia*.[1] As the cost of producing live-action features continues to rise, the obvious long-term economic benefits of animated features have not been lost on the studios. As Harvey Deneroff states in *The Animation Report*:

Yes, *Beauty and the Beast* benefited from the fact that animated features now cost less than the average live-action film; and yes it also benefited from the fact that the burden of residuals and profit participations was so much lower [greatly increasing the return to the studio]. But these factors, of course, are rather meaningless by themselves; after all, the lower residual and profit participations are nothing new for animation. What has changed is the realization that animation is not just for children. . . . The film's ability to capture both adults and children is now part of Disney's long-term strategy for all of its new animated features. . . . Other studios are already looking to imitate Disney's success in this field and are apparently planning to include animated musicals as part and parcel of their new strategies to appeal to the family market.[2]

In short, because it was seen by a very large audience, was taken seriously by critics, and has been extremely profitable—in the short term and undoubtedly over the long term—*Beauty and the Beast* has been broadly influential.

Clearly, the resurgence of cel has brought a marked shift in the way heads of studios, cable companies, and television networks think about animation. In the early 1980s, animation production at Disney was stagnant; a few cel animation houses were staying alive by supplying the Saturday morning market. Animation was a small ghetto in Hollywood. Now studio heads are rethinking animation as a capital-intensive, but potentially lucrative, mainstream commodity with a long shelf life and a variety of markets. In 1987 the theatrical re-release of *Snow White* grossed $46.6 million.[3] In 1992 *Pinocchio* was re-released in theaters *after* it sold 800,000 home video units in 1985 (Krause, 20).

Whether or not the current boom in animation continues, "it is clear that the industry will, after the inevitable bust, settle down to a much higher level of activity than it has ever seen in the past" (Deneroff, 1). For this study, the questions raised by the resurgence of animation in the 1990s are simple: Will Hollywood's traditional reliance on cel continue to the exclusion of other forms like clay? Or will clay benefit from the overall trend and enjoy further expansion? Where are current trends leading the medium?

Clay animation in the 1990s is no longer a rarity. But as we have seen, it is not now, nor has it ever been, a part of the Hollywood studio system in the way that cel animation has. The movie industry has grown comfortable with the cel technique, with its lower costs and more manageable production schedules, over the last six decades. Cel animation houses are concentrated in southern California, while clay continues to be more widely dispersed. The meager economic performance of *The Adventures of Mark Twain* has fostered doubts about clay's viability in the feature market, the primary area expected to enjoy continued growth.

EXPERT OPINIONS

So what is the future of clay animation in the next decade? Six experts offer their insights.

Tim Hittle, Independent Clay Animator

It seems pretty clear that computer animation will eventually take commercial work away from both stop-motion animation and from clay. Computer animation is getting cheaper. But it's like anything else: people will get sick of it if that's all they see. The problem is that the computer animation I see in festivals and on the tours is just based on the capability of the machine: "We can make this image, so let's just do it. It will be cool to look at." They don't think about story, or character, or anything else.

So I'm going to continue to work in clay. I'm going to make Jay Clay films for as long as I can, because it's cheap for me to do what I want to do with it. And I like the way it feels. There will always be a place for traditional clay animation, because it has its own look and feel.[4]

John Lemmon, Commercial Clay Animator

I really think clay will never come close to equaling cel animation in terms of finished minutes produced each year. I think cel will always be much more common than clay. Which is fine from my point of view, because it keeps clay fresh and unique-looking. For commercial clients, which are our bread and butter, they're just about guaranteed that they are going to be the only one in their market with a clay spot.

At the same time, I think the long-term future for clay is very bright. Clay is expensive, but viable in long-form entertainment. We have been looking at the possibility of doing a clay feature for some time now. Our long-term goal is to get into features and half-hour television specials.

For a feature, it would take you a certain amount of time to gear up, maybe 12 animators and support people for each . . . and even then we have projected two and a half years to animate a feature. So you need patient investors.

In terms of new techniques in clay, I think you will see more integration of clay and computer animation: clay characters against computer-generated backgrounds. I am sure people will always come up with new twists on the technique, like strata-cut or clay on glass. I am sure there will always be variations. But it's the same situation in cel: the important variable that distinguishes one project from another is not usually technique but the quality of the story, the expressiveness of the character, things like that. There's never been a clay feature that's really found the right narrative for the technique. The economics of clay prevents a lot of experimentation.[5]

Harvey Deneroff, Founder of the Society for Animation Studies and Publisher of *The Animation Report*

I don't see the difference in division of labor in cel versus puppet or clay animation as all that great, as a great obstacle to producing dimensionally animated features. There is obviously division of labor in both forms. But once the set is built and lit, a single animator goes in and does a whole scene. The big difference is that in cel there is nothing comparable to a single [dimensional] animator doing an entire scene. For stop-motion, that's where the savings come in.

But the real problem for producing a 3-D feature is the labor shortage. There are very few places that have the capability of doing a feature. In clay, the first place to look would be Will Vinton Productions. He has the capability to do a feature and wants to do a feature. John Mathews [a dimensional animator for Churchill Films] and Aardman Animations are probably capable of doing a feature. But the trade-off is that all of these companies would have to cut down on their regular commercial work because there just are not that many stop-motion animators out there.

You could possibly go to Eastern Europe to produce puppet animation, because they have that strong tradition there. But I suspect that their puppet animation would not work that well with American audiences; it's too simplified and stylized, and there's no real facial movement. Plus, nobody knows how to work with them, particularly the Russians. They aren't used to working on a Hollywood budget.

So to solve the labor shortage, you would basically have to start retraining cel animators in 3-D forms like clay. Which is possible, but you'd have the long start-up time like you did with *Roger Rabbit*. And with animated features, experienced production managers are almost nonexistent. So the general rule is: anybody who is doing their first animated feature will go over budget and over schedule. That would surely apply to clay.

The other big problem for *any* animated feature is that nobody knows how to handle them in distribution, outside of Disney and, to some extent, Twentieth Century-Fox with *Fern Gully*. Disney knows what they are doing. They don't automatically think of these films as children's pictures. They recognized the adult appeal of *Roger Rabbit* and *Beauty and the Beast*. So with a clay feature, one of your biggest jobs would be to educate the distributor.[6]

Linda Simensky, Director of Animation for Nickelodeon

I think there is a general belief in the animation community that clay is just at the beginning as a medium. They've figured out one way to do it, the Gumby or the Vinton way. Now clay is beginning to explore all sorts of new ways to enhance all sorts of visuals.

People know now how to do clay. Over the last 20 years, they've figured out the basic technical stuff. There is an obvious parallel with the development of cel. I think clay will go through the same steps, the way that true character animation developed in the 1930s. The next step is for clay figures to become real actors, for clay animators to bring true characterization to clay. They are just beginning to figure this process out. The past 20 years have laid the groundwork for clay to expand in these areas.

At Nickelodeon, we had some interesting experiences in the area of three-dimensional animation. We tested two model animation pilots. Kids kept referring to it as clay animation, and they did not like it that much. They thought it looked old-fashioned. So I don't know that kids are going to tune in every day to a clay animated television series.

For a children's audience, clay is a dual-edged sword. In some ways it's really mainstream, and in some ways it's just a little too strange. Clay is realistic in that it's three-dimensional. It's strange in that it moves in a much more fluid way. When you do metamorphosis with it, it's like it's *really happening*, it's almost too real for little kids. It seems to me that clay is confusing to many younger kids. It's like they both love it and don't get it.[7]

Joan Gratz, Independent Producer/Director and Clay Painter

Clay painting and [figurative] clay animation are two different things. I think of my technique as more like painting, and it certainly can be more abstract and more metaphorical. So there's a lot more to be done with it in the future. One would never assume that *painting* had been pushed as far as it can go, and I don't think I've pushed *clay painting* as far as it can go. What I want to do is continue to use this technique in less commercial, more personal ways. It seems appropriate for shorter works. I don't see myself or anyone else doing any feature films in [clay painting], because it is so labor-intensive.

On the other hand, traditional clay animation certainly can compete in the feature market. It can be done for about the same price as cel animation, or even a bit less. *The Adventures of Mark Twain* is not a good case to judge [the success of a clay feature] by, because they targeted it at a very young audience and it really fell down in terms of marketing. If you have an advertising budget and market it properly, [figurative] clay can be viable and competitive with cel.

Clay is becoming integrated with other techniques, and I think that's appropriate. The older Vinton studio films have a charm and unity that comes from the all-clay style. But now there's less focus on the raw material and more on the overall effect, which makes a lot more sense really. That's the direction that Aardman studios have always taken—using clay with other materials. That's really the direction the Vinton studio is moving towards, this idea of integrating clay with other techniques.[8]

David Daniels, Strata-cut Animator

The last 20 years have been spent proving that clay is viable. During that time, in the 1980s and on into the 1990s, the trend in animation generally has been the multilayering of all techniques, the integration of multiple levels of techniques in animation. Clay has been one part of that. Clay now functions as a graphic medium in the graphic environment. So, in the near future, clay will continue to be integrated in these multilevel techniques, as an element in the greater palette of animation.

In long form, the future of clay animation—and of three-dimensional animation generally—depends on the success of Tim Burton's feature *Nightmare before Christmas*. In that film, they are using puppet bodies with replacement faces that were sculpted in clay and cast. It's a good film, but the lip sync perhaps could be better if they resculpted the faces. The drawback to resculpting in clay is that it has a certain look, and it's a look that some people like and some people don't. But resculpting is always more articulate. It has more expression in the face, and that will always be clay's strength.

I think clay animation, as a pure art form in and of itself, will always be marginal—marginal in the sense that it will never be a mainstream, broad-based art form that everybody is doing, because it is so time-consuming. Clay is unique—it's like a special kind of rose, it's just not like every other variety.

But clay will be used as an element in computer modeling. Basically, you will build your character in clay, sculpt him into 20 or 30 or 40 different facial expressions, and digitize each one from all different angles. Then you have a digital map of facial movements that can be re-created and manipulated. They are already using clay in computer modeling. But the more easily computers can build a library repertoire of facial expressions, the more this [technique] will be used in character animation.

Computers will become sophisticated and cheap enough that you could use them in this hybrid form to make longer films. The [hybrid] process would ultimately give you more freedom and more longevity in manipulating the character. And the division of labor would finally be there for clay. You would have a lot of people employed as dimensional sculptors, but there would be fewer under-the-camera animators. The keys and in-betweens would be generated in the computer. This hybrid could be a more cost-effective way to animate in the long form, give a sense of dimensionality, and get around some of clay's limitations: the weight and the time you need to animate it.

But I think the real renaissance of three-dimensional clay will come when there is an available means of stereoscopic representation. The next generation of clay will blossom in 3-D, when there is a means to exploit the uniqueness of it, its dimensionality.[9]

CONCLUSION

The amount of clay animation produced in recent decades—the large output of the Vinton studio alone—has made figurative clay animation highly visible in the mass-media environment. And yet, over its entire history, clay animation has yet to produce an enduring, entertaining, internationally recognized character on the order of Mickey Mouse, Popeye the Sailor, or Bugs Bunny. That fact alone may account more for the way clay has developed in this century than any other factor.

In the last ten years, clay seems to have become more fashionable as an advertising medium, while longer clay narratives seem less prevalent in the post–California Raisin era. In the short term, the future of clay in the expanded market for animated features appears to be not only limited but linked to the success of other animation media, notably, Tim Burton's dimensional feature. In a future of more widely adopted three-dimensional delivery systems, the cost advantages of traditional cel animation are likely be outweighed by its inherent flatness, enhancing the future for dimensional animation.

Special techniques like strata-cut, clay painting, and animating clay on glass will no doubt continue to emerge in clay, but like most moving imagery, the future of clay animation seems linked to the computer. As various media—audio, video, text, still photos, and so forth—become digitally encoded, they converge at the computer as just another data file that can be manipulated, stored, and outputted in a variety of ways. Using clay objects to generate three-dimensional data files seems a clear-cut union of the two technologies, a model of hybridization that could be applied to a wide variety of animation techniques. If the computer becomes the place where all animators animate, the tool that all animators use to manipulate regardless of their "medium," then perhaps cel will no longer enjoy the cost advantages it has in the past. Whatever hybrid form of clay emerges, insofar as it uses the medium to "satisfy our spatial hunger" (as Clokey puts it) and to exploit the tactile, "funky" quality of the clay surface, it will remain true to the central aesthetic appeal that has driven the medium from the beginning.

As we have seen, clay is an art process that has its own potentials, is relatively easy to animate, and adapts to all kinds of incremental manipulation. Its potential for creating abstract visuals is matched by its natural affinity for clay figurative animation, in which the characters move in three-dimensional space, create their own perspective, and cast their own shadows. Beginners tend to capitalize on clay's accessibility, professionals on its expressiveness. From the earliest days of filmmaking, these potentials and the almost magical imagery generated by animated, moving clay have had a powerful appeal for artists, filmmakers, and audiences.

Around 1920, when cinema exchanged variety in the animated film for almost universal acceptance of the institutional modes of flat animation—slash and cel—it gained economy in production and established the conventions of the animated cartoon, which would become a familiar, enduring, and remarkably popular form of entertainment. Lacking the large-scale specialization and division of labor that can be brought to bear in the cel medium, clay has remained a secondary, though increasingly visible, animation technique since that time. But taken together, these conditions—its visceral visual appeal and its resistance to extensive division of labor—have ensured both the existence of the medium and its continued rarity compared with cel for the past seven decades. This situation seems unlikely to change in the near future. What remains to be seen is how new technologies—the computer and three-dimensional imaging technology—will fundamentally change animation and, in the process, change a medium that in essence remains the same animated sculpture that emerged in the early decades of motion pictures.

NOTES AND REFERENCES

Chapter One

1. Anonymous, "Les Trucs du cinématographe," *Lectures Pour Tous* (June 1908), reprinted in Donald Crafton, *Emile Cohl: Caricature and Film* (Princeton: Princeton University Press, 1990), 134–5, hereafter cited in the text. It is unclear what film is being described here by Arnaud, an early director at the Gaumont studio in Paris and a collaborator with Emile Cohl. In *Before Mickey: The Animated Film 1898–1928* ([Cambridge: MIT Press, 1984], 353 n. 25, hereafter cited in the text), Crafton indicates that the only Gaumont film released under this title was issued in December 1905. But later, Crafton states in *Emile Cohl* that the film described in this article is almost certainly *The Sculptor's Nightmare*. But could Arnaud be referring to the Edison film *A Sculptor's Welsh Rarebit Dream*, which was released two months prior to *Sculptor's Nightmare* and contains the same trick?

2. Crafton has touched on the changes over the years in the mystification of the animation process. In *Before Mickey*, he notes that some early animators who were making trick films, such as Méliès, argued for an oath of secrecy—much like that taken by members of the Syndicate of French Illusionists—regarding the single-frame process (30). Their fear was that audiences would no longer be interested in the films if the method of their creation was known. Ever since the cat has been out of the bag, animators have routinely tried to elevate their art by emphasizing in the popular press the tedious nature of the animation process, and even in the films themselves: the opening scenes of *Gertie the Dinosaur* and *The Sinking of the Lusitania* show huge stacks of drawings being prepared for shooting. Crafton has also pointed out that the recurring image of "the hand of the artist" in animated films is an attempt at the same sort of elevation. See Donald Crafton, "Animation Iconography: The 'Hand of the Artist,'" *Quarterly Review of Film Studies* 4 (Fall 1979): 409–17, hereafter cited in the text.

3. L. Bruce Holman describes the basic process for three-dimensional animation in the second section of his book *The History of Puppet Animation in Cinema: History and Technique* (Cranbury, N.J.: A. S. Barnes and Co., 1975), 49–79, hereafter cited in the text.

4. I am relying on the classification and descriptions of Fischinger's films presented by William Moritz in "The Films of Oskar Fischinger," *Film Culture*, nos. 58, 59, 60 (1974): 83.

5. Quoted in Richard Schickel, *The Disney Version: The Life, Times, Art and Commerce of Walt Disney* (New York: Avon, 1968), 161, hereafter cited in the text.

6. Leonard Maltin, *Of Mice and Magic* (New York: New American Library, 1980), 38, hereafter cited in the text.

7. Quoted in Barbara Vetter, "The Adventures of Mark Twain by Huck Finn," *American Cinematographer* (November 1985): 78, hereafter cited in the text.

8. For a description of Dayton's technique, see "Motion Picture Comedies in Clay," *Scientific American* 115 (16 December 1916): 553, hereafter cited in the text as "Comedies in Clay." On this issue, Art Clokey, the creator of Gumby, has said, "Using only clay or clay-covered set pieces gives Vinton's a certain appeal to the intellect, to the artist and adults. . . . We use a mix of mediums simply to get across a narrative" (Telephone interview with Art Clokey, 16 October 1982, hereafter cited in the text as "1982 Clokey interview"). For more on Clokey's technique, see chapter 6.

9. Alternatively, many animators will use a long lens, such as a 75mm for 16mm cameras, and simply move the tripod back ten feet or so from the set. If the angle is not too steep, this seems to lessen the effect of shooting down on the characters and gives closer shots of the characters. But the method results in flatter shots with less depth of field.

10. Like live-action filmmakers, animators will often simply "cheat" shots by placing characters wherever they want on the set to get the composition they need and controlling depth-of-field so that the background appears to match the other footage shot. Such cheating may eliminate the need to move the camera onto the set.

11. *The Old Mill* marked the studio's first extensive use of the multiplane camera—a large rostrum camera standing almost twelve feet high with up to six horizontal planes that the camera could "dolly" toward, a technical achievement for which the studio won an Academy Award. See David R. Smith, "Beginnings of the Disney Multiplane Camera," in *The Art of the Animated Image: An Anthology*, ed. Charles Solomon (Los Angeles: American Film Institute, 1987), 37–49. In some early test scenes for *Snow White*, clay was used to mold trees in relief, adding greater depth to these multiplane shots.

12. For a discussion of Vinton's aesthetic, see chapter 7.

13. Herbert Zettl has created a taxonomy of five basic sound functions: information, outer orientation (spatial orientation, time of day, season, and so forth), inner orientation (mood, internal states, and so forth), energy, and structure. For a complete description of these functions, see chapter 16 of his *Sight, Sound, and Motion: Applied Media Aesthetics*, 2d ed. (Belmont, Calif.: Wadsworth, 1990), hereafter cited in the text.

14. Susan Pitt, "Animation and the Creative Process," *Proceedings of the First Society for Animation Studies Conference*, 27–28 October 1989, Los Angeles (unpublished typescript), 1.

15. For a discussion of squash-and-stretch methods, see Frank Thomas and Ollie Johnston, *Disney Animation: The Illusion of Life* (New York: Abbeville Press, 1981), 47–69, hereafter cited in the text.

16. Sergei Eisenstein, *Eisenstein on Disney*, ed. Jay Leyda (London: Methuen, 1988), 22, hereafter cited in the text.

17. William Moritz, "Some Observations on Non-objective and Nonlinear Animation," in *Storytelling in Animation: The Art of the Animated Image*, vol. 2, ed. John Canemaker (Los Angeles: American Film Institute, 1988), 28–29, hereafter cited in the text.

18. Barry Bruce, animation workshop at the Second Annual UNC-G Film Festival, Greensboro, N.C., 1 April 1979, hereafter cited in the text as "Bruce workshop."

19. "Morphing," a computer extrapolation technique used in *Willow* (Ron Howard, 1988), *Terminator II* (James Cameron, 1991), and Michael Jackson's video "Black or White" (John Landis, 1991), capitalizes on this apparent violation of natural order and extends the magical quality of metamorphosis to nonanimated live-action footage.

20. William C. Carroll, *The Metamorphoses of Shakespearean Comedy* (Princeton: Princeton University Press, 1985), 4, hereafter cited in the text.

21. André Bazin, *What Is Cinema?* (Berkeley: University of California Press, 1967), 13–14.

22. Art Clokey, "Trimensional Animation" (unpublished typescript, 1977).

23. It is widely recognized that certain studios—notably, UPA and Zagreb—have honed the skill of *creatively* omitting details to such a fine art that their animation does not suffer for it; in fact, their simplicity is one of their strong points.

24. Telephone interview with John Lemmon, 15 July 1991.

25. Telephone interview with Joan Gratz, 9 September 1991, hereafter cited in the text as "Gratz interview."

26. Telephone interview with David Daniels, 20 October 1991. For an extended discussion of Daniels's work, see chapter 8.

Chapter Two

1. See, for example, John Canemaker, *Winsor McCay: His Life and Art* (New York: Abbeville Press, 1987), 46–47.

2. Winsor McCay, *Illustrating and Cartooning: Animation* (Minneapolis: Federal Schools Inc., 1923), 18, hereafter cited in text.

3. Constance Eileen King, *The Encyclopedia of Toys* (Secaucus, N.J.: Chartwell Books, 1978), 257.

4. Leslie Williams, "Visualizing Victorian Schooling: Art as Document and Propaganda," *Bucknell Review* 34, no. 2 (1990): 142.

5. William Harbutt, *Harbutt's Plastic Method and the Use of Plasticine in the Arts of Writing, Drawing, and Modelling in Educational Work* (London: Chapman and Hall, 1897), vii, hereafter cited in the text.

6. Denis Gifford, *British Animated Films, 1895–1985: A Filmography* (Jefferson, N.C.: McFarland & Co., 1987), hereafter cited in the text.

7. Charles Musser, *The Emergence of Cinema: The American Screen to 1907*, vol. 1 of *History of the American Cinema* (New York: Charles Scribner's Sons, 1990), 325, hereafter cited in the text.

8. *Edison Films*, no. 288 (July 1906), 21, contained in *Motion Picture Catalogs by American Producers and Distributors, 1894–1908*, microfilm ed., ed. Charles Musser (Frederick, Md.: University Publications of America, 1985), G–468, hereafter cited in the text as *Edison*.

9. Admiral Winfield Scott Schley was a commodore in the Spanish-American War who blockaded Santiago, Cuba, only to be superseded in command by Admiral W. T. Sampson. While Sampson was temporarily absent, Schley fought the battle of Santiago and defeated the Spanish fleet, prompting questions about who was responsible for that victory. Edwin S. Porter's earlier film, the three-shot *Sampson-Schley Controversy* (Edison, 1901), had capitalized on the uproar in the popular press when Schley requested that a court of inquiry look into the matter in 1901.

10. Charles Musser with Carol Nelson, *High Class Moving Pictures: Lyman Howe and the Forgotten Era of Traveling Exhibition, 1880–1920* (Princeton: Princeton University Press, 1991), 96, 114.

11. Howard Lamarr Walls, *Motion Pictures, 1894–1912, Identified from the Records of the United States Copyright Office* (Washington D.C.: Library of Congress, 1953), 54. I checked Ronald Maggliozzi's *Treasures from the Film Archives: A Catalog of Short Silent Fiction Film Held by FIAF Archives* and the UCLA Film Archives, the George Eastman House, and the Museum of Modern Art.

12. *The Moving Picture World* (22 February 1908): 148; citations from *The Moving Picture World* hereafter appear in the text.

13. Russell Merritt, "Dream Visions in Pre-Hollywood Film," in *Before Hollywood: Turn-of-the-Century Film from American Archives* (New York: Hudson Hills Press, 1987), 71, hereafter cited in the text.

14. *Biograph Bulletins 1896–1908*, comp. Kemp R. Niver (Los Angeles: Locare Research Group, 1971), 350, hereafter cited in the text as Niver.

15. Two of the busts in the film clearly bear the signature of the artist, but the name is illegible.

16. Though Bitzer had created double exposures to suggest miniature people as early as 1905 in *A Pipe Dream*, when he made *Sculptor's Nightmare* in April 1908 he had shot only one previous animation, *If You Had a Wife Like This* (in February 1908). This film was the first known Biograph film containing animation. A year earlier, Bitzer had collaborated on *The Tired Tailor's Dream* (shot in May 1907) with F. A. Dobson. Bitzer had also experimented with the backwards take in one previous film, *Princess in a Vase* (shot in February 1908), in which smoke from a princess's funeral pyre is drawn magically into a vase. Bitzer's early obsession with magic had led him in 1894 to take a job with the Magic Introduction Company, a purveyor of magic equipment owned by E. B. Koopman. When W. K. L. Dickson approached Koopman to produce a peep-show machine to rival the Kinetoscope, Koopman opened the American Mutoscope and Biograph Company on the same premises in 1895. Bitzer's interest shifted to film, but with his background in magic he was a logical choice to become a specialist in trick films. Erik Barnouw explores the role of the magician in early trick films in *The Magician and the Cinema* (New York: Oxford University Press, 1981), hereafter cited in the text.

17. Eileen Bowser, *The Transformation of Cinema 1907–1915*, vol. 2, *History of the American Cinema* (New York: Charles Scribner's Sons, 1990), 38, hereafter cited in the text.

18. Charles Musser, *Before the Nickelodeon: Edwin S. Porter and the Edison Manufacturing Company* (Berkeley: University of California Press, 1991), 69, hereafter cited in the text.

19. Noel Burch, *Life to Those Shadows* (Berkeley: University of California Press, 1990), 201 n16.

20. George C. D. Odell, *Annals of the New York Stage, 1843–1850*, vol. 5 (New York: Columbia University Press, 1931), 378, hereafter cited in the text.

21. David Devant, *My Magic Life* (London: Hutchinson and Co., 1931), 231.

22. Descriptions of *The Artist's Dream* and *The Artist's Dilemma* are found in *Edison*, G–480.

23. Paul Hammond, *Marvelous Méliès* (New York: St. Martin's Press, 1975), 90.

24. The scene described here does not appear in the print available from the National Film Archive of the British Film Institute.

25. None of the titles in the existing film name the imp figure.

26. The scene described here does not appear in the print available from the National Film Archive of the British Film Institute.

27. James Stuart Blackton, "A Glimpse in the Past," *The Moving Picture World* (10 March 1917): 1527.

28. A fairly detailed biography of Blackton can be found in Anthony Slide's *The BIG V: A History of the Vitagraph Company*, rev. ed. (Metuchen, N.J.: Scarecrow Press, 1987), 18–31.

29. The profound changes occurring in American life during the four decades prior to World War I brought a new awareness of, and demand for, sculpture. The captains of industry were building mansions in unprecedented numbers and lavishly adorning both house and garden with sculpture. Public squares, new civic architecture, financial houses, industrial headquarters, and sprawling exhibitions of the period incorporated the works from a new wave of American sculptors, among them, Augustus Saint-Gaudens, Karl Bitter, and Theo Alice Kitson. According to Roberta Tarbell's "Sculpture in America before the Armory Show: Transition to Modern" (in *Vanguard American Sculpture: 1913–1939* [New Brunswick, N.J.: Rutgers University Press, 1979], 1), the new awareness of sculpture in the United States was well established by 1910. At the annual exhibition of the National Academy of Design, the number of sculptures exhibited went from 13 in 1905 to 70 in 1907, to 167 in 1912, while the number of paintings shown did not increase correspondingly. The increased awareness of sculpture is also evidenced by the formation of the National Sculpture Society in 1893. By the 1920s, the society was one of the most vocal and influential arts organizations in the country.

In a related development, the late 1800s witnessed the rishing of the Arts and Crafts movement, a reaction to the decline of handmade goods brought about by industrialization; the movement contributed to the soaring production of handicrafts in Europe and America, including a dramatic increase in the number of potteries and potters operating around the country, particularly so-called art potteries, which produced lines of fancifully decorated ware. The use of clay as an animation medium prior to 1910 may be a reflection of two trends described here: an increased awareness of sculpture at the turn of the century and an increase in the available pool of labor for producing clay animated films—though the number of artists employed in clay animation never approached the number of graphic artists who found work in the cel animation industry.

30. Charles Seymour, *Tradition and Experiment in Modern Sculpture* (Washington, D.C.: American University Press, 1949), 23–27.

Chapter Three

1. Richard Koszarski, *An Evening's Entertainment: The Age of the Silent Feature Picture*, vol. 3, *History of the American Cinema* (New York: Charles Scribner's Sons, 1990), 172, hereafter cited in the text.

2. Joe Adamson, "A Talk with Dick Huemer," in *The American Animated Cartoon: A Critical Anthology*, ed. Gerald Peary and Danny Peary (New York: E. P. Dutton, 1980), 29–36.

3. Austin C. Lescarboura, *Behind the Motion Picture Screen* (1919; reprint, New York: Benjamin Blom, 1971), 316–22, hereafter cited in the text. *Dream Dolls* is also identified in Patricia Hanson, exec. ed., *The American Film Institute Catalog of Motion Pictures Produced in the United States: Feature Films, 1911–1920* (Berkeley: University of California Press, 1988), 228, hereafter cited in the text as *AFI Catalog, Feature Films, 1911–1920.*

4. Ephraim Katz, *The Film Encyclopedia* (New York: Perigee Books, 1982), 870.

5. Paul Dickson, *The Dickson Baseball Dictionary* (New York: Facts on File, 1989), 384, hereafter cited in the text.

6. *American Notes and Queries* (July 1948): 56.

7. "'Everywoman' Embellishes the Screen, Approaching More Nearly Spectacular Perfection Than Any Photofeature, Excepting David Wark Griffith's Film, 'Intolerance,'" *Exhibitor's Trade Review* (13 December 1919): 167.

8. Index card file, YMCA of the USA Archives, University of Minnesota.

9. *American Art Annual* 30 (1933) [edited by Alice McGlauflin] (Washington D.C.: American Federation of Arts, 1934), 487.

10. The first book is a guide to producing successful costume parties, charity bazaars, pageants, dinners, reunions, and amateur dramatic productions. The trappings for the social functions of the Society of Illustrators are featured throughout the text as illustrations. Watson Barratt, the husband of Dayton's coauthor and a magazine illustrator and longtime scene designer on and off Broadway ("Watson Barratt, Designer, 78, Dies," *New York Times* [8 July 1962]), is frequently identified as the designer of these sets and tableaux.

Long after their book collaborations in the 1920s, Louise Bascom Barratt, whose address in the 1940s was 15 West 67th Street, may have been neighbors with Helena Smith Dayton, since the Daytons were living in the same building from at least 1933 until Fred Dayton died in 1954. Louise Bascom Barratt was a magazine writer and edited *The New York Visitor*, the magazine of the New York Central Railroad, from 1936 until her death in 1942. Perhaps the two women had met through membership in the Society of Illustrators.

11. "Mrs. Helena Dayton," *New York Times*, 23 February 1960.

12. Howard Devree, "A Reviewer's Notebook," *New York Times*, 25 April 1943. The same show is also mentioned in "Art Notes," *New York Times*, 20 April 1943, and in *Art Digest* 17 (15 April 1943): 26.

13. "Fred Erving Dayton, Condé Nast Ex-Aide," *New York Times*, 30 October 1954.

14. In the article, Helena Smith Dayton's first name is mistakenly cited as "Helene." The article was rewritten into Lescarboura's *Behind the Motion Picture Screen* (309–16). The same photographs are used, though Dayton is not mentioned by name in the book.

15. *Motography* 18 (15 September 1917): 546. An article in *The Moving Picture World* ([2 February 1917]: 663) lists "S. & S. Photoplays, Inc., 1476 Broadway, New York City" among the educational producers. *AFI Catalog, Feature Films, 1911–1920* indicates that a company called "S & S Photoplays" distributed two feature films (nos. F1.1201 and F1.1905) in April 1918. Could this be the same company referred to in the *Motography* article as "S.S. Film Company"?

16. One month before the *Motography* blurb, on the theater page of the 12 August 1917 *New York Times*, a Strand Theatre ad featured an untitled "Educational" short on the bill with Marguerite Clark in *The Amazons*. Could the term refer to Dayton's short soon to *become* an official release of Educational Film Corporation?

17. "Strand Institutes Art Exhibits," *The Moving Picture World* (1 December 1917): 1301.

18. "Strand to Give Daily Concerts," *The Moving Picture World* (1 September 1917): 1359.

19. "Prominent Sculptor in Film," *The Moving Picture World* (24 November 1917): 1164. J. Charles Davis, Jr., was apparently the son of J. Charles Davis, whose obituary in the *New York Times* of 4 October 1919 indicates that Davis senior was for many years a press agent for Barnum & Bailey, as well as the manager of Milner's People's Theater in the Bowery and of the Fifth Avenue Theater, which became Proctor's.

20. By contrast, Eli Levitan's *Handbook of Animation Techniques* (New York: Van Nostrand Reinhold, 1979), a 300-page book overwhelmingly devoted to cel animation, treats stop-motion animation in five pages and puppet animation in three pages.

Chapter Four

1. See Donald Crafton's chapter in *Before Mickey*, "The Henry Ford of Animation: John Randolph Bray" (137–67), and Kristin Thompson, "Implications of the Cel Technique," in *The Cinematic Apparatus*, ed. Teresa de Laurentis and Stephen Heath (London: Macmillan, 1980), 106–20, hereafter cited in the text.

2. Cartoons were not only trivialized in the exhibition arena, but animators have found that the cel technique—as used in American studio animation—trivializes and restricts their creativity. The Disney animator Shamus Culhane calls cel "mind shackling," and after viewing a program of films by National Film Board of Canada artists one night, he was compelled to write: "How totally restrictive, constrictive, and dulling to freedom of expression the cel system has been. What a shock it was to realize that I have never enjoyed the excitement of making an entire film myself." See Shamus Culhane, "Frustration," in Canemaker 1988, 40.

3. Conrad Smith, "The Early History of Animation: Saturday Morning TV Discovers 1915," *Journal of the University Film Association* 29 (Summer 1977): 23.

4. Leonard Maltin identifies 14 "Out of the Inkwell" shorts from the Fleischer Brothers studio produced by John Randolph Bray from 1915 to 1920 and released in the *Paramount Screen Magazine*. After 1927 the series was called "Inkwell Imps." See Maltin, 358–59.

5. "The Inkwell Man," *New York Times*, 22 February 1920.

6. Michael Wassenaar, "Strong to the Finich: Machines, Metaphor, and Popeye the Sailor," *The Velvet Light Trap*, no. 24 (Fall 1989): 28.

7. Max Fleischer writing in a studio autobiography, cited in Leslie Cabarga, *The Fleischer Story* (New York: Nostalgia Press, 1976), ch. 2, p. 6.

8. Enid Welsford, *The Fool: His Social and Literary History* (London: Faber and Faber, 1935), 320.

9. Maurice Willson Disher, *Clowns and Pantomimes* (1925; reprint, New York: Benjamin Blom, 1968), 3–23.

10. Noel Burch, *Theory of Film Practice*, trans. H. R. Lane (Princeton: Princeton University Press, 1981), 17. Burch argues that offscreen space is divided into six segments. The four borders of the frame define four of those segments, and the fifth is a distinct space located behind the camera. The sixth segment includes the space existing behind the set.

11. The idea of a "punctured" background plane is found with variations throughout the series. In *Tantalizing the Fly* (between 1915 and 1920), Ko-Ko goes through the puncture and ends up on the back of the sheet of paper, and in *Ko-Ko the Kop* (1927), Ko-Ko moves through the puncture to a new cartoon space.

12. Index to *AFI Catalog, Feature Films, 1911–1920*. The topic of prehistoric cavepersons, who were related to dinosaurs in the public mind, was treated in films like *Twas Ever Thus* (Paramount, 1915), a film that connected scenes of a father opposing his daughter's marriage in prehistoric times, during the American Civil War, and in the present. Other films using the structure of the parallel story set in the prehistoric past were Cecil B. De Mille's melodrama *Adam's Rib* (1923) and Howard Hawks's comedy *Fig Leaves* (1926).

13. During the excavation, a remarkably complete skeleton of a sauropod was discovered and named *diplodocus carnegiei*, after the steel baron and benefactor of the museum. Carnegie, pleased with the designation, had a large number of castings of the skeleton made, then donated them to many major museums, disseminating this find to a wide audience throughout the world.

14. Edwin H. Clobert recounts the history of the discovery of dinosaur remains in America in *Men and Dinosaurs: The Search in Field and Laboratory* (New York: E. P. Dutton & Co., 1968), hereafter cited in the text.

15. The figures in *The Dinosaur and the Missing Link* have been incorrectly described by Oliver Goldner and George E. Turner (*The Making of King Kong: The Story Behind a Film Classic* [New York: A. S. Barnes and Co., 1975]) as "clay over jointed wooden skeletons" (41), but a close examination of the film shows what appear to be armatures wrapped in smooth latex. The human models show no cracking or crumbling or signs of repair at the armature joints, even though those joints are only thinly covered by the exterior material. The tiny fingers of the characters remain cleanly formed and show no signs of manipulation. Even when clay is carefully animated, such traces of manipulation are usually visible when viewed frame by frame. Moreover, both dinosaur and human figures have little mass: they are thin forms that maintain registration even when necks, arms, and legs are extended, whereas clay figures normally require more massive figures, particularly lower bodies, to support their upper body weight. Don Shay confirms this analysis in "Willis O'Brien: Creator of the Impossible" (*Focus on Film*, no. 16 [Autumn 1973]), identifying the figures as puppet armatures wrapped with thin sheet rubber (21).

16. Rudi Blesh, *Buster Keaton* (New York: Macmillan, 1966), 220.

Chapter Five

1. According to *The American Film Institute Catalog of Motion Pictures: Feature Films, 1961–1970* (New York: R. R. Bowker Co., 1976), Luce later coauthored and edited a 16mm motorcycle melodrama called *Wild Wheels* (Fanfare Films, 1969) and was associate producer for *Cain's Way* (M.D.A. Associates, 1970), a feature with John Carradine that made a connection between a motorcycle gang and Confederate marauders through flashbacks (138, 1228). *Cain's Way* was distributed under several titles, and some print sources credit Jack Hammond as associate producer.

2. Personal correspondence with Connie Tregillus, 28 December 1991, hereafter cited in the text as "C. Tregillus letter."

3. Leonard Tregillus's dissertation was entitled "A Study of the Kinetics of Electrode Reactions Associated with the Electrolysis of Dilute Amalgams" (University of California at Berkeley, 1950).

4. Unlike the Ranger, Mariner, and Surveyor missions to the moon, the Lunar Orbiter used film, not video, to capture images of the moon; the images were then read with an electron scanner for transmission to the earth. Bimat film was a slow, 70mm aerial film, insensitive to radiation fogging but susceptible to heat; it offered engineers greater resolution and weight savings over the magnetic storage media available at the time. "Bimat" refers to the developing process: a web film containing processing chemicals is pressed

against the exposed emulsion, and then through a diffusion-transfer process produces a positive image. The positive image stored on the web is then dried and scanned as needed to relay the data to earth.

5. Telephone interview with Connie Tregillus, 11 January 1992, hereafter cited in the text as "C. Tregillus interview."

6. Sheldon Renan, *An Introduction to the American Underground Film* (New York: E. P. Dutton, 1967), 83–84, hereafter cited in the text.

7. *1953 Educational Film Guide* (New York: H. W. Wilson Co., 1953), 812.

8. Unidentified catalog clipping from the files of Cecile Starr.

9. Unidentified catalog clipping from the files of Cecile Starr.

10. William Chapman, ed., *Films on Art 1952* (Washington, D.C.: American Federation of Arts, 1952), 129.

Chapter Six

1. John Izod, *Hollywood and the Box Office, 1895–1986* (New York: Columbia University Press, 1988), 134, hereafter cited in the text.

2. Douglas Gomery, *Movie History* (Belmont, Calif.: Wadsworth, 1991), 280.

3. Cy Schneider, *Children's Television: The Art, The Business, and How It Works* (Chicago: NTC Business Books, 1987), 18, hereafter cited in the text.

4. Slavko Vorkapich, "Cinematics: Some Principles Underlying Effective Cinematography," *Cinematographic Annual*, ed. Hal Hall (Hollywood: ASC Holding Co., 1930), reprinted in *Hollywood Directors 1914–1940*, ed. Richard Koszarski (New York: Oxford University Press, 1971), 257–58.

5. "He Calls It 'Ideagraphy,'" *New York Times*, 5 December 1937.

6. Louis Kaplan and Scott Michaelsen, *Gumby: The Authorized Biography of the World's Favorite Clayboy* (New York: Harmony, 1986), 1, hereafter cited in the text.

7. Telephone interview with Jim Danforth, 28 October 1982.

8. Personal correspondence with E. Roger Muir (the executive producer of "The Howdy Doody Show"), 6 January 1992. According to Muir, these early episodes included "Moon Trip," "Mirrorland," "Lost and Found," "Gumby on the Moon," and "Trapped on the Moon."

9. Stuart Fischer, *Kid's TV: The First 25 Years* (New York: Facts on File, 1983), 96.

10. See George Woolery, *Animated TV Specials: The Complete Directory to the First Twenty-five Years, 1962–1987* (Metuchen, N.J.: Scarecrow Press, 1989).

11. Karl Cohen, "Gumby," *Animation Magazine* 2 (Summer 1988): 8, hereafter cited in the text.

12. Telephone interview with Art Clokey, 28 April 1993, hereafter cited in the text as "1993 Clokey interview."

Chapter Seven

1. Claymation® was first used in 1978 in the documentary of that name; it was given official registered trademark status on 7 July 1981.

2. John Canemaker, "Redefining Animation," *Print* 33, no. 2 (March-April 1979): 60.

3. Other Academy Award–winning clay films are Jimmy Picker's *Sundae in New York*, Nick Park's *Creature Comforts*, and Joan Gratz's *Mona Lisa Descending a Staircase*.

4. Telephone interview with Will Vinton, 18 September 1979, hereafter cited in the text as "1979 Vinton interview." Vinton shares an architectural background with other animators (George Pal, for instance), while his interest in tinkering calls to mind the Fleischer brothers.

5. The set was originally constructed for a spot for Rainier Ale. *Mountain Music* marked the end of the collaboration between Vinton and Gardiner.

6. A matte shot—or more accurately here, a traveling matte—uses the optical printer to combine two or more film images into a single, composite image when the foreground image's position in the frame changes relative to the background. Traveling mattes in film are comparable to the familiar chroma key effect in television, in which two images are electronically "cut together" into a single composite. Thus, the matte process in film, unlike a super or double exposure, involves *selectively* printing different areas on a single piece of film. The Vinton studio generates mattes by front lighting and back lighting each foreground position in the scene to be matted.

7. Maxwell A. Smith outlines some of the indications that *The Little Prince* is autobiographical in *Knight of the Air* (New York: Pageant Press, 1956), 200, hereafter cited in the text.

8. Personal interview with Will Vinton, 22 February 1980, hereafter cited in the text as "1980 Vinton interview."

9. Rick Cooper, "Will Vinton and His Animated Shorts," *Design for Arts in Education* 84 (July-August 1983): 33. The filmography issued by the Vinton studio lists one less short (for a total of 11) and one more commercial (for a total of 10) produced through 1983.

10. Richard Bridgman, *Traveling in Mark Twain* (Berkeley: University of California Press, 1987), 1.

11. Vincent Canby, "Toy Twain," *New York Times*, 17 January 1986.

12. Stanley Kaufman, "Passions and Adventures," *New Republic* 193 (9 September 1985): 193.

13. Schickel outlines the scope of Disney's cultural production in the 1960s, well before Walt Disney World, the Disney cable channel, and Touchstone Pictures: "In 1966 Walt Disney Enterprises estimated that around the world 240,000,000 people saw a Disney movie, 100,000,000 watched a Disney television show every week, 800,000,000 read a Disney book or magazine, 50,000,000 listened or danced to Disney music or records, 80,000,000 bought Disney-licensed merchandise, 150,000,000 read a Disney comic strip, 80,000,000 saw Disney educational films at school, in church, on the job, and 6.7 million made the journey . . . to Disneyland" (10).

14. Disney animation has often been broadly and incorrectly characterized as "realistic" or, less problematically, "naturalistic." A typically naive description is found in Elizabeth Leebron and Lynn Gartley's *Walt Disney: A Guide to References and Resources* (Boston: G. K. Hall, 1979) in which the authors state, "[In Disney films the] world looked like the one outside the window and the figures moved as real animals and people moved" (10).

15. "Crossovers" and cycles increase the number of characters within a shot. In a crossover, inkers trace one set of character drawings onto the cel in more than one place to create two or three or more of the same figures moving in the same manner, but they often stagger the drawings a few frames out of sync with each other to create groups moving together, as in the four skeletons' dance sequence from *The Skeleton Dance* (1928). See Thomas and Johnston, 42–44.

16. Lewis Jacobs, "Walt Disney: Virtuoso," in *The Rise of the American Film: A Critical History* (New York: Harcourt, Brace and Co., 1939), 499.

17. Lewis Jacobs, "The Mobility of Color," in *The Movies as Medium*, ed. Lewis Jacob (New York: Farrar, Straus and Giroux, 1971), 190.

18. Thomas and Johnston include a wealth of background drawings in their book, but the four illustrations on pp. 246–47 suffice to demonstrate this range.

19. Laurel Wentz, "Raisins Dance in U.K. to Promote Sun-Maid," *Advertising Age* 58 (27 July 1987): 4.

20. William Feaver, *Masters of Caricature: From Hogarth and Gillray to Scarfe and Levine*, ed. Ann Gould (New York: Knopf, 1981), 85.

21. Alice Cuneo, "Sun-Maid, Dole Boost Raisins," *Advertising Age* 59 (10 October 1988): 44.

22. Telephone interview with Veronica Buxton of the Foote, Cone, and Belding Agency, 4 September 1991, hereafter cited in the text as "Buxton interview."

23. Michael Barrier, "The Clay's the Thing," *Nation's Business* 76 (December 1988): 57, hereafter cited in the text.

24. Will Vinton Productions, "About Will Vinton Productions" (unpublished studio release, 1991), 5.

Chapter Eight

1. Interview with Bruce Bickford, conducted at the Carolina Film and Video Festival, Greensboro, N.C., 22 March 1992, hereafter cited in the text as "Bickford interview."

2. Scenes from *Last Battle* appear in *The Amazing Mr. Bickford.*

3. Janet Maslin, "A One-Man Enterprise," *New York Times*, 21 December 1979, hereafter cited in the text.

4. *Variety Film Review* (New York: Garland, 26 December 1979).

5. Bruce Bickford, in *Baby Snakes.* The scene described here also appears in *The Amazing Mr. Bickford.*

6. Telephone interview with David Daniels, 13 September 1992.

7. Personal correspondence with David Daniels, 27 October 1991.

8. Herbert Schiller, *The Mind Managers* (Boston: Beacon Press, 1973), 24.

Chapter Nine

1. David Landis, "'Beauty' Sales Enchanting Disney," *USA Today*, 3 November 1992.

2. Harvey Deneroff, *The Animation Report* 1 (January 1992): 6.

3. Eliza Krause, "When You Wish úpon a Toon: How Disney Cleans up on Its Animated Classics," *Premier* (August 1992): 20, hereafter cited in the text.

4. Telephone interview with Tim Hittle, 2 November 1992.

5. Telephone interview with John Lemmon, 30 October 1992.

6. Telephone interview with Harvey Deneroff, 9 November 1992.

7. Telephone interview with Linda Simensky, 23 October 1992.

8. Telephone interview with Joan Gratz, 26 April 1993.

9. Telephone interview with David Daniels, 10 November 1992.

SELECTED BIBLIOGRAPHY

Books

Barnouw, Erik. *The Magician and the Cinema*. New York: Oxford University Press, 1981. An excellent short text on how magicians brought their methods into early trick films.

Biograph Bulletins 1896–1908. Compiled by Kemp R. Niver. Los Angeles: Locare Research Group, 1971. Advertisements and handbills issued by the American Mutoscope and Biograph Company, including several on early stop-motion trick films.

Bowser, Eileen. *The Transformation of Cinema 1907–1915*. Vol. 2 of *History of the American Cinema*. New York: Charles Scribner's Sons, 1990. Detailed document of the historical context of the introduction of clay animated trick films.

Canemaker, John. *Winsor McCay: His Life and Art*. New York: Abbeville Press, 1987. A comprehensive biography of a central figure in early animation.

———, ed. *Storytelling in Animation: The Art of the Animated Image*. Vol. 2. Los Angeles: American Film Institute, 1988. Articles and panel discussions on narrative/non-narrative approaches in a range of techniques other than clay.

Cabarga, Leslie. *The Fleischer Story*. New York: Nostalgia Press, 1976. Chatty adulation of the Fleischers. Has some good factual data and firsthand accounts of the studio's history.

Cholodenko, Alan, ed. *The Illusion of Life: Essays on Animation*. Sydney: Power Publications, 1990. Wide-ranging collection of papers applying poststructuralist approaches to animation theory.

Crafton, Donald. *Before Mickey: The Animated Film 1898–1928*. Cambridge, Mass.: MIT Press, 1984. Indispensable analysis of the interplay of artistic, social, cultural, and economic forces in silent animation.

———. *Emile Cohl: Caricature and Film*. Princeton: Princeton University Press, 1990. Meticulously researched biography of the artist and analysis of his work in historical perspective.

Gifford, Denis. *British Animated Films, 1895–1985: A Filmography*. Jefferson, N.C.: McFarland & Co., 1987.

Harbutt, William. *Harbutt's Plastic Method and the Use of Plasticine in the Arts of Writing, Drawing, and Modelling in Educational Work*. London: Chapman and Hall, 1897. Harbutt touts the advantages of his new modeling medium, and his illustrations give the suggestion of how clay might be animated in the future.

Holman, L. Bruce. *Puppet Animation in the Cinema: History and Technique.* A. S. Barnes and Co., 1975. Useful account of the aesthetics and practices of puppet animation, many of which are shared with clay animation.

Kaplan, Louis, and Scott Michaelsen. *Gumby: The Authorized Biography of the World's Favorite Clayboy*. New York: Harmony, 1986. Breezy book for fans that contains illustrations, synopses of the episodes in the first series, and an interview with Clokey.

Leyda, Jay, ed. *Eisenstein on Disney*. London: Methuen, 1988. Sergei Eisenstein's musings on the survival of totemism and animism in the work of Disney.

Lutz, Edwin G. *Animated Cartoons: How They Are Made, Their Origin and Development.* New York: Charles Scribner's Sons, 1920. An early how-to book that focuses on flat forms and rendering movement.

Maltin, Leonard. *Of Mice and Magic.* New York: New American Library, 1980. A useful survey that concentrates on the history of Hollywood studio animation, with substantive filmographies of the various Hollywood studios.

Musser, Charles. *The Emergence of Cinema: The American Screen to 1907.* Vol. 1 of *History of the American Cinema*. New York: Charles Scribner's Sons, 1990. Documents the historical context surrounding the introduction of the earliest clay "lightning sculpting" films.

———. *Before the Nickelodeon: Edwin S. Porter and the Edison Manufacturing Company*. Berkeley: University of California Press, 1991. An exhaustive reexamination of how Porter's work within the Edison studio advanced motion pictures.

———, ed. *Motion Picture Catalogs by American Producers and Distributors, 1894–1908.* Microfilm edition. Frederick, Md.: University Publications of America, 1985. Presents catalogs that are key sources of information on films made prior to 1908.

Peary, Gerald, and Danny Peary, eds. *The American Animated Cartoon: A Critical Anthology*. New York: E. P. Dutton, 1980. A collection of essays on the early history of animation, Disney, Hollywood studios, and contemporary animators.

Russet, Robert, and Cecile Starr. *Experimental Animation: An Illustrated Anthology*. 2d ed. New York: A. S. Barnes and Co., 1989. A survey of independent, abstract, non-narrative, and experimental animators, who are frequently marginalized in other studies.

Slide, Anthony. *The BIG V: A History of the Vitagraph Company*. Rev. ed. Metuchen, N.J.: Scarecrow Press, 1987. Contains a useful biography of James Stuart Blackton.

Smoodin, Eric. *Animating Culture: Hollywood Cartoons from the Sound Era.* New Brunswick, NJ: Rutgers University Press, 1993. Examines classic Hollywood cartoon discourse to understanding the interaction between government, the major studios, the popular press, theatrical exhibitors and the audience.

Schickel, Richard. *The Disney Version: The Life, Times, Art, and Commerce of Walt Disney.* New York: Avon Books, 1968. Readable biography and virulent critique of Disney's enormous output.

Solomon, Charles, ed. *The Art of the Animated Image: An Anthology.* Los Angeles: American Film Institute, 1988. An eclectic collection of essays on a range of techniques and animation issues.

Thomas, Frank, and Ollie Johnston. *Disney Animation: The Illusion of Life.* New York: Abbeville Press, 1981. Not the usual Disney picture book. Gives an insightful analysis of how the Disney aesthetic was created.

Walls, Howard Lamarr. *Motion Pictures 1894–1912, Identified from the Records of the United States Copyright Office.* Washington, D.C.: Library of Congress, 1953.

Woolery, George. *Animated TV Specials: The Complete Directory to the First Twenty-Five Years, 1962–1987.* Metuchen, N.J.: Scarecrow Press, 1989.

World Encyclopedia of Cartoons. Detroit: Gale Research, 1980.

Parts of Books.

Croy, Homer. "The Making of the Animated Cartoon." In *How Motion Pictures Are Made*, 308–27. New York: Harper and Brothers, 1918; reprint, New York: Arno Press, 1978. A snapshot of how the cel animation process was viewed shortly after its birth.

Koszarski, Richard. "Animation." In *An Evening's Entertainment: The Age of the Silent Feature Picture, 1915–1928*, vol. 3 of *History of the American Cinema*, 70–74. New York: Charles Scribner's Sons, 1990. Contains a short account of studio animation of the period.

Lescarboura, Austin C. "Cartoons That Move and Sculpture That Lives." In *Behind the Motion Picture Screen*, 302–22. New York: Scientific American Publishing, 1919; reprint, New York: Benjamin Blom, 1971. Includes a reprint of the article from *Scientific American* on Helena Smith Dayton and a section on Howard Moss's doll films.

Merritt, Russell. "Dream Visions in Pre-Hollywood Film." In *Before Hollywood: Turn-of-the-Century Film from American Archives*, 69–72. New York: Hudson Hills Press, 1987. Examines the logic of dream sequences in early motion pictures.

Thompson, Kristin. "Implications of the Cel Technique." In *The Cinematic Apparatus*, edited by Teresa de Laurentis and Stephen Heath, 106–21. London: Macmillan, 1980. Demonstrates how the cel technique limited the scope of the animated film in America.

Articles

Blackton, James Stuart. "A Glimpse in the Past." *The Moving Picture World* (10 March 1917): 1527–28. Blackton muses about his naive enthusiasm for his early trick film efforts.

Canemaker, John. "Redefining Animation." *Print* 33, no. 2 (March-April 1979): 60–71. Short survey of independent animation outside of Hollywood.

Cohen, Karl. "Gumby." *Animation Magazine* 2 (Summer 1988): 8. Outlines the production of the new "Gumby" series in 1988.

Cooper, Rick. "Will Vinton and His Animated Shorts." *Design for Arts in Education* 84 (July-August 1983): 29–33. A weak historical summary of the history of clay animation, followed by a snapshot of the Vinton studio prior to embarking on the *Mark Twain* feature.

Crafton, Donald. "Animation Iconography: The 'Hand of the Artist.'" *Quarterly Review of Film Studies* 4 (Fall 1979): 409–28. Clear-cut analysis of the significance of the enduring image of the "hand of the artist" in animated films.

"Motion Picture Comedies in Clay." *Scientific American* 115 (16 December 1916): 553. Description of Helena Smith Dayton's early clay animation work.

"Animated Sculpture Appears." *Motography* 18 (15 September 1917): 546. Short blurb on Helena Smith Dayton's work and its presentation to Governor Whitman of New York.

Fellman, Doug. "Twenty Nights in Clay." *American Cinematographer,* April, 1978. A look at the animation of Bob Gardiner for *Rolling Stone* magazine's tenth anniversary television special.

Frierson, Michael. "Clay Animation Comes Out of the Inkwell; The Fleischer Brothers and Clay Animation," *Animation Journal* 2, (Fall, 1993): 4–20. Focuses on the use of clay in *Modeling* in a journal devoted to scholarly analysis of animation.

Frierson, Michael. "The Invention of Plasticine and the Use of Clay in Early Motion Pictures," *Film History* 5, (June, 1993): 142–158. Recounts much of the information on early trick films contained here, within a strong issue devoted entirely to animation.

Hood, George. "Dialogue with a Plasticine Sculpitmator." *American Cinematographer,* April, 1978. Gardiner discusses and illustrates his clay techniques from the period.

McCarthy, Carrell and Paul Boyington. "Feats of Clay," *Super 8 Filmmaker,* 8 (December 1980): 19–25. A "how-to" article on using super 8 film to animate clay.

Palmer, Charles. "Cartoon in the Classroom." *Hollywood Quarterly* 3 (1947): 26–33. Describes the capacity of the drawn animation medium to present educational material.

Park, Nora. "Return to Oz." *American Cinematographer* (May 1985): 50–57. Discussion of the adaptation of the Claymation® process to achieve the special effects in this Disney film.

"Prominent Sculptor in Film." *The Moving Picture World* (24 November 1917): 1164. Announces the release of Helena Smith Dayton's work by Educational Film Corporation.

Shay, Don. "Willis O'Brien: Creator of the Impossible." *Focus on Film*, no. 16 (Autumn 1973): 18–48. Excellent short summary of the stop-motion animator's career; includes a detailed filmography.

Steffgen, Kim Alyse. "Vinton Studio Reaches Withering Heights with Raisins—and More!" *Animation Magazine* 2 (Spring 1989): 36–39. A profile of the Vinton Studio at the peak of "Raisinmania."

Verheiden, Mark. "The Making of *Closed Mondays*." *Cinefantastique* 4 (1975): 40–45. Detailed description of Gardiner and Vinton's methods in this early Claymation® film.

Vetter, Barbara. "The Adventures of Mark Twain by Huck Finn." *American Cinematographer* (November 1985): 74–90. Account of the Claymation® process adapted to the needs of feature film production.

'assenaar, Michael. "Strong to the Finich: Machines, Metaphor, and Popeye the Sailor." *The Velvet Light Trap*, no. 24 (Fall 1989): 20–33. An insightful analysis of the use of visual metaphor in "Popeye" cartoons.

SELECTED FILMOGRAPHIES

Leonard Tregillus

No Credit (Cinema 16, 1948)
Producers: Leonard Tregillus, Ralph W. Luce, and Jack Chambers
Running time: 6:00

Proem (A. F. Films, 1949)
Producers: Leonard Tregillus and Ralph W. Luce
Music: William Smith
Running time: 11:00

Odd Fellows Hall (A. F. Films, 1950)—live action and pixilation
Film by: Denver Sutton and Leonard Tregillus
Music: Don Sutton
Running time: 6:00

Casey at the Bat (1955)
Film by: Leonard Tregillus

Flashback (1955)
Film by: Leonard Tregillus

Hodge Podge (1955)
Film by: Leonard Tregillus

What Your Camera Can Do (1955)
Film by: Leonard Tregillus

Art Clokey
Original "Gumby" Episodes

Clokey Studio Personnel for the Original Episodes

Creator, writer, director, animator: Art Clokey
Writer, director, animator: Ray Peck

Writer, director, animator: Pete Kleinow
Art directors: Alfonson Eggleston, Verlyn Larson, and Melvin Wood
Story editor, treasurer: Ruth Goodell
Editor: Don McIntosh and Woodword Smith
Cameraman, editor: Colin Young
Animator, puppet maker: Jim Danforth
Artist, animator: Bob Danuser
Artist, animator, set builder: Roland Shutt
Writer, animator: Ralph Rodine
Animators: Doug Beswick, Bob Kesee, and Harry Walton
Lighting, production supervisor: Wady Medawar
Artists: Nick Kurdogla and Jerry Campbell
Music director: John Seeley
Dubbing: Bud Tolifson
Special effects: David Allen
Voice of Gumby and other voices: Dallas McKennon

Episodes from the Original Series Written and Directed by Art Clokey

"All Broken Up"
"Baker's Tour"
"The Black Knight"
"The Blockheads"
"The Blue Goo"
"Candidate for President"
"Chicken Feed"
"Dragon Witch"
"Eager Beavers"
"The Eggs and Trixie"
"Egg Trouble"
"Even Steven"
"The Ferris Wheel Mystery"
"Foxy Boxy" (written by Pete Kleinow)
"Gabby Auntie"
"G.F.D.(Gumby Fire Department)"
"The Glob"
"The Golden Gosling"
"The Golden Iguana"
"Good Knight Story"
"Goo for Gumby"
"Gopher Trouble"
"The Groobee"
"Gumby Business"
"Gumby Concerto"

"Gumby Crosses the Delaware"
"Gumby on the Moon"
"Gumby Racer"
"A Hair Raising Adventure"
"Hidden Valley"
"Hot Rod Granny"
"How Not to Trap Lions"
"In a Fix"
"In the Dough"
"The Kachinas"
"King for a Day"
"Lion Around" (written with Ralph Rodine)
"Lion Drive" (written with Ralph Rodine)
"Little Lost Pony"
"Lost and Found"
"The Magic Flute"
"The Magic Show" (written with Ralph Rodine)
"The Magic Wand" (written with Ralph Rodine)
"Making Squares"
"Mirrorland"
"Missile Bird"
"The Mocking Monkey"
"Moon Trip"
"Mysterious Fires"
"Northland Follies"
"Odd Balls"
"Outcast Marbles"
"Pigeon in a Plum Tree"
"Pilgrims on the Rocks"
"Point of Honor" (written by Ray Peck)
"Pokey Express"
"Pokey's Price"
"The Racing Game"
"Rain for Roo"
"Rain Spirits"
"The Reluctant Gargoyles" (written by Ray Peck)
"Ricochet Pete"
"Robot Rumpus"
"Sad King Ott's Daughter"
"Santa Witch"
"School for Squares"
"Scrooge Loose"
"The Siege of Boonesborough"

"The Small Planets"
"Son of Liberty "
"Too Loo"
"Toy Capers"
"Toy Crazy"
"Toy Fun"
"Toying Around"
"Toy Joy"
"Train Trouble"
"Trapped on the Moon"
"Treasure for Henry"
"Tree Trouble"
"Who's What?"
"The Witty Witch"
"Yard Work Made Easy"
"The Zoops"

Episodes from the Original Series Written and Directed by Ray Peck and Pete Kleinow

"Behind the Puff Ball"
"The Big Eye"
"A Bone for Nopey"
"Bully for Gumby"
"Dog Catchers"
"Do-It-Yourself Gumby"
"Dopey Nopey"
"Dragon Daffy"
"El Toro"
"Gold Rush Gumby"
"A Groobee Fight"
"Grub Grabber Gumby"
"Gumby Baby Sits"
"The Gumby League"
"Haunted Hot Dog"
"Hot Ice"
"Indian Challenge"
"Indian Country"
"Indian Trouble"
"A Lovely Bunch of Coconuts"
"Mason Hornet"
"The Moon Boggles"
"Moon Madness"

"Motor Mania"
"Mystic Magic"
"Of Clay and Critters"
"Piano Rolling Blues"
"Pokey Minds the Baby"
"Prickle's Problem"
"Prickle Turns Artist"
"Puppy Dog School"
"Puppy Talk"
"The Rodeo King"
"Shady Lemonade"
"Sticky Pokey"
"Stuck on Books"
"Super Spray"
"Tail Tale"
"This Little Piggy"
"Tricky Ball"
"Tricky Train"
"Turnip Trap"
"Weight and See"
"Wishful Thinking"

Clokey Studio Personnel for "The New Adventures of Gumby"

(A Primavision Production, 1988)
Producer, writer, director: Art Clokey
Supervising art director: Gloria Harman Clokey
Animation directors: Tom Gasek, Eric Leighton, and Harry Walton
Line producer: David Bleiman
Art director: Ken Pontac
Associate producer: Michael D. Hock
Music: Jerry Gerber
Editor: Lynn Stevenson
Trimensional animators: Kristine Albrecht, Michael Belzer, Stephen Buckley, Elizabeth Butler, Angine Glocka, Kurt Hanson, Timothy Hittle, Karen Kiser, Owen Klatte, Tony Laudati, Eric Leighton, Mark Peter Maggiore, Blake Martin, Lionel Orozco, Anthony Scott, Trey Thomas, Stephen C. Wathen, and Richard C. Zimmerman
Model makers and artists: Kirk Amidano, Dan Baldocchi, Cora E. Craig, Jay Davis Ltd. III, Norm DeCarlo, Damian J. Evans, Mike Fennell, Steve Fink, Victoria Fink, William D. Fink, Dane Fulkerson, Dick Gardner, Gene Hamm, Holly Harman, Fox C. Hughes, Martin McClure, Janet MacDuff, Marghe McMahon, Richard Miller, Dan

Morgan, Earle E. Murphy III, Shawn Nelson, Lynn Ritchie-Knez, Melissa Rockliff, Tom Rubalcava, Leonard Smith, Summer Swann, Hillary Van Austen, Hamilton Wendt, and Denis Yasukawa

Set coordinator: Mary J. Bradley
Production assistant: Kevin Reher
Production coordinators: Lesley Cardy and Stephanie Hock
Voice coach: Dallas McKennon
Lighting director: James Herrera
Still photography: Mindy Beede
Stage manager: James Belmessieri
Key grips: David McLaughlin and Chris Peterson
Production runners: Todd Davis and Jonathan Staggers
Postproduction coordinator: Jay Weinman
Audio postproduction: Focused Audio/Jeff Roth
Sound effects design: James Allen
Dialogue editor: Jamie Kibben
Audio transfers: Saul Zaentz Co., Sprocket Systems
Dialogue recording: The Plant/Ann Fry
Video transfers: Russian Hill
Film laboratory: Monaco Labs
Credit titles: Cinematte
Lorimar executive in charge: Scott Stone
Gumby's pal at Lorimar-Telepictures: Bob Bain

Episodes in "The New Adventures of Gumby" Written by Art Clokey

"Abominable Doughman"
"All Cooped Up"
"Arctic Antics"
"As the Worm Turns"
"Astrobots"
"Balloonacy"
"Band Contest"
"The Beetle and the Caterpillar"
"Best in the Block"
"The Big City"
"The Big Squirt"
"Birthday Party in the Middle Ages"
"Blocks in the Head"
"Children for Sale"
"Clayfully Yours"
"Clay Play"

"Command Performance"
"A Cottage for Granny"
"Denali Blues"
"Denali's House"
"A Dolly for Minga"
"Educational TV"
"The Elephant and the Dragon"
"The Fliver 500"
"Flying Carpets"
"Forbidden Mine," part 1
"Forbidden Mine," part 2
"For the Graduate"
"Fox Hunt"
"Fun Day"
"Funtasia"
"Geese Grief"
"Goo and the Queen," part 1
"Goo and the Queen," part 2
"Goo's Music Video"
"Goo's Pies"
"Great Mastodon Robbery"
"Guitar Magic"
"Gumbastic"
"Gumbitty Doo-dah" (by Kristine Albrecht, Kurt Hanson, Tim Hittle, Eric Leighton, and Mark Peter Maggiore)
"Gumbot"
"A Gumby Day"
"Gumby Music Video"
"Gumby's Circus"
"Gumby's Close Encounters"
"Hatching Out"
"High as a Kite"
"Humbug"
"Joker's Wild"
"Just Train Crazy"
"Kangaroo Express"
"Kid Brother Kids"
"Knightmare"
"Little Denali Lost"
"Little Lost Girl"
"Lost Arrow"
"Lost Birthday Present"

"Lost in Chinatown"
"Lost Treasure"
"Lotta Hot Air"
"Melon Felons"
"Merry-Go-Pumpkin"
"A Miner Affair"
"Minga's Follies"
"Minga Sitting"
"Mirror-Aculous Recovery"
"Moving Experiences"
"The Music Ball"
"My-O-Maya"
"Naughty Boy"
"Of Note"
"Ostrich Feathers"
"Picnic"
"The Plant"
"Pokey à la Mode"
"Prickle's Baby Brother" (written by David Bleiman)
"Proxy Gumby"
"A Real Seal"
"Rip Van Prickle"
"Robot Farm"
"Runaway Camel"
"The Search"
"Shrink-A-Dink"
"Skate Board Rally"
"Sleepytime Robbers"
"A Smashing Hit"
"Space Oddity," part 1
"Space Oddity," part 2
"Strange Circus Animals"
"Time Kapp-sule"
"Time Out" (written by Ken Pontac)
"To Bee or Not to Bee"
"Wickiups and Bullrushes"
"Wild Girls"
"Wild Horse"
"Wild Train Ride"
"The Wind Bag"
"Witch Way"
"Young Granny"

Will Vinton Productions

Note: The information below is as complete as possible, as generously furnished to me by Will Vinton Productions. Any information the studio was unsure of—such as exact running time, producer credit, and so forth—was not included. Some in-house promotional films, unreleased material, some nonclay works, and works contained in other works (for example, a music video within a television special) have not been listed.

Shorts, Packages, and Features

Culture Shock (1969)
Will Vinton and Bob Gardiner

Gone for a Better Deal (1970)
Written, produced, and directed by Will Vinton

Closed Mondays (1974)
Created by: Bob Gardiner and Will Vinton
Voices: Holly Johnson and Todd Oleson
Animation: Bob Gardiner and Will Vinton
Music: Billy Scream
Running time: 7:30

Mountain Music (1975)
Director: Will Vinton
Animation: Bob Gardiner, Kathy Hendricks, and Bevan Vinton
Music: Billy Scream and Paul Jameson
Running time: 8:15

Martin the Cobbler (Billy Budd Films, 1976)
Producer: Will Vinton
Director: Will Vinton
Executive Producer: Frank Moynihan
Screenplay and Adaptation: Tim Conner, Will Vinton
Set and Characters: Dick Allen, Barry Bruce, Kate Hendrickson, Don Merkt, Tom Samanen, and Will Vinton
Animation: Barry Bruce, Don Merkt, Tom Samanen, Will Vinton
Music: Billy Scream
Narration: Alexandra Tolstoy

Voices: Todd Oleson, Tom Early, Russ Fast, Joan Paglin, Linda Macentee, Holly Johnson, and Jack Shields
Running time: 27:00

Rip Van Winkle (Billy Budd Films, 1978)
Producer: Will Vinton
Director: Will Vinton
Executive producer: Frank Moynihan
Character design: Barry Bruce
Set design: Don Merkt
Production assistants: Rick Cooper and Tom Samanen
Screenplay and adaptation: Susan Shadburne
Animation: Barry Bruce, Joan C. Gratz, Don Merkt, and Will Vinton
Music: Billy Scream and Paul Jameson
Song and lyrics: Susan Shadburne
Narration: Will Geer
Voices: Tim Conner (Rip van Winkle), Bob Griggs, Bill Gratin, Jim Andrews, Marley Stone, Paul Jameson, and Billy Scream
Running time: 27:00

Claymation® (1978)
Director: Will Vinton
Screenplay and narration: Susan Shadburne
Animation: Barry Bruce, Don Merkt, and Will Vinton
Music and effects: Billy Scream and Paul Jameson
Production assistants: Rick Cooper, Dan Hoffman, Tom Samanen, Rick Johnson, and Mike McLeod
Running time: 17:00

Legacy (1979)
Director: Will Vinton
Producer: Will Vinton
Animation: Barry Bruce, Don Merkt, and Joan C. Gratz
Running time: 5:10

The Little Prince (Billy Budd Films,1979)
Producer: Will Vinton
Director: Will Vinton
Executive producer: Frank Moynihan
Character design: Barry Bruce

Set design: Don Merkt
Background design: Joan C. Gratz
Production manager: Rick Cooper
Story adaptation: Susan Shadburne
Animation: Don Merkt, Barry Bruce, Joan C. Gratz, and Will Vinton
Optical effects: Lookout Mountain Films: Pat O'Neil and Tim Shepard
Motion studies: TheatrElan
Music production: Susan Shadburne and Billy Scream
Casting: Character Actors
Voices: Cliff Robertson (Pilot), Michelle Mariana (Little Prince), Dallas McKennon (the Fox), Mel Suza (the Rose), Todd Oleson, Bob Griggs, Jan Conner, John Morrison, and Russ Fast
Running time: 27:00

Little Prince and Friends (1980)—feature release compilation of *Martin the Cobbler, Rip van Winkle,* and *The Little Prince*

Dinosaur (Will Vinton Productions/Pyramid Films, 1980)
Produced in Claymation® by: Will Vinton Productions
Screenplay: Susan Shadburne
Concept and visual design: Barry Bruce and Don Merkt
Animation: Joan C. Gratz, Barry Bruce, Don Merkt, and Matt Wuerker
Producer: Will Vinton
Voices: Michelle Mariana
Production manager: Rick Cooper
Story consultant: Don Roberts
Executive producer: David Adams
Running time: 13:00

The Christmas Gift (1980)
Director: Will Vinton
Producer: Will Vinton
Animation: Barry Bruce, Joan C. Gratz, Will Vinton, and Matt Wuerker
Running time: 8:00

Creation (1981)
Director: Will Vinton
Producer: Will Vinton
Clay painting: Joan C. Gratz
Running time: 9:00

The Diary of Adam and Eve (1981) (later included in *The Adventures of Mark Twain*)

The Great Cognito (1982)
Director: Will Vinton
Producer: Will Vinton
Animation: Barry Bruce
Additional Animation: William C. Fiesterman
Running time: 3:30

"Million Pound Note" (1983)—later dropped from *The Adventures of Mark Twain*

The Adventures of Mark Twain (1985)
Producer and director: Will Vinton
Executive producer: Frank Moynihan
Screenplay: Susan Shadburne
Character design: Barry Bruce
Set design: Don Merkt
Background design: Joan C. Gratz
Principal character animation: William C. Fiesterman (Becky Thatcher); Tom Gasek (Tom Sawyer and Dan'l Webster); Mark Gustafson (Huck Finn); Barry Bruce (Mark Twain); Craig Bartlett (Stormfield/ aliens); Bruce McKean (Airship)
Clay painting effects: Joan C. Gratz
Additional Claymation®: Don Merkt, Will Vinton, and Matt Wuerker
Assistant Claymators: Douglas Aberle, James McAllister, Joanne Radmilovich
Music (composition and arrangement): Billy Scream
Voices: James Whitmore (Mark Twain), Michelle Mariana, Gary Kruz, Chris Ritchie, John Morrison, Carol Edelman, Dallas McKennon, Herb Smith, Marley Stone, Wilbur Vincent, Wally Newman, Tim Conner, Todd Tolces, Billy Scream, Bob Griggs, Coward Wholesale Tomasek, and Sally Sopwith
Running time: 90:00

Festival of Claymation® (1986)—compilation, with original wraparound segments
Director: Will Vinton
Producer: David Altschul
Animation: Douglas Aberle, Gary Bialke, Lorah Conheim, and Will Vinton

Television Specials

A Claymation® Christmas Celebration (CBS Primetime Special, 1987)
Director: Will Vinton
Producer: David Altschul
Animation directors: Barry Bruce, Joan C. Gratz, Craig Bartlett, William C. Fiesterman, and Douglas Aberle
Animation: Vince Backeburg, Larry Bafia, Webster Colcord, Teresa M. Drilling, Chuck Duke, Thomas Gurney, Brad Johnson, Anthony LaMolinara, Michael McKinney, Tony Merrithew, Jeffrey Mulcaster, John Ashlee Prat, Robert C. Terrell II, Christina Sells, Mark Gustafson, Si Duy Tran, and Gary Bialke
Running time: 24:00

Meet the Raisins (CBS Primetime Special, 1988)
Director: Barry Bruce
Producer: Will Vinton
Lead animators: Douglas Aberle, Larry Bafia, Gary Bialke, Teresa M. Drilling, Mark Gustafson, Tony Merrithew, and John Ashlee Prat
Animators: Kristina Carol Ashley, Vince Backeburg, Kyle Bell, Aleisa Bloom, Jane Clugston, Webster Colcord, Chuck Duke, William C. Fiesterman, Thomas Gurney, Hal Hickel, Jerold Howard, Brad Johnson, Douglas Kelly, Sheila Lucas, Padraic Magin, Michael McKinney, Ray Nelson, Jr., Scott Norlund, Christina Sells, Robert C. Terrell II, Si Duy Tran, Doug Williams, and J. R. Williams
Running time: 29:00

The Raisins Sold Out (CBS Primetime Special, 1990)
Director: Will Vinton
Producer: Paul Diener
Lead animators: Douglas Aberle, John Ashlee Prat, Chuck Duke, Tony Merrithew, Jeffrey Mulcaster, and Doug Williams
Animators: Kyle Bell, Jane Clugston, Hal Hickel, Matt Isakson, Brad Johnson, Douglas Kelly (not listed in screen credits), Ray Nelson, Jr., and Christina Sells
Apprentice animators: Joel Brinkerhoff, Schell Hickel, Kellie Lewis, Jean G. Poulot, and Patricia Taylor
Running time: 28:00

Claymation® Comedy of Horrors (CBS Primetime Special, 1991)
Director: Barry Bruce
Producer: Paul Diener

Lead animators: John Ashlee Prat, Teresa M. Drilling, Chuck Duke, and Jeffrey Mulcaster
Animators: Kyle Bell, Aleisa Bloom, Joel Brinkerhoff, Jane Clugston, Thomas Gurney, Hal Hickel, Schell Hickel, Kellie Lewis, Ray Nelson, Jr., Jean G. Poulot, Si Duy Tran, and J. R. Williams
Apprentice animators: Mikhael Berenstein, Jeffrey Bost, Janet Karecki, Tracy Larson, Tim Tanner, and Bill Wagner
Running time: 24:00

A Claymation® Easter (CBS Primetime Special, 1992)
Director: Mark Gustafson
Producer: Paul Diener
Principal animators: Kyle Bell, Chuck Duke, Tony Merrithew, Ray Nelson, Jr., Jean G. Poulot, and John Ashlee Prat
Additional animation: Douglas Aberle, Jeffrey Bost, Joel Brinkerhoff, Mark Gustafson, Hal Hickel, and John Logue
Running time: 24:00

Clay Segments and Other Works

Trailer for *Bette Midler's Divine Madness* (1980)
Director: Will Vinton
Producer: Will Vinton
Animation: Barry Bruce, Joan C. Gratz, Don Merkt, Will Vinton, and Matt Wuerker
Running time: 3:25

Special effects for *Return to Oz* (Walt Disney Films/Silver Screen Partners II, 1985)
Director: Walter Murch
Producer: Paul Maslansky
Executive producer: Gary Kurtz
Screenplay: Walter Murch and Gill Dennis
Starring: Nicol Williamson, Jean Marsh, Piper Laurie, and (introducing) Fairuza Balk
Photography: David Watkin
Production designer: Norman Reynolds
Creature design: Lyle Conway
Clay animation: Will Vinton

Segments for *"Vanz Kant Danz"* (John Fogerty, 1985)—music video
Director: Will Vinton
Animation: William C. Feisterman, Douglas Aberle, Craig Bartlett, Mark Gustafson, Tom Gasek, Joan C. Gratz, and Bruce McKean
Running time: 5:15 (including live action)

Special effects for *Captain Eo*, a Disney 3-D theater film (1986)
Director: Will Vinton
Producer: David Altschul
Animation: Douglas Aberle

"Come Back, Little Shiksa," segment for an episode of the television series "Moonlighting" (ABC, 1987)
Director: Mark Gustafson
Producer: David Altschul
Animation: Mark Gustafson, Gary Bialke, and Lorah Conheim
Running time: 5:32

"Speed Demon," segment from "Moonwalker" (Michael Jackson, 1988)—music video
Director: Will Vinton
Animation: Douglas Aberle, Larry Bafia, Kyle Bell, Gary Bialke, Webster Colcord, William C. Fiesterman, Thomas Gurney, Matt Isakson, Brad Johnson, Michael McKinney, Tony Merrithew, Jeffrey Mulcaster, Ray Nelson, Jr., and Si Duy Tran
Running time: 11:00

"Cecille" segments for "Sesame Street" (Children's Television Workshop)

"Cecille" #1: "Intro" segment for "Sesame Street" (Children's Television Workshop) (1990)
Supervising director: Barry Bruce
Producer: Sue Conklin
Segment director: Teresa M. Drilling
Animation: Teresa M. Drilling
Running time: 0:20

"Cecille" #2: "Up Down In Out" segment for "Sesame Street" (Children's Television Workshop) (1990)
Supervising director: Barry Bruce
Producer: Sue Conklin
Segment director: Larry Bafia
Animation: Larry Bafia
Running time: 1:40

"Cecille" #3: "I Wanna Be Me" segment for "Sesame Street" (Children's Television Workshop) (1990)
Supervising director: Barry Bruce
Producer: Sue Conklin

Segment director: Douglas Aberle
Animation: Douglas Aberle
Running time: 1:50

"Cecille" #4: "Brushin' down the Doggies" segment for "Sesame Street" (Children's Television Workshop) (1991)
Supervising director: Barry Bruce
Producer: Sue Conklin
Segment director: Joel Brinkerhoff
Animation: Joel Brinkerhoff

"Cecille" #5: "The Game of Make Believe" segment for "Sesame Street" (Children's Television Workshop) (1991)
Supervising director: Barry Bruce
Producer: Sue Conklin
Segment director: Tony Merrithew
Animation: Tony Merrithew

"Cecille" #6: "I'm Gonna Get You" segment for "Sesame Street" (Children's Television Workshop) (1991)
Supervising director: Barry Bruce
Producer: Sue Conklin
Segment director: Teresa M. Drilling
Animation: Teresa M. Drilling
Running time: 2:00

Mesozoic (Smithsonian Institution, 1990)—permanent exhibit
Director: Michael McKinney
Producer: Marilyn Zornado
Animation: Michael McKinney
Running time: 1:07

Corn and Potato Show (Smithsonian Institution, 1991)—"Seeds of Change" exhibit
Director: John Logue
Producer: Marilyn Zornado
Animation: John Logue, Si Duy Tran, and Vince Backeburg
Running time: 2:15

Globeheads/Wasteheads (California Museum of Science and Industry, 1992)
Director: Larry Bafia
Producer: Marilyn Zornado

"Intro" animation: Ben Adams, Kyle Bell, and Joanne Radmilovich
"Faucet Dilemma" animation: Larry Bafia
"Down the Drain" animation: Ben Adams
"The Loop" animation: Kyle Bell
"Dust Bunnies" animation: Joanne Radmilovich
Running time: 0:56

Opening titles for *Brain Donors* (Paramount Pictures, 1992)
Animation director: Mark Gustafson
Producer: Paul Diener
Animation: Chuck Duke, William C. Fiesterman, Thomas Gurney, Mark Gustafson, Ray Nelson, Jr., Jean G. Poulot, and John Ashlee Prat

Closing titles for *Brain Donors* (Paramount Pictures, 1992)
Animation director: Skeets McGrew
Producer: Paul Diener
Animation: Douglas Aberle, Larry Bafia, and Schell Hickel

Adventures in Wonderland (Disney Channel, 1992)
Director: Barry Bruce
Producer: Paul Diener
Art director: John Longue
"The Cat and the Troll" animation: Si Duy Tran
"Dino-Floss" animation: Joel Brinkerhoff
"Eliot's China Shop" animation: Karen Hout
"Even Stephen" animation: Tracy Larson and Joel Brinkerhoff
"Freida, the Forgetful Witch" animation: Aleisa Bloom
"Humphrey and the Bloodhound" animation: Jeffrey Bost
"The Little Boy Who Cleaned His Room" animation: Schell Hickel
"Lost and Pound" animation: Vince Backeburg
"Morris, the Fearful Monster" animation: J. R. Williams and Si Duy Tran
"The Princess and the Three Frogs" animation: Mikhail Berenstein

"Adventures in Wonderland" (Disney Channel, 1992)
Director: John Logue
Producer: Paul Diener
Art director: Douglas Kelly
"The Bear Cycle" animation: Jim Dunn and Si Duy Tran
"A Boy and His Book" animation: Tracy Larson and Joel Brinkerhoff
"The Bug Ball" animation: J. R. Williams, Si Duy Tran, Thomas Gurney, and Ray Nelson, Jr.
"The Buttinsky Billy Goat" animation: Jeffrey Bost

"Casey, the Chameleon" animation: Schell Hickel and Joel Brinkerhoff
"The Copy Cat" animation: Ray Nelson, Jr.
"The Caveman Poet" animation: Schell Hickel and Ray Nelson, Jr.
"The Chicken or the Egg" animation: Tracy Larson
"The Cow Lullaby" animation: Jane Clugston
"Elbow Grease" animation: Webster Colcord
"Florence, the Fastest Inchworm" animation: Karen Hout
"The Goose Who Wouldn't Go South" animation: Thomas Gurney and Joel Brinkerhoff
"The Happy Ness Monster" animation: Jim Dunn, Tony Merrithew, Joel Brinkerhoff, and Jeffrey Bost
"The Jungle Gym" animation: Karen Hout
"King of Beasts" animation: Ray Nelson, Jr.
"Like Cats and Dogs" animation: Scott Norlund, Joel Brinkerhoff, and Ray Nelson, Jr.
"The Litterbug" animation: J. R. Williams and Jeffrey Bost
"Mouse Mountain" animation: J. R. Williams
"The Newshound Deadline" animation: Webster Colcord and Joel Brinkerhoff
"Old Dog, New Tricks" animation: Scott Norlund, Joel Brinkerhoff, and Jeffrey Bost
"Patience" animation: Vince Backeburg
"Peanut Juice" animation: Mikhail Berenstein
"Percy the Perfect Pig" animation: Karen Hout
"Phil the Grumpy Frog" animation: Vince Backeburg
"A Planet Called Clone" animation: Vince Backeburg
"The Spelling Bee" animation: Vince Backeburg
"Timmy's Toy Box" animation: Tracy Larson
"Tiny the Dinosaur" animation: Joel Brinkerhoff
"Try It You'll Like It" animation: Mikhail Berenstein
"White Christmas" animation: Larry Bafia, Chuck Duke, Jean G. Poulot, Joel Brinkerhoff, and Kyle Bell

"Adventures in Wonderland" (Disney Channel, 1993)
Director: John Logue
Producer: Mary E. Sandell
Art director: Douglas Kelly
"The Bat and Bird Buddies" animation: Joel Brinkerhoff
"Big Fish, Little Pond" animation: Joel Brinkerhoff
"The Cavegirl's Rock Collection" animation: Hal Hickel
"Charlie, the Cheating Cheetah" animation: Kyle Bell and Joel Brinkerhoff
"The Couch Potato" animation: Teresa M. Drilling
"Cow Competition" animation: Vince Backeburg

"The Do-Nothing Dogs" animation: Larry Bafia
"A Humorless Hyena" animation: John Ashlee Prat
"The Junk-Food Goat" animation: Kyle Bell
"The Kangaroo Who Jumped to Conclusions" animation: Jean G. Poulot
"Leader of the Pack" animation: Jeffrey Bost and Tony Merrithew
"The Lost Sheep" animation: Hal Hickel
"Money Doesn't Grow on Trees" animation: John Ashlee Prat
"The Prince's Shoes" animation: Mikhail Berenstein, Mikhail Tumelya, and Larry Bafia
"Rocky Raccoon" animation: Jean G. Poulot
"The Thoughtless Woodpeckers" animation: Tony Merrithew
"The Turtle and the UFO" animation: Si Duy Tran
"A Very Private Ant" animation: Vince Backeburg

"Hammer" (Children's Television Workshop, 1993)—computer animation for "Sesame Street"
Director: Barry Bruce
Producer: Paul Diener
Animation: Douglas Aberle, Barry Bruce, and Robert C. Terrell II

Television Commercials

Pacific Mountain Bartlett Pears (1975)
Running time: 0:30

Rainier Ale (1975)
Running time: 0:30

Soccer for Everyone (1975)

Levi's Youthwear (1978)
Director: Will Vinton
Producer: Will Vinton
Animation: Barry Bruce, Don Merkt, and Will Vinton
Running time: 0:30

Benjamin Franklin Savings & Loan (1981)
Director: Will Vinton
Producer: Will Vinton
Animation: Matt Wuerker
Running time: 0:30

Mr. Cheapskates Cereal (1981, never aired)
"Mr. Cheapskates"
Director: Will Vinton
Animation: William C. Fiesterman
Running time: 0:30

Quaker Bread (1981, never aired)
"Nobody Else"
Animation: Joan C. Gratz
Running time: 0:30

Illinois State Lottery (1982)
"Lucky Number II"
Director: Will Vinton
Producer: David Altschul
Animation: Tom Gasek and Mark Gustafson
Running time: 0:30

National Audubon Society (1982)—public service announcement
"Land of Nevermore"
Director: Tom Gasek
Animation: Tom Gasek and Joan C. Gratz
Running time: 0:30

Aim Toothpaste #1 (1983)
Director: Will Vinton
Producer: David Altschul
Animation: Douglas Aberle
Running time: 0:30

Nickelodeon (1983)
Director: Will Vinton
Producer: David Altschul
Animation: Joanne Radmilovich
Running time: 0:30

Scotsman Newspapers (United Kingdom, 1984)
"The Scotsman"
Director: Barry Bruce
Producer: David Altschul
Animation: Joanne Radmilovich
Running time: 0:30

Twizzlers Candy (1984)
"Mouth"
Director: Will Vinton
Producer: David Altschul
Animation: Craig Bartlett
Running time: 0:30

Aim Toothpaste #2 (1985)
"'A' Team with Mr. T."
Director: Will Vinton
Producer: David Altschul
Animation: Tom Gasek

Dallas Times-Herald Classified Ads (1985)
Director: Barry Bruce
Producer: David Altschul
Animation: Craig Bartlett, Tom Gasek, and Mark Gustafson
Running time: 0:30

John Deere (1985)
"Spring Sale"
Director: Will Vinton
Producer: David Altschul
Animation: Joanne Radmilovich
Running time: 0:30

Kentucky Fried Chicken #1 (1985)
"Overnight Experts"
Director: Barry Bruce
Running time: 0:30

Kentucky Fried Chicken #2 (1985)
"Part-time Experts"
Running time: 0:30

Kentucky Fried Chicken #3 (1985)
"Choices"
Animation: Tom Gasek and Mark Gustafson
Running time: 0:30

Kraft Noodles (1985)
"Rockers 'n' Rollers"
Director: Will Vinton
Producer: David Altschul
Animation: Douglas Aberle, William C. Fiesterman, and Bruce McKean
Running time: 0:30

Alka Seltzer Antacid (1986, never aired)
Director: Will Vinton
Producer: David Altschul
Animation: Mark Gustafson and Joan C. Gratz
Running time: 0:30

American Bank (1986)
"Disappearing Blanket"

Beneficial Finance (1986)
"Claymanager"
Animation: William C. Fiesterman
Running time: 0:30

California Egg Commission (1986)
"Mr. Egghead"
Animation: William C. Fiesterman
Running time: 0:30

California Raisin Advisory Board #1 (1986)
"Late Show"
Director: Will Vinton
Producer: David Altschul
Animation: William C. Fiesterman, Gary Bialke, and Douglas Aberle (and Tony Merrithew for Canadian version)
Running time: 0:30

California Raisin Advisory Board #2 (1986)
"Lunch Box"
Director: Will Vinton
Producer: David Altschul
Animation: Mark Gustafson, Gary Bialke, and William C. Fiesterman
Running time: 0:30

Cap'n Crunch Cereal (1986, never aired)
"Soggies"
Director: Will Vinton
Producer: David Altschul
Animation: Mark Gustafson and Craig Bartlett
Running time: 0:30

Circus Fun Cereal #1 (1986)
"Marching"
Director: Will Vinton
Producer: David Altschul
Animation: Douglas Aberle and Mark Gustafson
Running time: 0:30

Circus Fun Cereal #2 (1986)
"Nightstand"
Director: Will Vinton
Producer: David Altschul
Animation: Douglas Aberle and Mark Gustafson
Running time: 0:30

Circus Fun Cereal #3 (1986)
"Tabletop"
Director: Will Vinton
Producer: David Altschul
Animation: Douglas Aberle and Mark Gustafson
Running time: 0:30

Domino's Pizza #1 (1986)
"Pizza Puncher"
Director: Barry Bruce
Producer: David Altschul
Animation: Barry Bruce and Douglas Aberle
Running time: 0:30

Domino's Pizza #2 (1986)
"Noid Intro"
Director: Barry Bruce
Producer: David Altschul
Animation: Barry Bruce and Craig Bartlett
Running time: 0:30

Domino's Pizza #3 (1986)
"Hot and Delicious"
Director: Barry Bruce
Producer: David Altschul
Animation: Craig Bartlett, Mark Gustafson, and Tony Merrithew
Running time: 0:30

Hershey's Chocolate Bar (1986)
"One of the All-time Greats"
Director: Barry Bruce
Producer: David Altschul
Animation: Joan C. Gratz
Running time: 0:30 (with other footage)

Kentucky Fried Chicken #4 (1986)
"Circles"
Running time: 0:30

Kentucky Fried Chicken #5 (1986)
"Fresh Chicken"
Director: Joan C. Gratz
Animation: Joan C. Gratz
Running time: 0:30

Kentucky Fried Chicken #6 (1986)
"Tough Chicken"
Running time: 0:30

Kentucky Fried Chicken #7 (1986)
"Flying"
Running time: 0:30

Kentucky Fried Chicken #8 (1986)
"Icicles"
Director: Joan C. Gratz
Animation: Joan C. Gratz
Running time: 0:30

Kentucky Fried Chicken #9 (1986)
"Crumble"
Animation: Mark Gustafson
Running time: 0:30

KOMO Radio (1986)
Directors: Skeets McGrew and Tom Gasek
Animation: Tom Gasek
Running time: 0:30

Nike (1986)
"Shoes for Kids"
Director: Craig Bartlett
Animation: Craig Bartlett
Running time: 0:30

Aquarius Isotonic Drink #1 (Japan, 1987)
"Isotonic"
Director: Skeets McGrew
Producer: David Altschul
Animation: Joan C. Gratz and Douglas Aberle
Running time: 0:30 (with other footage)

Aquarius Isotonic Drink #2 (Japan, 1987)
"Water in the Desert"
Director: Skeets McGrew
Producer: David Altschul and Marilyn Zornado
Animation: Bruce McKean and Jim McAllister
Running time: 0:30 (with other footage)

California Raisin Advisory Board #3 (1987)
"Playing with Your Food"
Director: Will Vinton
Producer: David Altschul
Animation: Mark Gustafson, Chuck Duke, and Tony Merrithew
Running time: 0:30

Domino's Pizza #4 (1987)
"Dome of Quality"
Director: Barry Bruce
Producer: David Altschul and Marilyn Zornado
Animation: Craig Bartlett and Tony Merrithew
Running time: 0:30

Domino's Pizza #5 (1987)
"Time Bomb"
Producer: Marilyn Zornado
Animation: Mark Gustafson, Gary Bialke, and Tony Merrithew
Running time: 0:30

Domino's Pizza #6 (1987)
"Trapdoor"
Director: Barry Bruce
Producer: Marilyn Zornado
Animation: Craig Bartlett and Tony Merrithew
Running time: 0:30

Domino's Pizza #7 (1987)
"Monolith"
Director: Barry Bruce
Producer: Marilyn Zornado
Animation: Tony Merrithew
Running time: 0:30

Domino's Pizza #8 (1987)
"Joker"
Director: Barry Bruce
Producer: Marilyn Zornado
Animation: Tony Merrithew
Running time: 0:30

Hardee's Restaurants #1 (1987)
"Grapevine"
Director: Will Vinton
Producer: David Altschul
Animation: Douglas Aberle, Tony Merrithew, Ian Shadburne, and James Logan
Running time: 0:30

Hormel/Spam (1987)
"Dress up Spam"
Producer: David Altschul
Animation: William C. Fiesterman
Running time: 0:30

Sun-Maid Raisins #1 (1987)
"Late Show"
Animation: No new animation; recomposited footage from original "Late Show."

California Raisin Advisory Board #4 (1988)
"Raisin Ray"
Director: Mark Gustafson
Producer: Marilyn Zornado
Animation: Mark Gustafson, Chuck Duke, Vince Backeburg, and Anthony LaMolinara
Running time: 0:30

Contact Cold Medicine (1988, never aired)
"Sudafed" and "Actifed"
Director: Barry Bruce
Producer: Marilyn Zornado
Animation: Teresa M. Drilling and John Logue
Running time: 0:30

Dole Frozen Fruit Bars (1988)
"In the Mood"
Director: Mark Gustafson
Producer: Marilyn Zornado
Animation: Vince Backeburg, Larry Bafia, Lorah Conheim, Chuck Duke, and Padraic Magin
Running time: 0:30

Domino's Pizza #9 (1988)
"Wizard"
Director: Barry Bruce
Producer: Marilyn Zornado
Animation: Tony Merrithew
Running time: 0:30

Domino's Pizza #10 (1988)
"Silver Screen"
Director: Skeets McGrew
Producer: Marilyn Zornado
Animation: Si Duy Tran, Tony Merrithew, and John Ashlee Prat
Running time: 0:30

Domino's Pizza #11 (1988)
"Noid Video"
Director: Skeets McGrew
Producer: Marilyn Zornado
Animation: Mark Gustafson and Kyle Bell
Running time: 0:15

Domino's Pizza #12 (1988)
"Noid Freud"
Director: Skeets McGrew
Producer: Marilyn Zornado
Animation: Kyle Bell
Running time: 0:10

Domino's Pizza #13 (1988)
"Extra, Extra"
Director: Skeets McGrew
Producer: Marilyn Zornado
Animation: Craig Bartlett
Running time: 0:30 (with other footage)

General Foods/Tang Drink Mix #1 (1988)
"Store"
Director: Craig Bartlett
Producer: Marilyn Zornado
Animation: Craig Bartlett, Larry Bafia, and Webster Colcord
Running time: 0:30

General Foods/Tang Drink Mix #2 (1988)
"Refrigerator"
Director: Craig Bartlett
Producer: Marilyn Zornado
Animation: Larry Bafia and Webster Colcord
Running time: 0:30

Hardee's Restaurants #2 (1988)
"Concert"
Director: Will Vinton
Producer: Marilyn Zornado
Animation: Tony Merrithew, John Ashlee Prat, and Teresa M. Drilling
Running time: 0:30

Hardee's Restaurants #3 (1988)
"Warm-up"
Director: Will Vinton
Producer: Marilyn Zornado
Animation: Tony Merrithew
Running time: 0:15

Kentucky Fried Chicken #10 (Canada, 1988)
"Raisin Men"
Director: Skeets McGrew
Producer: Marilyn Zornado
Animation: John Logue and Jean Clugston
Running time: 0:30 (with other footage)

Post Raisin Bran Cereal #1 (1988)
"Big Stars"
Director: Will Vinton
Assistant director: Chuck Duke
Producer: Marilyn Zornado
Animation: Chuck Duke, Webster Colcord, and Vince Backeburg
Running time: 0:30

Purina Grrravy Dog Food #1 (1988)
"Bombs Away"
Director: William C. Fiesterman
Producer: Marilyn Zornado
Animation: Chuck Duke, Lorah Conheim, and Doug Williams
Running time: 0:15

Purina Grrravy Dog Food #2 (1988)
"Flowers in the Desert (Indian)"
Director: William C. Fiesterman
Producer: Marilyn Zornado
Animation: William C. Fiesterman and Christina Sells
Running time: 0:15

Sun-Maid Raisins #2 (1988)
"My Girl"
Director: Tom Gasek
Producer: Marilyn Zornado
Animation: Tom Gasek and Elizabeth Butler
Running time: 0:30

Switzer Licorice Candy (1988)
"Frankie and the Switzers"
Director: John Logue and Skeets McGrew
Producer: Marilyn Zornado
Animation: Craig Bartlett, Webster Colcord, and John Logue
Running time: 0:30

Tagamet Ulcer Medicine (1988)
"Heartburn"
Director: Barry Bruce
Producer: Marilyn Zornado
Animation: John Ashlee Prat and Teresa M. Drilling
Running time: 0:30

American Academy of Pediatric Physicians (1989)—public service announcement
"The Shocking Adventure of Casual T. Cat"
Director: Mark Gustafson
Producer: David Altschul
Animation: Mark Gustafson, Jeffrey Mulcaster, Doug Williams, and Robert C. Terrell II
Running time: 0:30

Beecham's #1 (United Kingdom, 1989)
"Cough Caps Clock"
Director: Barry Bruce
Producer: Marilyn Zornado
Animation: Teresa M. Drilling and Thomas Gurney
Running time: 0:30

California Raisin Advisory Board #5 (1989)
"Locker Room"
Director: Mark Gustafson
Producer: Marilyn Zornado
Animation: Jerold Howard, Doug Williams, and Robert C. Terrell II
Running time: 0:30

California Raisin Advisory Board #6 (1989)
"Intermission"
Director: Mark Gustafson
Producer: Marilyn Zornado
Animation: Larry Bafia, Jerold Howard, and Si Duy Tran
Running time: 0:30

California Raisin Advisory Board #7 (1989)
"Michael Raisin"
Director: Will Vinton
Producer: David Altschul
Animation: Douglas Aberle, Kristina Carol Ashley, Vince Backeburg, Larry Bafia, Kyle Bell, Gary Bialke, Aleisa Bloom, Webster Colcord, Chuck Duke, Mark Gustafson, Hal Hickel, Jerold Howard, Brad Johnson, Douglas Kelly, Tony Merrithew, Jeffrey Mulcaster, John Ashlee Prat, and Christina Sells
Running time: 0:30 (theatrical version is 1:00)

California Raisin Advisory Board #8 (Japan, 1989)
"Zun!"
Director: Skeets McGrew
Producer: Marilyn Zornado
Animation: Aleisa Bloom, Jane Clugston, Thomas Gurney, Hal Hickel, Matt Isakson, Brad Johnson, Sheila Lucas, Scot Norlund, and Christina Sells
Running time: 0:30

Domino's Pizza #14 (1989)
"Mad Scientist"
Director: Skeets McGrew
Producer: Marilyn Zornado
Animation: Tony Merrithew, Kyle Bell, and Thomas Gurney
Running time: 0:30

Domino's Pizza #15 (1989)
"Remote Control"
Director: Skeets McGrew
Producer: Marilyn Zornado
Animation: Tony Merrithew and Kyle Bell
Running time: 0:10

Domino's Pizza #16 (1989)
"Yo Domino's"
Director: Skeets McGrew
Producer: Marilyn Zornado
Animation: Kyle Bell (and Craig Bartlett for "Dome of Quality" footage)
Running time: 0:30

Fuji Videotape (1989)
"The Presentation"
Director: Barry Bruce
Producer: Marilyn Zornado
Animation: Chuck Duke, Jeffrey Mulcaster, Webster Colcord, Doug Williams, Ray Nelson, Jr., and Vince Backeburg
Running time: 0:30

General Foods/Tang Drink Mix #3 (1989)
"Mom"
Director: Mark Gustafson
Producer: Marilyn Zornado
Animation: Chuck Duke and Webster Colcord
Running time: 0:30

General Foods/Tang Drink Mix #4 (1989)
"Allowance Promo"
Director: Larry Bafia
Producer: Marilyn Zornado
Animation: Kyle Bell and Larry Bafia
Running time: 0:30

Hardee's Restaurants #4 (1989)
"Mouth Promo"
Director: Skeets McGrew
Producer: Marilyn Zornado
Animation: Larry Bafia, Webster Colcord, Alesia Bloom, and J. R. Williams
Running time: 0:30

Kamol Baume Ointment #1 (France, 1989)
"Le Secrétaire"
Director: Barry Bruce
Producer: Marilyn Zornado
Animation: Michael McKinney
Running time: 0:15

Kamol Baume Ointment #2 (1989)
"Le Rugbyman"
Director: Barry Bruce
Producer: Marilyn Zornado
Animation: Vince Backeburg, Hal Hickel, and Sheila Lucas
Running time: 0:10

Kamol Baume Ointment #3 (1989)
"Le Déménageur"
Director: Barry Bruce
Producer: Marilyn Zornado
Animation: Larry Bafia, J. R. Williams, Hal Hickel, and Jerold Howard
Running time: 0:15

Oregon Arts Commission (1989)
"Check-off for the Arts"
Director: Barry Bruce
Animation: J. R. Williams and Webster Colcord
Running time: 0:30 (with other footage)

Pacific Gas and Electric Weatherization Program (1989)
"House of Clay"
Director: Teresa M. Drilling
Producer: Marilyn Zornado
Animation: Teresa M. Drilling
Running time: 0:30

Post Raisin Bran Cereal #2 (1989)
"Honeymooners"
Director: Will Vinton
Producer: Marilyn Zornado
Animation: Jeffrey Mulcaster, Chuck Duke, Webster Colcord, Gary Bialke, and Douglas Kelly
Running time: 0:30

Post Raisin Bran Cereal #3 (1989)
"Raisin Search I, II, and III"
Director: Mark Gustafson
Producer: Marilyn Zornado
Animation: No new animation; animation from "Big Stars" recut with stills.

Seven-Eleven Slurpee (1989)
"Animotion"
Director: Barry Bruce
Producer: Marilyn Zornado
Animation: Doug Williams
Running time: 0:10

WMMS FM Radio (1989)
"Buzzard"
Director: Skeets McGrew
Producer: Marilyn Zornado
Animation: Brad Johnson
Running time: 0:10

Alpo Treats and Biscuits (1990)
"Animated Dan"
Director: Barry Bruce
Producer: Marilyn Zornado
Animation: Vince Backeburg, Alesia Bloom, Thomas Gurney, and Hal Hickel
Running time: 0:30

American Library Association (1990)—public service announcement
"Raisin Rap"
Director: Skeets McGrew
Producer: Marilyn Zornado
Animation: Larry Bafia, Webster Colcord, and Brad Johnson
Running time: 0:30

Carlos the Fifth Chocolate Bar (Mexico, 1990)
"Carlos V Tag"
Director: Skeets McGrew
Producer: Marilyn Zornado
Animation: Douglas Aberle and Larry Bafia

Charmin Bathroom Tissue (1990, never aired)
"Baby Store"
Director: Mark Gustafson
Producer: Marilyn Zornado
Animation: Vince Backeburg, Jerold Howard, and Tony Merrithew
Running time: 0:30

Dinosaur Grahams (1990)
"Pop-up"
Director: Mark Gustafson
Producer: Marilyn Zornado
Animation: Larry Bafia, Webster Colcord, Hal Hickel, Douglas Kelly, and Michael McKinney
Running time: 0:30

Federal Express (Canada, 1990)
"La Transformation"
Director: Skeets McGrew
Producer: Sue Conklin
Animation: John Logue and Larry Bafia
Running time: 0:30

Fritos Rowdy Rustler BBQ Chips (1990)
"Picnic"
Director: Mark Gustafson
Producer: Marilyn Zornado
Animation: Larry Bafia, Alesia Bloom, Jerold Howard, J. R. Williams, and Robert C. Terrell II
Running time: 0:30

Met Life Insurance (1990)
"Logo"
Director: John Logue
Producer: Marilyn Zornado
Animation: John Logue, Scott Norlund, and Karen Hout
Running time: 0:10

Portland Trailblazers Basketball (1990)
"Blazer Billboard"
Director: Mark Gustafson
Producer: Paul Diener
Animation: Chuck Duke, Hal Hickel, and Ray Nelson, Jr.
Running time: 0:30

Showtime Cable Network (1990)
"Holiday Logo"
Director: Joan C. Gratz
Producer: Sue Conklin
Animation: Joan C. Gratz

Tetley Tea (United Kingdom, 1990)
"Any Umbrellas"
Director: Skeets McGrew
Producer: Marilyn Zornado
Animation: Karen Hout, Brad Johnson, Robert C. Terrell II, and Christina Sells
Running time: 0:30

United Airlines (1990)
"Natural"
Director: Joan C. Gratz
Producer: Sue Conklin
Animation: Joan C. Gratz
Running time: 0:30

Bay Cable Co-op #1 (1991)
"It's Alive"
Director: Skeets McGrew
Producer: Sue Conklin
Animation: Douglas Aberle, Joel Brinkerhoff, and Hal Hickel
Running time: 0:30

Bay Cable Co-op #2 (1991)
"TV Turn On"
Director: Skeets McGrew
Producer: Sue Conklin
Animation: Vince Backeburg
Running time: 0:30

Beecham's #2 (United Kingdom, 1991)
"Hot Lemon"
Director: Barry Bruce
Producer: Marilyn Zornado
Animation: Teresa M. Drilling and Christina Sells
Running time: 0:30 and 0:15

California Raisin Advisory Board #9 (1991)
"Robot"
Director: Mark Gustafson
Producer: Paul Diener
Animation: Tony Merrithew, Chuck Duke, Hal Hickel, Joel Brinkerhoff, and Schell Hickel
Running time: 0:30

Hardee's Restaurants #5 (1991)
"American Gothic"
Director: Will Vinton
Producer: Paul Diener
Animation: Douglas Aberle, Larry Bafia, Joel Brinkerhoff, Hal Hickel, John Logue, and Jean C. Poulot
Running time: 0:30

Macleans Toothpaste (United Kingdom, 1991)
"Castle"
Director: Barry Bruce
Producer: Marilyn Zornado
Animation: Larry Bafia, Teresa M. Drilling, Jean G. Poulot, Christina Sells, and Schell Hickel
Running time: 0:30 and 0:15 (no clay)

Nestles' Candy (France, 1991)
"Crunch"
Director: Skeets McGrew
Producer: Marilyn Zornado
Animation: Webster Colcord, Jean G. Poulot, and J. R. Williams
Running time: 0:30

Pacific Bell Spanish Yellow Pages #1 and #2 (1991)
"La Transformation"
Director: Skeets McGrew
Producer: Marilyn Zornado
Animation: Thomas Gurney and Si Duy Tran

Pacific Bell Spanish Yellow Pages #3 (1991)
"Date"
Director: Skeets McGrew
Producer: Marilyn Zornado
Animation: Thomas Gurney and Douglas Aberle
Running time: 0:30

Pacific Bell Spanish Yellow Pages #4 (1991)
"Wedding"
Director: Skeets McGrew
Producer: Marilyn Zornado
Animation: Thomas Gurney and Douglas Aberle
Running time: 0:30

Ralston Purina/Teenage Mutant Ninja Turtles (1991)
"Turtle Song"
Director: Will Vinton
Producer: Marilyn Zornado
Animation: Kyle Bell and Tony Merrithew
Running time: 0:30

Samon Energy Drink #1 (Japan, 1991)
"Running Business Man"
Director: Skeets McGrew
Producer: Marilyn Zornado
Animation: Douglas Aberle, Hal Hickel, and Christina Sells
Running time: 0:30 (with other footage)

Samon Energy Drink #2 (Japan, 1991)
"Rap Dance"
Director: Skeets McGrew
Producer: Marilyn Zornado
Animation: Tony Merrithew, Hal Hickel, Schell Hickel, and Si Duy Tran
Running time: 0:15 (with other footage)

Sunkist Wacky Players Candy #1 (1991)
"Slam It Home"
Director: Barry Bruce
Producer: Marilyn Zornado
Animation: Douglas Aberle, Joel Brinkerhoff, and Jerold Howard
Running time: 0:30

Sunkist Wacky Players Candy #2 (1991)
"Autograph"
Director: Barry Bruce
Producer: Marilyn Zornado
Animation: Tony Merrithew, Douglas Aberle, Hal Hickel, Larry Bafia, Jerold Howard, and Teresa M. Drilling
Running time: 0:30

Takeda C-1000 (Japan, 1991)
"Surfing Couple (Hechara)"
Director: Skeets McGrew
Producer: Sue Conklin
Animation: Douglas Aberle, Larry Bafia, and Hal Hickel
Running time: 0:30 (with other footage)

Typhoo Tea #1 (United Kingdom, 1991)
"Try It"
Director: Mark Gustafson
Producer: Marilyn Zornado
Animation: Joel Brinkerhoff, Chuck Duke, Hal Hickel, and Ray Nelson, Jr.
Running time: 0:30; three 0:15 teasers

Zany Zone #1, #2, and #3 (1991)
"Zany Zone"
Director: Skeets McGrew
Producer: Sue Conklin
Animation: William C. Fiesterman

Burger King (1992)
"Membership Front"
Director: Skeets McGrew
Producer: Mary E. Sandell
Animation: Tony Merrithew and Jean G. Poulot
Running time: 0:30 (with other footage)

Cadbury's (United Kingdom, 1992)
"Mad on a Fruit and Nut Bar"
Director: Mark Gustafson
Producer: Marilyn Zornado
Animation: Douglas Aberle, Kyle Bell, Hal Hickel, Ray Nelson, Jr., and John Ashlee Prat
Running time: 0:30

California Raisin Advisory Board #10 (1992)
"Raisin Breakfast"
Director: Mark Gustafson
Producer: Paul Diener
Animation: Tony Merrithew, Chuck Duke, Joel Brinkerhoff, and Jean G. Poulot
Running time: 030

Cypress Gardens (1992)
"Butterfly Symphony"
Director: Joan C. Gratz
Producer: Marilyn Zornado
Animation: Joan C. Gratz
Running time: 0:30

Eagle Vision (1992)
"Pedestal"
Director: Skeets McGrew
Producer: Marilyn Zornado
Animation: Douglas Aberle
Running time: 0:30 (with other footage)

Eat 'n' Park (1992)
"Smiley Cookie"
Director: Skeets McGrew
Producer: Marilyn Zornado
Animation: John Ashlee Prat
Running time: 0:30

Giggle Wiggle Game (1992)
"Giggle Wiggle"
Director: Skeets McGrew
Producer: Marilyn Zornado
Animation: Douglas Aberle
Running time: 0:30 (with other footage)

Harpic (United Kingdom, 1992)
"You're the One I Want"
Director: Skeets McGrew
Producer: Marilyn Zornado
Animation: Larry Bafia, Chuck Duke, Christina Sells and Joel Brinkerhoff

Kellogg's Pop-tarts (1992)
"Bladerunner"
Director: David Daniels
Producer: Zilpha Yost
Animation: Dan Ackerman, Ben Adams, Tom Arndt, Amy Blumstein, Webster Colcord, Hal Hickel, Schell Hickel, Karen Hout, and Michael O'Donnell
Running time: 0:30 (mostly photo cutout)

Mini Cheddars (1992)
"Life," "Statistics," "Mouse," and "Cheddar"
Director: Skeets McGrew
Producer: Marilyn Zornado
Animation: Kent Burton
Running time: 0:20 (no clay)

Norfolk Southern Railroad (1992)
"Horse of a Different Color"
Director: Barry Bruce
Producer: Paul Diener
Animation: Larry Bafia, Teresa M. Drilling, Hal Hickel, and John Ashlee Prat
Running time: 0:30 (no clay)

Pinkifou (1992)
"Invasion"
Director: Skeets McGrew
Producer: Marilyn Zornado
Animation: Douglas Aberle, Hal Hickel, and Jean G. Poulot
Running time: 0:30

Play Doh #1 (1991)
"Doc"
Director: Skeets McGrew
Producer: Marilyn Zornado
Animation: Teresa M. Drilling and Webster Colcord
Running time: 0:30 (with other footage)

Play Doh #2 (1992)
"Trio (Fun Sounds)"
Director: Skeets McGrew
Producer: Marilyn Zornado
Animation: Webster Colcord
Running time: 0:30 (with other footage)

Play Doh #3 (1992)
"Jewelry"
Director: Skeets McGrew
Producer: Marilyn Zornado
Animation: Christina Sells
Running time: 0:30 (with other footage)

Play Doh #4 (1992)
"Bugs"
Director: Skeets McGrew
Producer: Marilyn Zornado
Animation: Webster Colcord
Running time: 0:30 (with other footage)

Play Doh #5 (1992)
"Baby"
Director: Skeets McGrew
Producer: Marilyn Zornado
Animation: Douglas Aberle and Teresa M. Drilling
Running time: 0:30 (two versions with other footage)

Ritz Bits #1 (1992)
"Pizza"
Director: Will Vinton
Producer: Bruce McKean
Animation: Larry Bafia, Jean G. Poulot, Tony Merrithew, and Joel Brinkerhoff
Running time: 0:15

Ritz Bits #2 (1992)
"Nacho"
Director: Will Vinton
Producer: Bruce McKean
Animation: Douglas Aberle, Chuck Duke, and Kyle Bell
Running time: 0:15

Typhoo Tea #2 (United Kingdom, 1992)
"Dairy Cow"
Director: Mark Gustafson
Producer: Marilyn Zornado
Animation: Chuck Duke and Tony Merrithew

Typhoo Tea #3 (United Kingdom, 1992)
"Sky Diver"
Director: Mark Gustafson
Producer: Marilyn Zornado
Animation: Chuck Duke and Tony Merrithew

Butterfinger BBs (1993)
"Gnarly Party"
Director: Skeets McGrew
Producer: Marilyn Zornado
Animation: Tony Merrithew and Schell Hickel

Independent Commission against Corruption (Hong Kong, 1993)
"ICAC"
Director: Barry Bruce
Producer: Mary E. Sandell
Animation: Teresa M. Drilling
Running time: 0:30

Kellogg's Frosted Flakes (1993)
"Monsters"
Director: Barry Bruce
Producer: Marilyn Zornado
Animation: Webster Colcord
Running time: 0:30 (with other footage)

Pacific Bell (1993)
"Flipbook"
Director: Mark Gustafson
Producer: Paul Diener
Animation: Tony Merrithew and Ben Adams
Running time: 0:30

Pacific Bell Spanish Yellow Pages #5 (1993)
"Grau"
Director: Skeets McGrew
Producer: Marilyn Zornado
Animation: Douglas Aberle and Chuck Duke
Running time: 0:30

Pacific Bell Spanish Yellow Pages #6 (1993)
"Optometrista"
Director: Skeets McGrew
Producer: Marilyn Zornado
Animation: Douglas Aberle and Chuck Duke
Running time: 0:30

Pacific Bell Spanish Yellow Pages #7 (1993)
"Mapas"
Director: Skeets McGrew
Producer: Marilyn Zornado
Animation: Douglas Aberle and Chuck Duke
Running time: 0:30

Pacific Bell Spanish Yellow Pages #8 (1993)
"Tortilleria"
Director: Skeets McGrew
Producer: Marilyn Zornado
Animation: Douglas Aberle and Chuck Duke
Running time: 0:30

Pacific Bell Spanish Yellow Pages #9 (1993)
"Fiesta"
Director: Skeets McGrew
Producer: Marilyn Zornado
Animation: Douglas Aberle and Chuck Duke
Running time: 0:30

Pacific Bell Spanish Yellow Pages #10 (1993)
"Estadios"
Director: Skeets McGrew
Producer: Marilyn Zornado
Animation: Douglas Aberle, Chuck Duke, and Schell Hickel
Running time: 0:30

Scott's Fertilizer (1993)
"Scott's Fertilizer"
Director: Skeets McGrew
Producer: Paul Diener
Animation: Vince Backeburg
Running time: 0:30 (with other footage)

Sugus (1993)
"Train"
Director: Skeets McGrew
Producer: Marilyn Zornado
Animation: Douglas Aberle and Larry Bafia
Running time: 0:30

Tyco (1993)
"Lickin' Lizzards"
Director: Mark Gustafson
Producer: Paul Diener
Animation: Jeffrey Bost
Running time: 0:30 (with other footage)

Bruce Bickford
Segments in Features, Compilations, and Shorts

Baby Snakes (Intercontinental Absurdities, 1979)
Producer and director: Frank Zappa
Camera: Robert Leacock, Phil Parmet, and Richard Pearce

Editor: Frank Zappa
Assistant editor: Laura Whipple
Cast: Tex Abel, Angel, Adrian Belew, Bruce Bickford, Dale Bozzio, Terry Bozzio, Chris, Warren Cucurullo, Ron Delsener, David Ditkowich, Diva, Roy Estrada, French the Poodle, Bill Harrington, Klaus Hundsbichler, Janet the Planet, John, Phil Kauffman, Robert Leacock, Ed Mann, Tommy Mars, Chris Martin, Kerry McNabe, Nancy, New York's Finest Crazy Persons, Patrick O'Hearn, Phil Parmet, Richard Pearce, Ms. Pinky's Larger Sister, Joey Psychotic, Brian Rivera, John Smothers, Donna U. Wanna, Peter Wolf, and Frank Zappa
Running time: 166:00

The Amazing Mr. Bickford (Intercontinental Absurdities, 1987)
Writer, producer, and director: Frank Zappa
Associate producer: Jill Silverthorne
Animation scenarios: Bruce Bickford and Frank Zappa
Animation photography: Bruce Bickford and Karl Krogstadt
Clay, cardboard, and line animation: Bruce Bickford
Editing: Booey Kober
Telecine: Joe Finley
Music: Frank Zappa (all compositions published and controlled by Munchkin Music [ASCAP])
Conducting: Pierre Bouley (Ensemble Intercontemporain)
Conducting the London Symphony: Kent Nagano (London Symphony Orchestra)
Postproduction facility: Pacific Video
Special video equipment: Sony Broadcast
MPI Home Video/It's a Honker Home Video

Prometheus' Garden (1981–88)
Photography, animation, clay figures, set design, construction, and story: Bruce Bickford
Music composition and recording: Bill Bagley
Negative cutter: Janice Findley
Equipment: George Bickford, Jeff Gerson, and John Nonnenmacher
Running time: 28:00

Works-in-Progress
15 minutes of clay animation (1988–present; rough edit)
20 minutes of line animation (1970–91; pencil tests)

David Daniels
Shorts and Segments in Other Works

For "Pee Wee's Playhouse"
"Penny Cartoons"
"Allen" (1986)
"Kids' Rights" (1986)
"My Room" (1986)
"Christopher Columbus" (1987)
"The Declaration of Independence" (1987)

Peter Gabriel's music video "Big Time" (excerpt, 1987)

Jackson Five music video "ABC" (excerpt, 1988)

MTV promo "Idiot Box" (1990)

Commercials

California Lottery (1990)
"Pot 'o' Gold"
"White Room"
"7–11–21"

Honda (1990)
"Metamorphosis"

Hi-C (1991)
"Stomping Banana Berry"

Kellog's Pop-tarts (1992)
"Bladerunner"
(For Will Vinton Productions, see p. 248)

APPENDIX

Shot List for *The Sculptor's Nightmare*
(The print used for this description is from the Library of Congress.)

Shot	Scope	Description
1	LS*	A group of men sits at a table debating the upcoming presidential election; they hold signs over a bust of Teddy Roosevelt to indicate their preferred candidate. They argue and exit the room in haste.
2	LS	A female model poses for a sculptor in his studio. The men burst in to hire him to make busts of their respective candidates. They pay him a large sum of money and mill about, destroying the sculptor's studio and his work-in-progress. Elated by his newfound wealth, the sculptor gestures to the model to come celebrate with him.
3	LS	The sculptor and model go to a restaurant. The sculptor drinks excessively, and his boisterous behavior annoys the other diners. A matronly woman enters, outraged at the sculptor. She drags the model out. The police arrive to haul the sculptor away.
4	LS	Two policemen put the sculptor in a jail cell.
5	LS	The sculptor collapses onto a bed and falls asleep. Three pedestals appear—one at a time—in the middle of the room. Each pedestal has a mound of clay on top of it.

*See end of Appendix for List of Abbreviations.

Shot	Scope	Description
6	MS	The three mounds of clay mold themselves into heads of the candidates, each with a nameplate underneath—"Fairbanks," "Taft," and "Bryan." The heads come alive, mouths and eyes moving. Fairbanks has a wineglass moving to and from his mouth. Taft smokes a cigar.
7	LS	Continues shot 5. The sculptor wakes and finds the busts. Amazed (and still a little drunk), he takes the wineglass and the cigar. He begins to drink; the wineglass, cigar, busts, and pedestals disappear. As he lies down and sleeps, one pedestal with a mound of clay appears in the cell.
8	MS	The clay molds itself into a teddy bear, which becomes animated. The bear molds into a mound and then re-forms as the head of Teddy Roosevelt, with a nameplate reading "Teddy" underneath.
9	LS	The sculptor wakes to find the bust. Surprised, he goes to touch it. The bust and pedestal disappear, and the sculptor returns to sleep.

Shot List for *Chew Chew Land; or, The Adventures of Dollie and Jim*
(The print used for this description is from the British Film Institute.)

Shot	Scope	Description
1	LS	In a classroom, an unidentified boy stands at the blackboard doing a problem. As a prank, he puts a piece of gum on the teacher's chair. The teacher enters and sits on the gum. She believes Dollie is responsible for the prank and pulls her up to the board. (*Title:* "Jim takes the blame.")
2	LS	Continues shot 1. Jim claims he is responsible for the prank and is sent to the board in Dollie's place. The teacher dismisses class but keeps Jim after. (*Title:* "Waiting!")

Shot	Scope	Description
3	LS	Dollie waits outside school holding a bouquet for Jim.
4	LS	Jim works diligently after school until the teacher dismisses him.
5	LS	Jim finds Dollie on the school steps. She gives him the flowers, and they walk off together.
6	LS	Jim walks Dollie home. (*Title:* "Sweethearts.")
7	LS	Continues shot 6. Jim tries to kiss Dollie. She runs inside, laughing.
8	LS	Jim walks home. (*Title:* "Jim's dream of Chew Chew Land.")
9	MS	Jim goes to sleep. An imp named Wriggles appears and startles Jim. Wriggles points at the window and jumps out of it.
10	MS	Wriggles lands on the ground and motions for Jim to follow. He then conjures up Dollie.
11	LS	Jim jumps out the window.
12	MS	Continues shot 10. Jim lands on the ground. Wriggles leads Jim and Dollie off.
13	LS	Wriggles makes a plant magically disappear into the ground, leaving a large hole. Wriggles jumps into the hole and motions for them to follow. They do.
14	LS	Wriggles skips through an underground cave. Jim and Dollie enter, amazed.
15	LS	Wriggles stands before the mouth of a cave and begins to conjure a vision.
16	CU	A plant magically sprouts from a twig, and its leaves quickly unfurl one after another.

Shot	Scope	Description
17	LS	Continues shot 15. Wriggles conjures another piece of magic.
18	CU	Three sticks of gum appear. A ball of clay rolls in and "absorbs" one of the sticks of gum. Small lumps of clay build up into a head. The head comes to life and smiles.
19	LS	Continues shot 17. Jim and Dollie laugh and chew gum. Wriggles sneaks away. Dollie notices that he is gone. Scared, she exits. Jim is left confused. A bright light flashes.
20	MS	Continues shot 9. Jim wakes in his bed.

Shot List for *Swat the Fly*

(The print used for this description is from the Em Gee Film Library, Reseda, California.)

Shot	Scope	Description
1	MS	A mound of clay molds itself into a large bust. (*Title:* "Frenchy 'Strikes Out.'")
2	MS	Continues shot 1. A fly lands on Frenchy's nose. He wiggles his nose to dislodge the fly. The fly moves to his eyebrow. Frenchy wiggles his eyebrow. The fly moves to his ear. Frenchy wiggles his ear. (*Title:* "Lord Algy Endeavors 'Y' Know.'")
3	CU	Continues shot 2. Frenchy's head returns to a mound of clay and then molds itself into a different head—Lord Algy. A fly lands on Lord Algy's nose, then on his eyebrow. Trying to dislodge the fly, Algy drops his monocle. The head changes to a different shape. (*Title:* "O'Brien 'Sacrifices.'")
4	CU	Continues shot 3. The fly lands on O'Brien's nose. He wiggles his nose. The fly then moves to his forehead, eyebrow, mouth, and then back to his nose. O'Brien is unsuccessful in dislodging the fly. The artist's hand enters the frame and swats the fly, crushing the nose in the process. The hand then rips the entire nose off of the head. (*Title:* "The End.")

Shot List for *Modeling*
(The print used in this description is from the Library of Congress.)

Shot	Scope	Description
1	MCU	Animator's (Max's) hands with pen; dips in inkwell.
2	MCU	Hands draw a series of circles.
3	MCU	Hands "pour" the circles off the back page into pen.
4	MCU	Hands move the "filled" pen back to the drawing board.
5	MCU	Hand draws a rainbow shape that leads a group of drops to metamorphose into Ko-Ko. (*Title:* "Why don'tcha use fresh ink when you draw me? I've got no more pep than a snail under ether.")
6	CU	Ko-Ko yawns.
7	MS	Max admonishes Ko-Ko on the drawing board. (*Title:* "No stalling now—brace up—show some life!")
8	CU	Hand on drawing board flicks Ko-Ko over, who continues to yawn. Hand prods him again.
9	LS	Crandall works at another easel. The Gentleman enters and sits.
10	MS	Crandall uncovers a clay bust that is a caricature of the Gent.
11	CU	Crandall rotates the bust, showing its exaggerated features.
12	M2Sh	Gent and bust for comparison.
13	CU	Hands touch up the bust.
14	CU	Ko-Ko is knocked about by the hand, continues to yawn.

Shot	Scope	Description
15	M2Sh	Gent looks disapprovingly at bust. (*Title:* "No, no—that won't do!")
16	MCU	Gent taps the large nose of the bust.
17	MCU	Crandall responds. (*Title:* "Well what's the matter with it?")
18	MCU	Gent rotates the bust. (*Title:* "Why it looks exactly like me!")
19	MCU	Continues shot 18.
20	3Sh	Gent poses. Crandall begins to resculpt the bust and shouts to Max in the next room.
21	MS	Max turns, holding Ko-Ko pinned against the drawing board. (*Title:* "I'll be over just as soon as I put some pep into this clown!")
22	MS	Continues shot 21.
23	LS	Hand draws skates on Ko-Ko and a lake for him to skate on.
24	MS	Max exits to help Crandall.
25	MS	Max enters Crandall's workspace.
26	3Sh	Max and Crandall discuss bust.
27	2Sh	Gent with bust, looking annoyed.
28	LS	Ko-Ko skates unsteadily.
29	MS	Gent looks on disapprovingly as Max and Crandall sculpt.
30	LS	Ko-Ko pratfalls and skates; skates toward camera and sticks out tongue.
31	MS	Same as shot 26.

Shot	Scope	Description
32	LS	Ko-Ko skates out beyond "Danger" sign toward hole in ice; flings sign. It boomerangs back and hits him. Ko-Ko figure-skates a cartoon carving of the Gent onto the ice.
33	CU	Gent poses for sculpture.
34	LS	Continues shot 32. Cartoon dissolves away. Bear enters, steals hat. Ko-Ko chases it into ice house. Their fight flings a cow onto ice. Cow falls through ice; climbs out with calf, and they exit. Bear and Ko-Ko wrestle in the ice house. Ice house breaks apart. Ko-Ko jumps into stovepipe. They battle and exchange snowballs. Ko-Ko rolls huge snowball that envelops the bear. Ko-Ko sculpts the ball into a bust of Gent (:56).
35	2Sh	Gent with bust; points at Ko-Ko's bust.
36	2Sh	Max and Crandall turn to look. Max flings a wad of clay at Ko-Ko.
37	LS	Wad hits Ko-Ko, who rolls and ends up upside down with clay on his head.
38	MS	Max returns, sits by drawing board. Crandall and Gent follow.
39	LS	Hand flips Ko-Ko over. Ko-Ko skates with clay on head; wads it up; flings it toward the camera.
40	CU	Gent pulls wad off eye.
41	3Sh	Max and Crandall try to help Gent.
42	LS	Ko-Ko skates toward camera (repeats shot 30). Ko-Ko dives in hole to escape Max and Crandall.
43	MS	Max, Crandall, and Gent try to fish Ko-Ko out of the hole.

Shot	Scope	Description
44	MS	Ko-Ko skates out onto desk from behind the board; skates over books like a ski jump.
45	LS	Ko-Ko lands on office floor.
46	LS	Ko-Ko skates across rug, right to left.
47	LS	Ko-Ko skates across rug, right to left; shimmies up Gent's cane.
48	LS	Ko-Ko continues up cane.
49	LS	Ko-Ko climbs "onto" bust (as photo background).
50	LS	Max continues to fish for Ko-Ko. Crandall and Gent exit.
51	LS	Ko-Ko hides "in" the mouth of the clay bust (photo background).
52	LS	Gent reenters to continue sculpture.
53	3Sh	Crandall, Gent, and bust.
54	CU	Gent resumes pose.
55	CU	Clay bust; the nose begins to wiggle.
56	CU	Same as shot 54. Gent turns and is frightened.
57	CU	Same as shot 55. Nose continues to wiggle.
58	CU	Crandall turns and is shocked.
59	MS	Gent falls off stool.
60	CU	Clay-covered Ko-Ko wiggles out of nose and down the bust.
61	2Sh	Crandall enters; grabs Max to show him the amazing sight.

Shot	Scope	Description
62	MS	Same as shot 48. Clay blob wiggles down the real cane.
63	MS	Same as shot 4. Clay blob continues to wiggle down and across floor.
64	3Sh	Crandall, Max, and Gent stare in astonishment. Eyeline movement, left to right.
65	MS	Clay blob wiggles in circle, left to right.
66	MS	Clay continues to wiggle, then "stands up and looks around."
67	3Sh	Same as shot 64. The men all try to grab the blob.
68	CU	Three men's hands wrestle with the blob.
69	3Sh	Same as shot 67. They "pick up" the blob.
70	3Sh	The three men stand up thinking the blob is in hand.
71	LS	Ko-Ko skates on the rug. They did not capture him.
72	3Sh	Same as shot 70. Gent shoves Crandall and exits in disgust.
73	MS	Gent turns to curse them.
74	LS	Gent picks up hat and shakes his fist; picks up a wad of clay.
75	2Sh	Max and Crandall shout back at him.
76	LS	Same as shot 74. Gent hurls the clay at them.
77	2Sh	Same as shot 75. Crandall ducks. Max hit in head with clay (pop-in).
78	LS	Same as shot 74. Gent exits.

Shot	Scope	Description
79	LS	Ko-Ko skates, left to right.
80	LS	Same as shot 78. Crandall helps Max remove the clay.
81	MS	Same as shot 44. Ko-Ko skates back behind drawing board.
82	LS	Same as shot 78. Continues. Crandall helps Max remove the clay.
83	LS	Ko-Ko pops up and down out of the ice hole.
84	LS	Same as shot 78. Crandall and Max point to Ko-Ko.
85	MS	Ko-Ko jumps off the board.
86	MS	Ko-Ko flies into inkwell; pulls top onto bottle with pincers.
87	CU	Max uncorks inkwell and pours out ink. Fade to black.

Shot List for *Monsters of the Past*

(The print used for this description is from the International Museum of Photography, George Eastman House.)

Shot	Scope	Description
		(*Title:* "Monsters of the Past, Pathe Review, 5–28.")
		(*Title:* "Ten million years ago, when the world was young, giant reptiles ruled the earth.")
1	LS	Brontosaurus eats and wags tail in simple slow movements. (*Title:* "These mighty beasts were busy writing their own chapter in the sands of time.")

Shot	Scope	Description
2	LS	Brontosaurus wags tail. (*Title:* "And the sands reveal another chapter.")
3	MS	Backwards take shows animated bones lying in sand coming together into dinosaur skeleton. (*Title:* "From these fossils, the sculptor, *Virginia May,* can reconstruct the dinosaurs of the past.")
4	WS	Reverse take; May stands at sculpture stand and "builds" a tyrannosaurus rex. (*Title:* "The king of the tyrant reptiles; *Tyrannosaurus Rex.*")
5	WS	Continues shot 5. (*Title:* "He was many times larger than our modern elephant.")
6	2sh	T-rex and elephant face each other; elephant wags tail and ears. (*Title:* "And was the greatest flesh eater of all times.")
7	LS	T-rex steps on carcass and breaks off leg; bends to eat carcass.
8	MCU	Match cut; T-rex chews flesh. (*Title:* "Another monster from the past.")
9	LS	Triceratops enters. (*Title:* "He was a peaceful vegetarian until attacked.")
10	MCU	Triceratops wags his tail and eats vegetation. (*Title:* "His deadly enemy, the King of Reptiles.")
11	LS	T-rex stands.
12	CU	T-rex; his nostrils flare.
13	LS	Continues shot 11. T-rex hops and runs.
14	LS	Triceratops shakes and chews a branch off a bush. (*Title:* "A heavyweight championship fight ten million years ago.")
15	LS	They enter and growl at each other.

Shot	Scope	Description
16	MLS	T-rex kicks up his feet.
17	CU	Continues shot 12.
18	LS	T-rex hops and attacks triceratops, drawing blood. (*Title:* "The King of Reptile's huge size was against him in battle.")
19	LS	Triceratops impales T-rex, who writhes on the ground. (*Title:* "The new champion.")
20		Triceratops steps up to T-rex; he looks and wags his tail. (*Title:* "Pathe Exchanges.")

GLOSSARY

Armature any device (usually internal) used to support the weight of an animated three-dimensional figure and hold it in a fixed position during stop-motion photography. Armatures can be made of unsophisticated materials, such as tin foil and wire, or sophisticated machined parts like ball-and-socket joints.

Backwards take a single run of the camera in which the film is moving backwards. Also, any take producing a similar effect by inverting the camera and shooting with the camera running forward, then reversing the orientation of the take in editing the film so that the image is projected tail-to-head (and, as a consequence, base side out).

Cel animation film animated by using drawings on clear celluloid, overlaid on a background drawing.

Claymation® the registered trademark covering films produced using the clay animation techniques of the Vinton studio.

Clay animation film animated using soft modeling material as the raw material. Typically, clay films use nonhardening materials such as plasticine, though traditional pottery clay has been used.

Clay painting animating clay by smearing soft modeling material on a flat surface and filming the process frame by frame.

Fairing slowly increasing incremental movements as an action accelerates, and slowly decreasing incremental movements as an action decelerates, in order to mimic natural phenomena and avoid jerky movements.

Flag opaque or translucent material attached to a rod that can be positioned in front of a lighting instrument to control where the beam falls.

Inky dinky a small (dinky) incandescent (inky) lighting instrument.

Lightning sketch, lightning sculpting originally, a vaudeville entertainment in which the artist rapidly produced a series of drawings (or changes in those drawings) to illustrate a narrative. During the early silent period, the lightning sketch routine was often filmed; the rapidity and surprise effect produced by the transforming drawings was augmented by undercranking, stop-motion substitution, or animation of the routine. Lightning sculpting produces the same effects using sculpture instead of drawings.

Lip sync the simultaneous presentation of mouth movements and the corresponding character dialogue. In animation, shooting lip sync is not a recording process—as it is in live action (that is, the camera records the image of the moving mouth while a synchronous recording of the dialogue is captured on tape)—but involves generating mouth positions to match an existing track.

Live-action film the largest class of films, live action is shot primarily using people or other nonanimated subjects, and with the camera usually running at sound speed (24 frames per second). To the animator, the term denotes any nonanimated film—that is, those films that are not produced by frame-by-frame manipulation of the material in front of the camera.

Log sheet the description of the action to be filmed, with some indication of the timing and duration of the action. Log sheets vary in degree of precision. In films animated to a sound track recorded and logged during preproduction, the log sheet records the precise breakdown of the relevant sounds at each frame in the film. In more loosely animated works, the log sheet may indicate what action occurs at a given point in time (for example, "around :02 seconds later, the character stands").

Mag, magnetic film (16mm or 35mm) magnetic audiotape in the same format as 16mm or 35mm film, with the same perforations and width to facilitate its synchronization with the picture.

Metamorphosis literally, "changing forms." Metamorphosis is a central theme in all forms of animation.

Mise-en-scène originally a French theater term meaning, literally, "put into the scene." In film, the term refers to the entire arrangement and movement of visual elements before the camera—sets, objects, characters, light and dark areas, and so forth—as well as the camera's position, angle of view, lens usages, and so forth.

Multiplane camera an animation camera developed at the Disney studio in the 1930s that allows the separate animation of several levels of cels placed at different distances from the lens to suggest depth and parallax movement in the foreground, middle ground, and background.

Pencil test in drawn animation, an early sketch of the action that is photographed to test the timing and flow of the action.

Periscopic lens a specialized lens that functions like a periscope, displacing the camera's point of view from its body, allowing shooting at extreme angles, even with the use of miniatures on a tabletop set. Often called a snorkel lens.

Pixilation from the root words, *pixy* and *tintillated*, a form of three-dimensional animation in which people and everyday objects are used as the raw material. Pixilation often describes the eccentric, comic effect of rapid motion generated by the single-frame camera.

Plasticine a nonhardening modeling material that suspends clay and pigment in a mixture of oil and wax. Plasticine was first developed by William Harbutt in England around 1895.

Popping in, popping out an effect based on the stop-motion substitution effect wherein a character or object instantaneously appears in the frame (pops in) or disappears from it (pops out). The effect can be produced when a continuously running camera is stopped and restarted, or at any point during frame-by-frame animation.

Postproduction all filmmaking activities that take place after the actual shooting is completed. Postproduction in animation is limited because, unlike live action, the labor involved precludes the production of multiple takes.

Puppet animation film animated using free-standing, articulated puppets. Typically, puppet films use padded, clothed figures, although there are many different forms, including George Pal's "Puppetoons," which were animated using carved wooden figures with replacement faces, arms, legs, and so forth.

Preproduction all filmmaking activities that take place before the actual shooting begins. Preproduction in most animated films is extensive, with detailed storyboards, prerecording, and logging of the sound track.

Presynchronization recording and logging a frame-by-frame count of the audio track on mag film so that imagery can be generated that precisely synchronizes to that track; often called "shooting to the track."

Probe lens a non-telephoto lens configured in a very long, narrow diameter tube that allows extension of the camera's point of view into difficult-to-reach areas (such as a tabletop set).

Production all filmmaking activities that take place during shooting. Production in most animated films involves shooting the raw material frame by frame, as dictated by the log sheet.

Registration maintaining the rigid spatial relationship between the camera and the animated subject—objects, drawings, and so forth—to avoid unwanted jumping and jitter from one frame to the next. In cel animation, registration is achieved through careful construction of the artwork using a peg bar and punched cels that fit over the pegs. In clay and other forms of three-dimensional animation, everything within the camera's view must be either firmly attached to the set or sufficiently rigid to hold position long enough to shoot a frame of film. Armatures give clay characters the ability to move and rigidly pose at intervals, thus maintaining registration during filming.

Rostrum camera a generic term for an animation camera rigidly mounted above a table, used for shooting flat artwork, sand, clay relief sculptures, and so forth.

Rotoscope a device, patented by the Fleischer brothers, that facilitates drawn animation by projecting live-action footage onto a drawing table frame by frame so that the animator can trace the frames of movement.

Snoot a metal cone placed on the front of a lighting instrument to narrow its beam.

Squash and stretch techniques that give animated characters a more rubbery, fluid mode of movement; developed primarily at the Disney studio in the early sound era. Typically, a ball drawn striking a bat is slightly flattened (squashed) as it strikes the bat, and slightly elogated (stretched) as it leaves the bat, mimicking the natural phenomenon and producing more natural movement.

Stop-motion animation the category of three-dimensional films, made frame by frame, in which "motion" is achieved by photographing a series of "stopped" positions. The term covers the same techniques as dimensional animation, but also refers to dimensional animation incorporated as special effects in live-action films.

Stop-motion substitution effect an effect used in live-action films wherein a camera running at normal speed is stopped, a change is made in some area of the camera's field of view, and then it is restarted. The resulting change happens rapidly, producing a magical or comical effect. Méliès explored the potential uses of this effect. The same principle is at work in stop-motion animation, though the camera is being advanced frame by frame.

Storyboard a series of images produced to represent individual shots of the key action to be filmed. A storyboard is usually considered essential in animation to visualizing the film in preproduction, saving unnecessary labor during production.

Strata-cut a dimensional animation technique in which plasticine loaves are constructed, placed before a camera, and sliced; the camera records each layer of imagery as it changes.

Studio cartoon cel-animated short films produced or released by the major Hollywood studios between the 1920s and the 1960s. The studio cartoon typically runs around seven minutes, features a known animated star, and is fast paced, entertaining, and humorous.

Sync block a standard tabletop editing device, positioned between rewinds, that holds strands of film and mag tape using sprocketed wheels, so that picture and sound can be manipulated in sync and footage can be counted.

Three-dimensional animation animation techniques that use three-dimensional objects in front of the camera. Specific forms include puppet animation, clay animation, and pixilation.

Trick film films from the early silent period that usually establish a narrative premise in live action and then exploit the magical effects that can be produced using the stop-motion substitution effect and single-frame photography. The works of Méliès and Blackton contain well-known examples of this type of film.

INDEX

Page numbers in *italic* refer to photo illustrations.

THE AUTHOR

Michael Frierson is an assistant professor in the Broadcasting/Cinema Division of the Department of Communication and Theater at the University of North Carolina at Greensboro. While studying radio, television, and film at the University of Michigan, he wrote his doctoral dissertation on an experimental educational animated film, *Write Write*, which he coproduced for the Fund for the Improvement of Post Secondary Education. With his wife, Martha Garrett, he has produced clay animated films for Children's Television Workshop's "Square One Television" and for Nickelodeon. He has served as an associate producer for "Mardi Gras 1992," a high-definition television program for NHK in Japan. Currently, he is completing an hour-long film documentary on the life and times of the New Orleans photographer Clarence John Laughlin.

Clay Animation: An Animated Anthology
Produced by Michael Frierson

Michael Frierson brings together a representative sample of the clay animated films featured in this book in *Clay Animation: An Animated Anthology*. Rare clay films not in circulation elsewhere make this a useful companion to the book and valuable for the animation fan or collector.

For a complete description of this VHS tape and ordering information, send a self-addressed stamped envelope to:

Little Man Productions
P.O. Box 5411
Greensboro, North Carolina
USA 27435-5411